DISASTERS AND THE SMALL DWELLING

DISASTERS AND THE SMALL DWELLING

Perspectives for the UN IDNDR

Edited by

YASEMIN AYSAN

Director, Disaster Management Centre
Oxford Polytechnic

and

IAN DAVIS

Deputy Director, Disaster Management Centre
Oxford Polytechnic

from Routledge

First published by James & James (Science Publishers) Ltd. in 1992

This edition published 2013 by Earthscan

For a full list of publications please contact:

2 Park Square, Milton Park, Abingdon, Oxfordshire OX14 4RN
52 Vanderbilt Avenue, New York, NY 10017

Routledge is an imprint of the Taylor & Francis Group, an informa business

First issued in paperback 2018

© 1992 James and James Science Publishers Ltd

British Library Cataloguing-in-Publication Data

Disasters and the small dwelling:
Perspectives for the UN IDNDR.
I. Title II. Aysan, Yasemin III. Davis, Ian
363.3

ISBN 978-1-873936-07-8 (hbk)
ISBN 978-1-138-38414-9 (pbk)

Conference Sponsored by

Disaster Management Centre

National Center for Earthquake
Engineering Research

Titles of related interest from James & James Science Publishers

Hydrology of Disasters. O. Starosolszky and O.M. Melder (eds). ISBN 0–907383–50–5

Power, Choice and Vulnerability: A case study in disaster mis-management in South India, 1977–88. Peter Winchester. ISBN 1–873936–05–2

Hazard Management and Emergency Planning: Perspectives on Britain. D.J. Parker and J.W. Handmer (eds). ISBN 1–873936–06–0

Typeset by Columns Design and Production Services Ltd, Reading

Contents

Acknowledgements   ix

1 Introduction   1
   YASEMIN AYSAN and IAN DAVIS

2 Conference on 'Disasters and Small Dwelling':
   Opening Speech   5
   MICHEL F. LECHAT

3 Disasters and the Small Dwelling – Process, Realism and
   Knowledge: Towards an Agenda for the IDNDR   8
   IAN DAVIS and YASEMIN AYSAN

4 Review of Twelve Years' Experience of Disasters and
   Small Dwellings   23
   FRED CUNY

5 The Global Vulnerability   30
   GUSTAVO WILCHES-CHAUX

6 Materials and Construction Techniques for Disaster
   Protection   36
   ROBIN SPENCE

7 Disaster Prevention and Mitigation in Latin America
   and the Caribbean: Notes on the Decade of the 1990s   45
   STEPHEN BENDER

CONTENTS

8 Problems in Post-Disaster Resettlement: Cross
   Cultural Perspectives   58
   ANTHONY OLIVER-SMITH

9 The Socio-Cultural and Behavioural Context of
   Disasters and Small Dwellings   67
   RUSSELL R. DYNES

10 A View of the Role of NGOs in Natural Disaster Work   72
    REINHARD SKINNER

11 Cross Cultural Disaster Planning: The Alice Springs
    Flood   77
    JOHN HANDMER

12 Disasters and Housing Policy for Rural Bangladesh   88
    DAVID OAKLEY

13 Choice of Technique: Housing Provision by NGOs
    the 1988 Floods in Bangladesh   97
    JOHN BORTON and TONY BECK (with JANE PRYER,
    NAUSHAD FAIZ, NURUL ALAM and MIKE CHAUHAN)

14 Floods in Bangladesh: Vulnerability and Mitigation
    Related to Human Settlement   110
    HUGH BRAMMER

15 Earthquake Reconstruction for Future Protection   119
    ANDREW COBURN and IGNACIO ARMILLAS

16 Hazards Mitigation and Housing Recovery: Watsonville
    and San Francisco One Year Later   127
    MARY C. COMERIO

17 The Reconstruction of Kalamata City after the 1986
    Earthquake: Some Issues on the Process of Temporary
    Housing   136
    MIRANDA DANDOULAKI

18 Diasaster Aid: Equity First   146
    ERIC DUDLEY

19 Introducing Disaster Mitigation in a Political Vacuum:
    The Experiences of the Reconstruction Plan Following
    the Alto Mayo Earthquake, Peru, 1990   162
    ANDREW MASKREY

20 Wind Effects on the Tongan 'Hurricane House'   175
    GREG REARDON

CONTENTS

21 Disaster Resistant Construction for Small Dwellings
    in Solomon Islands   183
    CHARLES BOYLE

22 Occupant Behaviour in Earthquakes   189
    MANSOUR RAHIMI

23 Rebuilding of Fao City, Iraq: A Case of Central
    Government Post-war Reconstruction   194
    SULTAN BARAKAT

24 La Zurza: A Unique Experience in the Integral Urban
    Development of Santo Domingo, Dominican Republic   207
    DAVID SCOTT LUTHER

25 Housing in El Salvador: A Case Study   218
    DÉBORA VÁSQUEZ VELÁSQUEZ

26 Mitigation Program Selection and Evaluation:
    Assessing Effectiveness   224
    PATRICIA A. BOLTON

27 Assessment of the Iranian Earthquake 20 June 1990:
    A Field Report   231
    PATRICK STANTON (with RODERICK JARVIS,
    MICHAEL MARCHANT and ROBERT POVERY)

Conclusions   256

Index   261

Acknowledgements

The 'Disasters and the Small Dwelling' Conference, held at Oxford Polytechnic, in September 1990, was jointly organised by the National Centre for Earthquake Engineering Research (NCEER) of the University at Buffalo and the Disaster Management Centre (DMC) of Oxford Polytechnic. We are particularly grateful to Jelena Pantelić, Assistant Director of NCEER, for supporting the idea and thoroughly overseeing its promotion and execution. The financial contributions of the NCEER made it possible for the USA participants to attend the Conference and introduce many new perceptions. Deborah Plotnik, Research Assistant at the NCEER, facilitated the links with us and the USA groups prior to the Conference, and Patricia Coty, of the same centre, prepared a bibliography on Small Dwellings. We are thankful for their patience and thoroughness.

Many of the contributors to the Conference and to this volume have been known to us through their works over the years. We are grateful to them for sharing their experiences with the participants and revising their papers for the final publication. We are also thankful to the agencies and organisations who supported their travel and attendance.

When the idea of reviewing the progress in the subject since the 1978 Conference of the same title and venue was conceived, contributors to the original meeting were contacted. Those who were available provided the much needed continuity and 'institutional memory' on the progress of the last twelve years. In this respect we are grateful to John Seaman, Frederick Cuny, Allan Taylor, Ken Westgate, Paul Oliver and Robin Spence for making the effort.

Both the Conference and the production of this volume have been made possible by a large group of people. The staff from the Disaster Management

ix

ACKNOWLEDGEMENTS

Centre worked long hours to help run everything smoothly. Fatiha Haddar was central to all stages of this undertaking from the organisational to academic matters. Miranda Dandoulaki made valuable contributions to programming and discussion papers. Elaine Smith undertook the difficult task of following up correspondence and typing the minutes of the discussion session. Sylvia Eaton typed the late additions to the volume. Alistair Cory and Daniel Perez-Selsky provided the very essential day to day support to the Conference. Andy Clayton transcribed the tapes and helped to produce the index for this volume. Paul Oliver reviewed some of the discussion sessions. Apart from the DMC staff, Gustavo Wilches-Chaux and Peter Winchester provided continuous support before, during and after the Conference through discussion in shaping both the meeting and the inputs. Our sincere thanks to all of them.

Finally, we wish to convey our gratitude to many staff from Oxford Polytechnic who made arrangements with accommodation, catering and other facilities for us and our guests.

There are many others, colleagues, past students and local people from different parts of the world who are too numerous to mention, but nevertheless they have been central to shaping our perceptions of this subject. We owe much of what we know to them; our gratitude to all of them for enlightening us.

Yasemin Aysan
March 1992

CHAPTER 1

Introduction

YASEMIN AYSAN

Disaster Management Centre
Oxford Polytechnic, UK

The events of the last decade demonstrate that despite the availability of a wider selection of building materials and technologies in both rural and urban parts of developing countries, small dwellings continue to be vulnerable to disasters. Safer building materials and technologies are either not affordable by the most vulnerable communities, or are at times misused, increasing the damage risk in disasters. Building codes and other structural mitigation seem to have little impact in reducing their vulnerability as small dwellings seldom benefit from such measures. The question to ask at this point is why, with considerable knowledge of building damage and many technical tools to reduce it, very little improvement is made in increasing the safety of such buildings to natural disasters?

Low perception of disaster risk by the public and the lack of a 'safety culture' are often mentioned as reasons. However, it is not easy to expect the rural and urban poor to invest in protecting their dwellings against rare and destructive disaster events while their priorities may lie in economic survival or better health and education. Andrew Maskrey highlights this point in his case study from Alto Mayo in Peru where the discussions held at the Regional Assembly only two weeks after a major earthquake revolved around the problems of rice and maize growers rather than reconstruction of the damaged towns. In urban areas, low income people may choose to invest very little in building better structures, not because they do not know how to, or are irresponsible, but because they feel that the Government can forcibly remove them. So, as a consequence, they invest in those assets that they can take with them – such as television, refrigerators and stoves. The case study by David

Scott-Luther discusses how this phenomenon contributed to increased vulnerability to landslides in the Dominican Republic.

Knowing how to, but choosing not to invest in improving the safety of their homes, is one attitude that might be taken by low-income communities. However, with money available, loss of a local knowledge base due to the migration of skilled builders from rural into fast-growing urban areas, and the limited understanding of new materials and construction techniques, can equally increase the risk to small dwellings. In many developing countries those who have the building skills to earn money in cities are rapidly joining the urban labour markets. Often employed in engineered buildings, skilled and unskilled 'builders' are becoming part of a new and complex construction process where opportunities to understand the principles of new technologies and building materials relative to disaster risk are virtually non-existent. Mistakes that could have been avoided, often at no extra cost, if the principles were understood, are rapidly becoming transferred into small urban dwellings and back into the disaster-prone rural areas. Charles Boyle's paper on the Solomon Islands highlights the dangers of employing partially understood 'urban' technologies in cyclone-prone villages. If used properly, such new construction techniques and materials may have reduced damage to buildings and loss of life.

The impact of urbanisation in increasing vulnerability is not only limited to the depletion of skills in rural areas and the misuse of transferred technologies. The United Nations suggests that 80% of the growth in population in the next few decades will be urban. Already cities of several hundred thousand inhabitants are found in regions which until recently were sparsely populated. Spitak in Armenia and the cities in Iran, which suffered major damage in the recent earthquakes, display the risks induced by the concentration of population in areas where natural hazards previously had no measurable impact. In addition, the need to build rapidly in response to increased demand for housing, often reduces safety standards to a minimum, as the two earthquakes tragically revealed.

In existing urban centres where the disaster risks are already known, population growth is still beyond the control of authorities. Over the last 30 to 40 years, growth in cities of developing nations has been so rapid that it is equivalent to an entire new city built on the periphery or over the old city every 10 to 15 years. Peripheries are often inhabited by the urban poor who live in sub-standard small dwellings and land prone to landslides and floods. Such informal housing, built on flood plains or steep, loose slopes, was worst hit by Hurricane Gilbert and the floods that followed in Jamaica.

According to the official report published by the United Nations Economic Commission for Latin America – (ECLA) – and the World Bank, 60,000 homes were destroyed by the earthquake in El Salvador, of which 50,600 were informal. Already occupying illegal land or rented property these groups were the victims of an urban economic and political crisis which is common to many cities in Latin America. In her contribution on El Salvador, Déborah Vásquez-Velásquez identifies both land tenure and inadequate income due to lack of permanent employment as reasons for vulnerability and obstacles to speedy post-disaster reconstruction.

During the 1978 'Disasters and Small Dwelling' Conference, due to its rural focus, ownership and availability of land were not discussed extensively. A decade later, the high number of urban disasters has radically shifted this focus. Representing different types of disasters and levels of development, both in Greece and Bangladesh land became one of the key factors for effective post-disaster reconstruction. As explained in Miranda Dandoulaki's paper, the delays in the provision of housing after the Kalamata earthquake in Greece were partly due to the complex legal process of land acquisition. The extensive research carried out by Tony Beck and John Borton in Bangladesh concludes that following the 1988 floods, most of the Overseas Development Administration (UK) funded housing projects, run by the NGOs, benefited those who owned land. This automatically excluded those households without land tenure, generally acknowledged to be the poorest group in Bangladesh.

Population increase in urban areas not only highlights the risk to the informal housing sector and the landless but also to those who occupy the historic and old urban cities. Once well built and maintained, such areas in developing countries which have been changing hands from the upper- and middle-class landlords, and in the case of, for example, Colombia from the ownership of Church to lower-income tenants, are now gradually deteriorating due to neglect. Both in Popoyán and Mexico City such historical building stock suffered considerable earthquake damage. Again in both cities, post-earthquake reconstruction focused upon the restoration of buildings as well as the gentrification of the old centres in an attempt to safeguard future maintenance to the houses. Maintenance of the old building stock appears to be an equally difficult task in the USA. As discussed in Mary Comerio's paper on the Loma Prieta earthquake, the US building codes were inadequate to control the quality of old housing stocks both in downtown San Francisco and in Watsonville, a small town located 150 miles south of the city.

The examples discussed in this volume highlight a significant change in the definition of small dwelling in the last decade from traditional rural buildings to a more diverse spectrum of urban, rural, traditional, non-traditional, historical and informal housing. Moreover, case studies from a wide range of countries display the fact that neither vulnerability nor post-disaster reconstruction of small dwellings can be addressed solely as a physical problem. A 'home' is always more than a structure; it is a place of security, symbol of status, reflection of social values and expression of aspirations. For many a home is also a workplace.

It is this broadest context of 'small dwelling' as a metaphor for an artefact, an economic entity, a social and cultural unit that the papers in this volume are addressed in relation to the disaster events of the last decade. We hope that the insights of the contributors will facilitate a more comprehensive understanding of the vulnerabilities of 'small dwellings' and appropriate solutions to reduce them.

CHAPTER 2

Conference on 'Disasters and the Small Dwelling': Opening Speech

MICHEL F. LECHAT

CRED, University of Louvain, Brussels,
School of Public Health, Belgium

Reflections

We are back in Oxford 12 years after the First International Workshop on Disasters and the Small Dwelling, which a number of us attended, and ten years before the completion of the International Decade for Natural Disasters Reduction. Where are we? Where are we coming from? Where are we driving at? Over the last decade or two, considerable progress was achieved in the global approach to disasters, more specifically natural disasters.

First, natural disasters of whatever type have become increasingly recognized as part of a system. A system in a continuous time-frame, from prevention to long-term rehabilitation, through warning, impact, rescue and coping mechanisms, relief. This reductionist approach made it possible to generalize experience – no disaster was a unique event any more, from which no lesson can be drawn. It also provided a general format for designing and evaluating intervention at the various stages. Hence the concept of disaster management, which became widely accepted.

Second, the emphasis shifted from post-facto improvisation to pre-disaster preparedness. This was mainly as a result of studies – both theoretical and in the field – carried out by a limited number of individuals, relief officers, field workers, scientists in their specific disciplines – architects, social scientists, geographers, engineers, economists, epidemiologists among others.

Third, it became clear that disaster management is an interdisciplinary affair, no sector being independent of the others. Hence, the necessity for integrated planning.

Fourth, and finally, it was realized that natural disasters are closely related to development. An obstacle to development that could also be an opportunity, a challenge and a spearhead.

I cannot resist here the temptation to recall some old memories common to many of us. Not only Oxford 1978, but also the London Technical Group, LTG, in the early 1970s and the prominent figure of our late friend, John Rivers; the National Academy of Science Committee on Disaster Assistance, Washington, 1976–78, under the chairmanship of Russell Dynes, a pioneer in the field; the ongoing collaboration of the Oxford Polytechnic Disaster Management Centre to our courses in Brussels; the adventurous launching of a most successful scientific journal, *Disasters*, by John Seaman.

All of this contributed to changing attitudes. The point I want to make is: those were mostly spontaneous initiatives often carried out on shoe-string budgets by a limited number of individuals. Now, not only have the attitudes changed, but also disaster management has become a most respectable discipline. Thus, the time has come for the implementation of new concepts. For the second phase we enter the UN International Decade for Natural Disasters Reduction, 1990–99 (IDNDR).

The Future

To make a long story short, following a suggestion by Frank Press, the President of the US National Academy of Science, at the 8th International Congress of Earthquake Engineering in 1984, and on the basis of a Report by an International Group of 25 experts specially appointed by the UN Secretary General, the Decade was officially proclaimed by the UN General Assembly in December 1989. I shall not get into details. Sufficient to say that among the main goals of IDNDR are: the application of existing scientific and technical knowledge for disaster reduction; the fostering of scientific and engineering endeavours aimed at closing critical gaps in knowledge – that is research; the dissemination of technical information for the assessment, prediction and mitigation of disasters; technical assistance and technology transfer; education and training. In a nutshell, what we were striving for during the last two decades, and what this Conference is all about.

No doubt the United Nations system, the UN Secretariat together with the specialized agencies, is the right body to market these concepts and make them operational on a global, planetary scale. Regarding the structure recommended in the Report, an IDNDR Secretariat has already been established in Geneva, to work in close co-operation with UNDRO, the Office of the United Nations Disaster Relief Coordinator.

This Secretariat will serve as a most powerful catalyst. For playing this role, however, two major aspects of IDNDR which percolate through the report of the Group of Experts should be kept in mind.

First is the development of knowledge and technology. The Decade originated from an initiative by the scientific community and represents a great opportunity to strengthen the interface between this community and the world 'at large. This opportunity goes beyond natural disasters. It could serve as a precedent; it should not be lost.

Second, the Decade is not a new body. It is an idea, an umbrella, an opportunity. It will be what everyone of us does with it, for good or bad. The Report by the Experts stresses the importance of National Committees. It is high time that these Committees were formed, with the appropriate input from scientific people.

Large-scale marketing, however, has its dangers. Institutionalisation is not the least of these. New stereotypes, looking at visibility more than at achievements, trading at words rather than facts. This is a normal trend in the bureaucratic ecology.

Here is one crucial role the academies and the universities could and should play, through conferences like this one, in support of the IDNDR structure. That is: bringing together people for trying out new ideas, experimenting outside of the tracks, following risky ways rather than safe procedures, exploring innovative avenues of research and not marching according to rituals, being concerned more with products than processes, keeping serendipity alive – all these are the responsibilities of informal scientific groups towards and within IDNDR. Still more important, by attracting new and young people to the field, meetings like this one will prepare them to ever reinvent disaster management, beyond 1999, when, hopefully, the Decade will have been successfully completed.

CHAPTER 3

Disasters and the Small Dwelling – Process, Realism and Knowledge: Towards an Agenda for the International Decade for Natural Disaster Reduction (IDNDR)

IAN DAVIS and YASEMIN AYSAN

Disaster Management Centre
Oxford Polytechnic, UK

Introduction

The Disasters and the Small Dwelling Conference held in Oxford in 1990 was conceived as a long-term follow-up to a previous conference on the same topic also held in Oxford Polytechnic in 1978. During this meeting a conference paper was produced that outlined three priority concerns, with the need for:

'a deeper understanding of the coping abilities of disaster survivors'

'the reduction of vulnerability in disaster-prone areas'

'more effective intervention by outside groups' (Davis 1981)

Therefore we want to do some stocktaking in this paper by reviewing developments during the past decade in these critical issues as well as in other matters that had not emerged in 1978.

A review of progress in any complex, rapidly evolving subject is an ambitious task. Whilst the aim is to be objective it is inevitable, in a subject that is severely under-researched, that many of the observations that follow are calculated guesswork based on assumptions rather than research findings. Therefore, in the absence of hard data, the following text can best be described as working hypotheses that need to be tested under various conditions.

It is also clear that the view of any subject is determined by the position of the authors. Our standpoints have varied from undertaking research, acting as consultants to Governments, NGOs and various UN agencies and assisting in training in these topics. This has occurred within a framework of disaster management in courses focused on staff needs at various levels ranging from local communities to ministerial levels. Whilst we acknowledge the limitation of our 'academic view', we have aimed to balance this bias by working with local counterparts in virtually all fieldwork and consultancy.

This paper is structured around three closely interrelated issues: 1, the need for the entire subject to be seen within a much wider set of dimensions than is frequently the case; 2, the necessity of realism in policy formulation and implementation; 3, the development, retention and application of knowledge.

Through a critical appraisal of these issues the paper will identify a series of key issues relative to shelter, low-income housing and settlement that will merit further developments during the International Decade for Natural Disaster Reduction (IDNDR).

Increasing Awareness of the Processes of Risk Reduction and Shelter Provision

Gaps in vulnerability analysis

During the past decade there has been a continual neglect of social criteria which have been persistently undervalued in favour of physical dimensions. Whilst there has been a growing concern to undertake hazard mapping and vulnerability analysis, these tasks have been largely confined to the exposure of low-income dwellings to hazards as seen from an engineering standpoint as opposed to the wider perspective of a physical planner, social/development worker or economist.

From this narrow physical perspective the following elements of buildings have been well covered: siting and settlement patterns, configuration, number of stories, structure, materials, detailed design and level of maintenance. These are all vital aspects of the vulnerability of any dwelling but they do not cover the exposure of building occupants and their livelihoods to hazards.

Social, or human, vulnerability analysis will need to include several critical issues:

- density of building occupancy
- the level of an individual's perception of risk
- the effectiveness of local disaster preparedness planning
- occupations and livelihoods relative to hazards, (for example within flood-prone areas the livelihoods of farmers are closely related to the incidence of

9

flooding in both negative and positive terms, both as potential irrigation and as a threat to crops and livestock)
- economic recoverability
- social groups and communities with special needs due to specific conditions which make them particularly vulnerable: physical handicaps, certain age categories, single parent families
- economic level of the inhabitant
- ownership of property
- function of the building, including its use during different times of the day
- attachment to the place (i.e. resistance to move to safer places due to social, economic or cultural reasons).

Up to the present time these socio-cultural and economic aspects of vulnerability analysis remain largely undeveloped territory. There is still minimal literature on the subject, a lack of an agreed assessment methodology and little experience concerning the most effective way to link such data with physical elements to produce a balanced holistic understanding which can lead to effective risk assessment and mitigation measures (Anderson and Woodrow 1989).

'Human Vulnerability Analysis' is also a prerequisite to the development of medical preparedness pre-planning for types of anticipated injury and numbers of casualties. In the case of earthquakes it is vital to know precisely where the greatest number of casualties are likely to occur. This risk assessment will need to review the adequacy of local health infrastructure and the local capacity for search and rescue. Therefore there is a need for the medical professions to encourage staff to develop, and transfer specialized expertize in the use of epidemiological methods to determine injury and death estimates relative to natural hazards. This need has relevance to the 'building community' since a high percentage of earthquake casualties are caused by building collapse. Information on injury prediction can be used both in justifying expenditure on protective measures as well as in hospital contingency planning. The progress on this subject, much coming from research in the USA and Japan, is the produce of the last decade and needs wide dissemination (NOJI 1989).

Changes in the vulnerability of small dwellings and their occupants

During the 1980s it became clear from various studies that the vulnerability of small dwellings to potential hazard impact is a dynamic process with continual changes taking place to both the structures as well as their occupants, which may reduce or improve their safety. Some of the reasons for these changes include the following factors:

- changes in hazards; e.g. the impact of a river that changes its course due to environmental or other reasons

- the impact of broad 'macro-forces'; e.g. warfare, urbanization, deforestation, population growth
- the condition of buildings; e.g. deterioration of old building stock
- modifications to a house by its owner or occupants; e.g. sub-division of buidings into tenements
- aspirations to use new materials and technologies without an understanding of the risks introduced; e.g. migrants from rural areas moving to towns who switch their building habits from traditional to new materials and construction techniques
- retrofit measures to improve the safety of a building
- implementation of building codes and use of safer materials and technologies.

The issue, therefore, concerns the necessity for risk assessment to be regarded as a continuous process to cope with such changing patterns of vulnerability. Then there is also a need for longitudinal research with a detailed evaluation, over time, of the impact of changes to dwellings on their vulnerability to various types of hazard. From such a study advice could be offered in two directions: firstly, to the owners or occupiers of dwellings as part of community-based public awareness programmes, and secondly, to professionals and authorities in Government and NGO groups on how this awareness of vulnerability might affect the design of new dwellings, or the organization of strengthening programmes of existing buildings.

The adoption of 'sustainable development' policies and programmes can be regarded as an attempt to ensure development patterns which allow a mutual process of adaptation between environment and human communities. The basis of these development models will operate in a dual manner: the assumption that the environment will not be a hazard for the community, and that the community will not pose a hazard for the natural environment. Work is needed from environmental groups to explore further the impact of communities in reducing or increasing vulnerability, particularly in relation to the buildings and settlements.

During the IDNDR there needs to be a concerted effort to expand the techhiques of vulnerability analysis from its present narrow technical scope to become a multi- and inter-disciplinary pursuit, with dwellings, however humble, being regarded as homes, fragments of a community, work settings, economic asssets, development opportunities as well as physical structures of mud, bricks and mortar.

Loss estimation

A further aspect of vulnerability analysis concerns the process of 'Loss Estimation'. This involves the estimation of casualties and property losses in terms of:

- anticipated deaths and injuries, and how they are likely to affect the recovery process

11

- direct losses to property such as the cost of replacing a dwelling
- the impact of indirect losses, such as the loss of production, or unemployment resulting from the destruction of a workplace.

Gradually there has been the growing awareness of the importance of indirect losses, and the need for mitigation to be developed to protect such economic priority sectors. The knowledge gained from economic appraisal of risk can become a key element in benefit cost appraisal techniques which, thus far, has been a neglected tool in the development of disaster mitigation within developing countries (Anderson 1990).

Considering shelter and housing as processes to support, as opposed to products to be delivered

It is important to note that the terminology is critical in emphasizing the process view. Thus the terms 'sheltering' or 'housing', used as verbs, implying an active creative process, are suggested in preference to such nouns as 'shelter', or 'housing programmes' with more passive associations. The expanded perception of sheltering and housing as processes involving many people and agencies inevitably leads to the need for a broad consideration of the elements that contribute to risk reduction and recovery. These will include the social, cultural, economic, political, ecological and developmental dynamics that constrain the processes of sheltering or housing families. The distinction in terminology has been thoroughly considered in a study of sheltering following disasters in the USA (Quarantelli 1982).

Agencies, the professions who serve them, and the private sector all have good reasons to regard the shelter needs of disaster survivors as being the question, and a series of products – e.g. tents, prefabs and caravans – as being the obvious answer. During the 1980s a series of disasters have continued to indicate the limitations of this view. If a 'process view' is taken then this opens the way to consider voluntary evacuation, the temporary occupation of existing buildings, improvisation of shelters by survivors from available debris, and the provision of unavailable tools and materials to enable 'sheltering' to occur.

The role of designers

Whilst the design of a 'Universal Shelter' to suit all cultures, climates and hazards was dismissed as totally unviable in the UN study of 'Shelter after Disaster' (UNDRO 1982) there has been no shortage of attempts to pursue this dream in the intervening years.

It has proved very difficult for architects and industrial designers to recognize the limitation to their capacity to assist constructively in the shelter field. In addition many Governmental and NGO officials have also pursued the quest for 'instant shelters'. It is now clear that any major disaster with extensive media exposure of the plight of families living in makeshift accommodation (as occurred in the Kurdish/Iraq Crisis of 1991) results in the widespread, simplistic assumption that an instant, universal shelter unit is needed and is an effective solution.

The issue proves yet again that stereotypical opinions and entrenched attitudes are not easily influenced by the documentation of research findings. In the sector of post-disaster assistance there is a very high level of staff turnover, and frequent politicization of decision making in the face of technical advice. Therefore key issues will need to be continually restated and unsuccessful examples of post-disaster shelter provision need to be widely disseminated.

Training of small builders in safe housing

During the past 12 years a number of projects have taken place in Guatemala, El Salvador, Colombia, Yemen, South Pacific, the Caribbean, Peru, India, Vietnam, and the Philippines in the training of local builders in improved construction. Different teaching approaches and safety measures have been adopted in such programmes, and thus far no critical comparison has been undertaken to review their long-term effectiveness or sustainability. This cross-cultural comparison and appraisal is needed before further programmes are undertaken.

In addition the various organizations' financial and operational approaches used in these programmes need to be evaluated, findings disseminated and lodged in an accessible venue to allow future project managers to avoid 'reinventing the wheel' with extensive duplication of efforts.

A new project has recently been formulated with the support of the UK Overseas Development Administration (ODA) that aims to do some stocktaking to consider the effectiveness of the various programmes that have occurred since the mid-1979s, and outline some future directions in this critically important subject (DMC 1992).

Temporary accommodation for families without housing loss following earthquakes

Following any major earthquake some dwellings will be damaged, but will remain inhabitable. However with persistent aftershocks there are serious risks for people sleeping in such dwellings, since the weakened structure may easily collapse in severe aftershocks to cause further casualties. The public is often reluctant to go back to their houses for a considerable length of time due to the fear of aftershocks.

Previous studies of emergency shelter needs have often underestimated this special sheltering category which requires further analysis. However pending

13

further study it is already aparent that shelter policies within preparedness plans must recognize this need and plan accordingly.

Cultural dynamics of post-earthquake shelter and housing

After a typical disaster there is a strong desire on the part of the authorities to restore normality, to clear away the mess, to rehouse families who lost their homes, to improve safety, and to rebuild the economy. Such processes are largely physical activities that can be observed, measured and photographed, and as such are very important to politicians. However, there are a whole series of equally critical social, psychological and cultural recovery processes to be undertaken in parallel with more tangible activities, but these are often seriously neglected. Many relate to shelter and housing and include such concerns as:

- restoration of the social and cultural identity of the settlement
- factors which relate to the location of post-disaster shelters and settlements relative to their previous location, the workplace and economic activities of the inhabitants, and the social and cultural patterns of neighbourhoods
- the therapeutic value of families that have suffered losses being involved in decision-making on aspects of reconstruction that concern them, and their participation in the physical rebuilding process
- the size of plots on which houses are placed to enable future adaptations and growth to facilitate social and economic security of the families
- consideration of not only the technical aspects of reconstruction but also the social and cultural acceptability of sites, designs, materials etc. to the occupants (Aysan and Oliver 1987).

Mitigation and future urban development

Specific attention should be drawn to the importance of *integrating* other areas of Government and community policies (at all levels) with policies for disaster prevention and reduction. In other words policy conflicts should be identified and mechanisms for reducing them should be focused upon to ensure that the conditions for disaster are not exacerbated by policies designed to pursue other priorities (Parker 1991).

Any development plan has to incorporate risk reduction measures and vice-versa any disaster mitigation programme has to incorporate long-term development issues. This reality is a key issue that needs to be continually brought before Governments allocating land to cope with the twin pressures of rapid urbanization and population growth. Therefore much more effort is needed to incorporate disaster preparedness and mitigation measures into programmes such as the upgrading of squatter settlements and urban and rural housing projects.

An implication for agencies and development planners is to link risk reduction strategies to long-term development plans which emphasize balanced growth, and ecologically sound habitation for human settlements.

In the above topics an attempt has been made to look at some of the 'processes' that need to be studied if risks are to be reduced or effective shelter (or sheltering) is to occur.

The needs are: to recognize and plan within a dynamic situation in both pre- and post-disaster situations; to consider shelter and housing as a complex process, largely managed by the surviving community, needing support but not to be supplanted by external bodies.

The Need for Realism in Disaster Planning for Shelter and Housing

Risk assessment

The starting point for realistic disaster planning is an accurate assessment of risks and resources. If either risks or resources are over or underestimated officials rapidly move into the world of 'Alice in Wonderland', but it is a rather more dangerous world than Lewis Carroll's version.

Due to the political dynamics that require tangible evidence of concern, donor countries as well as non-Governmental organizations have traditionally been more enthusiastic to invest in visible mitigation and preparedness *measures* rather than to devote money to the vital process of risk *assessment*. Therefore Governments and NGO groups need encouragement to consider spending a considerable ratio of their disaster assistance allocations on ways to analyse and monitor hazards and ever changing patterns of vulnerability. To be effective this process has ultimately to occur at the local level.

Without such proper risk analysis it is possible that precious funds may be wasted on inappropriate forms of protection. Typical examples could include: levels of protection which may be unrealistically high or low, failure to recognize particularly dangerous locations and mitigation that fails to take account of the most dangerous hazards whilst addressing lesser risks to satisfy powerful sectional interests.

Resource assessment is the complementary process that should follow risk assessment. This review will need to include an examination, in all vulnerable areas, of such resources as cash, goods, expertise, leadership, disaster preparedness, enabling legislation, appropriate local institutions and local 'coping abilities'.

Advice may be needed on how to undertake this type of assessment, but in addition it is vital that disaster-prone countries are made aware of the likely type and scale of assistance that may be forthcoming from assisting bodies.

IAN DAVIS and YASEMIN AYSAN

Realistic standards for risk reduction

Since global vulnerability is increasing due to such macro-forces as urbanization, deforestation and population growth, the range of mitigation measures, however useful and essential, are unlikely to have a significant effect on the overall global reduction of casualties and property losses. In addition it may be the case that resources are reducing for this protection due to tight constraints on aid budgets. Therefore, standards of mitigation need to be focused and realistic. Three approaches are suggested:

1. Prioritization of intervention areas; e.g. high-risk areas, buildings, groups
2. Reduction of utopian standards, costing too much, or too high a ratio of the cost of a given building, to a lower standard of protection, possibly aiming for safe collapse, where appropriate (the Core-House project in the Philippines, where one section of the dwelling, used for sleeping purposes, is stronger than other sections is a useful example of this process)
3. Aiming for standards of safety that are not only affordable but also acceptable to the occupants of vulnerable buildings and areas.

Frequent, low damage potential or infrequent high damage potential disaster risk

Advice is needed to establish the most effective focus for disaster reduction effort. E. Gruntfest and J. Huber of the University of Colorado have posed the question whether Governments should address more frequent events as well as the rare, devastating disasaters that capture public attention:

When there are limited resources the question has to be faced whether it is reasonable and cost effective in all cases to protect against extremely rare events when perhaps more lives can be saved by reducing the risk from more common environmental extremes (Gruntfest and Huber 1991).

The answers to such dilemmas may lie within the process of economic analysis using a cost-benefit approach, but a recent study indicated that as yet very few countries in these regions are using economic appraisal techniques in risk assessment (Asian Development Bank 1991). The issue relates to economic viability of protection standards of a small dwelling in terms of a complex equation that relates the lifespan of a building to a hazard return period.

Realistic understanding of rural and urban variables

It has been frequently noted that much of the literature on 'Disasters and the Small Dwelling' has had a strong rural bias, therefore without the participants to the 1978 conference recognizing the bias, advice was offered that was particularly appropriate to rural conditions with tacit, and largely false

16

assumptions that land was universally plentiful and that dwellings were likely to be occupied by their owners.

It took the major earthquakes in Mexico City and San Salvador, in 1985 and 1986, to bring home the harsh economic vulnerability of highly congested urban areas with vulnerable tenant occupiers of dwellings of uncertain safety, landless families living in squatter settlements and the key issue of inequitable patterns of land tenure. Fred Cuny wrote on these variables in 1987 and suggested that the problem of the loss of property and reconstruction in such contexts was primarily an economic problem:

[T]he majority of people affected are the poor. For the poor, disasters represent lost property, jobs, and economic opportunity. In real terms they can represent an enormous economic setback. Therefore, reconstruction assistance should be designed to: relieve the economic strain and reduce the cost of reconstruction; inject capital into the community; create employment opportunities; [and] support and strengthen existing economic enterprises (Cuny 1987).

Therefore, in the light of rapid urbanization pressures, there has been an important corrective emphasis in the past decade to focus on urban vulnerability in lieu of the previous preoccupation with rural conditions. Long overdue attention has been given to poor quality urban housing, whether within high rise tenements, inner city areas or squatter settlements in detailed planning. This expanded focus will draw in the issue of rented property, landlessness and the consequence of pressure on available safe land.

Realism in the re-allocation of resources

Disaster studies have tended to follow finance and political interest, therefore it is not surprising that immediate shelter provision, as an integral element of relief provision, has always occupied the 'high profile' position in the priority of Governments and has thus attracted far greater interest than reconstruction.

Despite an important study of Reconstruction Planning in the mid-1970s (Haas, Kates *et al.* 1977) there has been minimal serious study of Post-Disaster Reconstruction needs. A conference on the subject was held in the National Centre for Earthquakes Engineering Research in 1989 with the collaboration of the Disaster Management Centre of Oxford Polytechnic.

It is hoped that further study of reconstruction will follow and that it will identify – through analysis of a range of case studies – what resources were needed at what stage of reconstruction. Conversely it will be equally vital to learn negative lessons that concern the implication of cash or material resources *not* being available at critical phases of recovery and reconstruction.

The very tight constraints of disaster mitigation require an extremely realistic appraisal of the asssociated problems. This section of our paper has emphasized the need for realism in lieu of false optimism. This approach is likely to find favour with authorities with limited resources to deploy in order to achieve maximum results.

The Need to Develop, Retain and Apply Knowledge

Currently research in the field of disaster planning in developing countries is very limited and what there is tends to be concentrated on understanding hazards such as the massive US$ 140 million research programme in progress in Bangladesh to understand the dynamics of flood action as a prelude to a concerted programme of international assistance to reduce flood risk throughout the country. In the field of building, with certain notable exceptions, research has followed investment priorities. Therefore there has been extensive research on the performance of engineered structures to resist seismic or high wind forces.

In the sphere of disaster assistance, whilst there is a rapid increase in the development of national centres to coordinate disaster response, as well as a wide range of new training initiatives, there is a very serious research gap.

For example, during the past decade it is probable that millions of dollars have been spent on emergency shelter and temporary housing. Further millions have also been spent on the housing of refugees. The policies that have been followed in both cases have probably been based on advice contained in guidelines which were based on fragments of research rather than on any comprehensive and systematic research programmes. We had the privilege to be associated with both the UNDRO guidelines on 'Shelter after Disaster' as well as the guidelines on 'Refugee Assistance', and in both cases the documents were based on limited evidence that relates to knowledge gained during the 1970s not the 1980s.

The implications of this situation are very serious, since current policies and procedures may be erected on assumptions and limited evidence, with a possible consequence of waste, inappropriate assistance and the risk of unnecessary human distress.

Transfer of useful knowledge

First impressions would suggest that there is likely to be minimal value in transferring ideas that relate to small dwellings and shelter from the First to the Third World. However it is clear that despite obvious resource differentials, there are some aspects in the management of 'domestic hazards' in Europe, Australia, Japan and North America that relate to much poorer countries.

There is some need to document the experience from 'the developed countries' in a format that provides usable ideas on such aspects as: the development of legislation to promote building byelaws; the role of insurance in mitigation; data collection; warning systems; coordination of related bodies; risk assessment techniques; structural and non-structural mitigation measures including community awareness programmes.

Whilst this documentation may well be known to sections of the 'in-country' scientific community it is unlikely to be familiar to policy makers developing local preparedness plans. By adopting a case-study approach a candid appraisal could be undertaken of both negative as well as positive learning experiences.

Commonalities and differentials

Whilst there are the obvious differences between hazard types and their impact characteristics, there are also important similarities. Therefore a generic approach is needed in scientific enquiry on ways to reduce risks that continually looks for opportunities to establish linkages whenever they are appropriate. For example, the experience of warning systems for flood risk may be transferable to cyclone prone areas and the development of safety legislation, and land use planning controls to reduce seismic risk may provide lessons that are applicable to the development of a legal framework to reduce flood impact.

Perhaps the IDNDR will break down some professional barriers and thus facilitate this transfer of ideas between 'hazard communities' as well as between the frequently isolated worlds of research, policy development and practice.

Application of existing knowledge

Whilst new research is always required it is important to determine why so much knowledge concerning preparedness and mitigation relative to small dwelling safety is lost, or is known but not put into practice. An understanding of the constraints and opportunities to the implementation of existing knowledge can be valuable in focusing future research to practical ends.

A critical review of this question could reduce some of the very serious wastage of research findings and free blockages. Procedures could be developed to preserve institutional memories within Governments/NGOs in order to implement existing, well proven measures to reduce risks.

Conclusion

Policy changes within the field of Disaster Management mainly reflect:

- the impact of politics, at local, national and international levels
- funding priorities that can change as frequently as the tide
- fashionable areas of interest for donors

• the direct learning experiences of a given agency in a past disaster situation.

These factors do not inspire an optimistic view that the coming decade will be an advance on the previous twelve years that were reviewed in the 'Disasters and Small Dwelling' conference.
There are certain conclusions to be made:

• the non-Governmental Development Agencies have largely vacated the field of low-cost housing or reconstruction planning. This widespread withdrawal has been made on the grounds of cost – but the policy needs to be reappraised since Governments may benefit from the challenge of NGO innovation
• in view of frequent politicized decision-making in shelter and housing provision, technical advice, based on well researched findings, is absolutely vital in all aspects of this subject
• more resources are needed in the field of preventative action and long-term reconstruction. Some of this may be relocated from resources allocated to excessive provision of temporary shelter and temporary housing
• a priority issue concerns training at all levels: improvements are needed in technical training of public officials in such matters as the assessment, management and evaluation of shelter and housing requirements.

Returning to the opening quotation of 1978, it is apparent that there is *still* a need to promote the three primary concerns. But in the intervening years the problem has increased. *Now* there are infinitely more disaster victims (and survivors) due to population and urbanization pressures and patterns of shelter and housing provision. This paper has made a plea for mitigation, shelter and housing to be seen within a broad context, described in this paper as a 'process view'; realism is needed to avoid delusion and failure and the lack of research in these uncharted areas poses a very serious problem.

IDNDR offers the opportunity to focus on these topics. They may not be particularly glamorous subjects for funding agencies and Governments and agencies, but we firmly believe that if these issues are addressed during the decade, lives will be saved, distress reduced and the property of unfranchised occupants of small dwellings protected.

Acknowledgements

Since 1978 we have worked within the Disasters and Settlements Unit (DSU), which changed its name in 1987 to the Disaster Management Centre (DMC). During the decade we have greatly valued the support and insights of many students and colleagues who have contributed to various aspects of this subject – they include:

Andy Clayton, Alistair Cory, Joy Cypriano, Miranda Dandoulaki, Fatiha

Haddar, Andrew Maskrey, Wu Qingzhou, Stuart Lewis, Paul Oliver, Mokhtar Paki Pudnek, Gustavo Wilches-Chaux and Peter Winchester.

Since 1982, over 200 participants from various disaster-prone countries have attended the Disaster Management Workshops run by the DMC at Oxford Polytechnic. Their experiences have been invaluable in shaping our perception of the subject.

References

ANDERSON, M.B. and WOODROW, P.J. (1989), 'A Framework for Analyzing Capacities and Vulnerabilities', *Rising from the Ashes, Development Strategies in Times of Disaster*, Westview Press, Boulder and San Francisco and UNESCO, Paris.

ANDERSON, M.B. (1990) *Analyzing the Costs and Benefits of Natural Disaster Responses in the Context of Development*, Environmental Working Paper No. 29, The World Bank, Washington DC, USA.

AYSAN, Y. and OLIVER, P. (1987) *Housing and Culture after Earthquakes: A Guide for Future Policy Making on Housing in Seismic Areas*, Prepared for the Overseas Development Administration (ODA), Oxford Polytechnic, Oxford.

CUNY, F.C. (1987) 'Sheltering the Urban Poor: Lessons and Strategies of the Mexico City and San Salvador Earthquakes', *Open House International* (3): 16–20.

DAVIS, I. (ed.) (1981) 'Disasters and Settlements: Towards an Understanding of the Key Issues', *Disasters and the Small Dwelling*, Pergamon Press, Oxford, UK.

DAVIS, I. and GUPTA, S.P. (1991) 'Vulnerability Analysis', *Disaster Mitigation in Asia and the Pacific*, Asian Development Bank (ADB), Technical Background Paper.

GRUNTFEST, E. and HUBER, J. (1991) contribution to *An Appraisal of Priority Concerns for the International Decade for Natural Disaster Reduction (IDNDR)*, DMC and Flood Hazard Research Centre, Middlesex Polytechnic. (Unpublished)

HAAS, E., KATES, R.W. and BOWDEN, M.J. (1977) *Reconstruction Following Disaster*, MIT Press, Cambridge, Mass., USA.

NOJI, E.K. (1989) 'Training in Search and Rescue Teams for Constructal Collapse Events: A Multi-disciplinary Approach', *Modern Disaster Medicine*, Proceedings of the Asian-Pacific Conference on Disaster Medicine, Herusu Publishing Co. Inc.

PARKER, D. (1991) contribution to *An Appraisal of Priority Concerns for the International Decade for Natural Disaster Reduction (IDNDR)*, DMC and Flood Hazard Research Centre, Middlesex Polytechnic. (Unpublished)

QUARANTELLI, E.L. (1982) *Sheltering and Housing After Major Community Disasters: Case Studies and General Observations*, Federal Emergency Management Agency, Washington DC, USA. (Lucid discussions on Terminology, Emergency Sheltering, Temporary Sheltering, Temporary Housing, and Permanent Housing are on pages 73–80.)

UNDRO (1982) 'Section 3.6: Shelter Strategies', *Shelter after Disaster: Guidelines for Assistance*, United Nations, New York.

Note

Disaster Management Centre (DMC). In March 1992 a meeting was convened in Oxford to review international progress in the field of Building Improvement Programmes. This was part of a joint DMC and Cambridge Architectural Research (CAR) project funded by the Overseas Development Administration (ODA).

CHAPTER 4

Review of Twelve Years' Experience of Disasters and Small Dwellings

FRED CUNY

INTERTECT, USA

Introduction

This paper provides a framework for looking at the question of disaster and the small dwelling; we need to get beyond just thinking about world housing and small buildings and looking at housing for the poor. This paper looks at milestones or lessons and talks about some of the gaps that still exist, then examines some research and action priorities for the next decade.

Some of our concepts of a few years ago are getting grey and some of our attitudes are getting stale. One of the problems in the last few years is that there haven't been a lot of new recruits or new ideas coming in. Who are the people that are challenging us, as we challenged Russel and other people? One problem is that we haven't engaged the young people who come in. There are some notable exceptions – people like Jolyon Leslie and others who have been out with Oxfam and other groups. But a lot of the same names keep reappearing in the last decade: we need to get some new blood now. There's also been a major shift since 1978 when the action was with the local NGOs who were doing the really exciting stuff on housing. They were trying to bring in social anthropological issues and scale the attention down to realistic approaches. That seems to have died out, and there's more emphasis now on Governments picking up the housing field. There's been some very interesting programmes – Gustavo Wilches-Chaux and Popayán probably being the key ones. There have been many others that have been led by Governments which picked up on some of the ideas of the NGOs, but NGOs are no longer the centre of the action and Governments are becoming aware and taking interest. It is ultimately their responsibility to provide the funding so that more people can take advantage of the different types of programme. We have to restructure our thinking about how Governments work and find new ways to involve NGOs and Governments in a better dialogue. This is going to be difficult, given the problems of many of the Governments we have to deal with in the Third World.

Another shift is that we are moving to economic based programmes, because of the USA and other western countries pushing for more market orientated economy in many of the formerly socialist countries and those that had ties with the East. More of the interesting housing is market driven. We want to number the role of the market in the housing system, and how we intervene through markets without dealing directly with the builders perhaps, but try to make more materials available through alternate ways.

There is a shift of emphasis away from rural areas to urban areas, largely because this is where the disasters were situated; for example in the 1970s the disaster of Guatemala was predominantly a rural disaster. In the 1980s the disasters were Popayán, an urban area, the Armenian earthquake, which has been essentially Spitak, though there were associated rural areas, and Mexico City: all were predominantly urban problems. So most of the emphases have been changing to providing housing for the poor in the urban zone.

Another major change is the increasing use of computers, which has enabled us to focus on the need for information gathering. We used to decry the problems of people not getting enough information and now we're getting almost an information overload. The problem has been to use computers in a way that enables us to support decisions. Work has been done at OAS to try and increase the familiarity of all the groups with what you can do with such a simple system, the databases and so forth. However, we don't forget the people in the process.

A further major shift has been the decline of emphasis on urban building. In the 1978 papers on disasters everyone was focusing on the Doby; out of that grew the conference in 1981 on urban buildings in seismic areas. A research programme at different levels funded the Doby network, and there was a lot of emphasis on trying to improve low quality buildings. However we weren't able to sustain interest, Governments weren't interested in finishing it and people didn't want that sort of housing. The emphasis moved to cement block houses. People want block structures, because they perceive them as being safer, of better material and so forth. There is also more work on the periphery: people are no longer focusing on the house and on the way they provide the house. They're looking at the associated areas of the economics of housing and the risks associated with it, and a lot of work is going into the broader areas without focusing on the central object. We don't find as much interest in looking at housing *per se* as there was ten years ago.

People want to look at the whole community, how it works and how it provides housing and homes to people. This does reflect the growing awareness of the socio-economic and political environment in which we

24

operate. However, we must also continue to look at the structure itself, at ways to improve it and at ways of getting that information to the people who need it, when they need it.

Milestones

If you look back over the last ten years there have been some very interesting milestones in terms of programmes.

Popayán

Popayán was probably the best example of where ideas from previous disasters were incorporated. Gustavo did a fantastic job in bringing together a good team, of training them quickly, of getting out to the field and helping people build houses. And the Government took responsibility for a housing-education approach, getting information to people, putting decision-making in their hands and giving them the technical support to pull off the upgrading of structures. This was a real milestone that encouraged everyone.

Yemen

Yemen proved that NGOs can still have an impact. It was a good programme that produced a lot of technical papers, together with a validation of some concepts and a questioning of old concepts. It focused attention on the issue of the maintenance of buildings, that buildings are never static – if you build an earthquake resistant house one year, then ten years later because of modifications it may no longer be earthquake resistant: what is the role of ageing in buildings? Yemen was an excellent bit of work and it is another one we need to look at.

Mexico City

The Mexico City, and to a lesser extent, the San Salvador earthquakes were also milestones, in terms of what happened in the state of the art. We began focusing here on the problem of urban tenements, structures that are not owned by the poor but by a few very wealthy slumlords. How do we assemble land? How do we address these problems? How do we provide the financing? We learned some very painful lessons about expropriation in Mexico City. Unfortunately we learned that you don't do it in El Salvador – you're going to create problems. It opened far more questions than we've been able to answer and is a milestone for looking at that type of problem in other countries.

FRED CUNY

Armenia

Armenia wasn't really a milestone as far as small buildings were concerned, except in one area, and that is when the mass-produced, high-rise buildings failed, it forced a scaling down of the type of architecture used in reconstruction. This is an interesting area that we should be looking at. People in Armenia will no longer accept high-rise buildings that are shoddily built, and the Government has been forced to build smaller lower rise buildings. Even today, Armenians are not happy with the four-storey buildings that they have – they would like to have single-storey, detached buildings. How do we meet those needs after a major catastrophe like Armenia? Many countries in the same zone on both sides of the Soviet border also have similar building types that could be vulnerable.

Lastly in terms of milestones are the continuing conflicts around the world – Lebanon, Afghanistan, Sri Lanka, Iran–Iraq. We learned a lot there about how difficult it is to provide reconstruction when wars continue. In Sri Lanka we decided not to do relief programmes but go directly into reconstruction while the war was still under way, and try to identify areas of relative tranquility where we could provide resources to use reconstruction as a means of reducing the number of people who might be involved in a conflict. It may appear close to pacification but we were able to put 100,000 people back to work and begin a reconstruction process indirectly by the jobs and economic approach. We need to look more at dealing with conflicts and how we cope with reconstruction afterwards, especially in a situation where hundreds of homes have been destroyed.

Governments simply do not have the resources to rebuild those houses – there's got to be self-help, self-financed reconstruction effort, and we need to know a lot more about this: there are some good case studies of those conflicts mentioned.

Progress Report of Last Decade

I mentioned several major problems that I saw in 1978, which I'll now review quickly and see what progress has been made.

The first problem was the failure to understand the complexities relating to housing and shelter. In 1978 we were talking about architecture, and how to build a better house, and advocating more of a human approach. In 1990 we're still talking about the human element but more and more we're looking at economic questions. Probably because of the shift in political regimes, people are looking more at market driven societies and market driven housing systems: we need to go back and look at the entire process.

In 1978 there was a search for a universal housing solution, trying to find the shelter that everyone would be able to use in different parts of the world. In

1990 most of the organisations have some sort of universal programme to find a framework under which we can provide housing around the world. AID, ODA, UNDP and others are now trying to come up with a programmatic framework for providing disaster assistance. This is a very dangerous thing just like the universal solution for architecture – it's not going to work. We need people who can work with Governments and in the local society, who can say this is really the best way to approach the problem, given the social and economic fabric.

In 1978, another problem was the failure to distinguish between natural disasters and conflict, and that approaches designed for shelter after war were often used to provide shelter in the aftermath of disasters. It's still a problem, for example in Armenia, with the attempt to provide tents which were useless, then different types of shelter, and so on, but there is a scaling down of that type of thing. What they've moved on to is not necessarily better. AID no longer gives tents, they give plastic, but there is a rethinking here and we are beginning to see some change.

In 1978 there was a failure to understand the linkages between disasters and development. In the 1990s everyone is talking about disasters and development. It has become a popular phrase and a lot of books are being written about it. However, the same old programmes are sometimes being justified as development programmes when in fact they are the same thing: what do we mean by development? What do we mean by the process of housing?

In 1978 there was a failure of agencies to cooperate and share data. The whole trend has been to form consortiums, especially among the NGOs, and it has been very positive in every field except housing. In famine and food supply operations, everybody's sharing resources and personnel and integrating their services. But when it comes to a major earthquake, each agency still wants to go out and build its own houses and complexes. This is a major problem that NGOs have and one of the reasons they are not as active: they do two or three programmes, spend a lot of money and get a few structures and then they are out of business. When someone evaluates it and tells them what a terrible job it is, they give up on it.

In 1978 people didn't take a very sophisticated approach to the problems of housing and community development; they wanted to simplify it to a point where it was virtually meaningless. This is declining. People are now talking about integrated programmes. We need more work to make these programmes truly integrated and also need to be looking at more indirect ways of reaching people. But the expertise is now there and it has been one of the good things about the work.

Evaluations are not carried out frequently enough and are not carried out with criteria that really mean anything. Some evaluations recently were worthless. You've got to have a clear understanding that if you're going in to evaluate a building you've got to look at the concepts. The biggest problem is that it threatens people, especially people who've done it for the first time.

They feel proud of what they've done and then someone comes in with this tough evaluation and starts asking questions and nobody wants to hear the answers.

Gaps in the system

Some of the 1978 gaps in the system still exist and are very serious.

The first is an overall failure of the humanitarian system. In 1978 we talked about the problems of reaching people. Today, the biggest problem is that this system itself is about to collapse. There are so many needs that we don't have enough people at a local and international level who are willing to dedicate themselves to this area, and if you look at the international humanitarian architecture, it's falling apart. There are so many gaps, so many people fall through the system. For example housing handled by AID, where the office of housing doesn't do housing. What it does is that it guarantees housing through arranging market loans for people or Governments to come and borrow money. And there's been a real problem trying to get the US Government's aid programme actually to deal with the construction of buildings, building standards and building codes. Some NGOs promote services in a very limited area; the big UN bureaucracies are very slow and allow a lot of people to fall through the cracks, and certain target groups such as displaced persons don't fall into anybody's category. There are major gaps in our system and we need to rethink the whole humanitarian architecture that we have and make it more responsive to people's needs.

The second thing we need in this system failure is a better way for Governments and NGOs to interface. Right now there's an almost adversarial relationship between them. In every country I'm working in, NGOs are having problems. The UN doesn't give them much support, in fact the UN likes to push them out and use them as a lightning rod to see how much strike they can get. And sometimes they get struck pretty hard. A number of NGOs have been kicked out of countries because they were trying to help people: it's going to continue to be a problem. We have to find a better way of protecting the NGOs and find ways of getting Governments to react in a more positive manner to them so that the expertise that's there can get into Government programmes.

Research institutions are still not properly focused. There is certainly a need for far more information on sociological and economic aspects but there are still some areas within the structural aspects where we need more information. The decade has been a general failure in trying to focus people, by taking a much more 'shot-gun' approach to the situation. It's going to be up to us to focus the institutions.

Declining NGO inputs is another gap. NGOs have failed in this decade to continue to push in the area of housing. It's also, to a large extent, because of declining contributions world-wide to NGOs and a problem of the types of structures that encourage that sort of thing. They don't have the resources they did. However, there's been a real abandonment of many of the things that started in the 1970s, and NGOs need to be putting some money into research and questioning their programmes and evaluating them.

A gap mentioned earlier is the need for new blood. Not necessarily here among us but what about the Third World? Where are we going to get these people involved in the problem? Where are the people who are going to follow Gustavo, the people who are going to be coming out of Mexico? How do we capture these people, bring them into the system and let them develop local solutions?

Another gap is urban reconstruction. Unfortunately, we've still not redressed the major problems of land, the questions of urban areas, how to capacitate people to build sophisticated structures or have control over the building process. There's been some interesting proposals though many have been shot down by Governments or the bureaucracies at UN level. The problem of urban disasters, especially in the earthquake area, is going to be a major one for us to contend with in the upcoming decades. Vulnerability is increasing at a phenomenal rate. Major cities in Latin America today are categorised as an earthquake risk if they are on the western side of Central America. Large areas of Asia are under earthquake risk, many of which are not recognised. For example many people think there is no earthquake risk in Dhaka, but there have been some tremendous earthquakes in there. If you look at the types of buildings they have, the low quality masonry structures, then if there is an earthquake in the wet season, when there is a lot of loose soil on the surface, there would be major problems in Dhaka, probably hundreds of thousands of people killed or injured. We need to be focusing on how we're going to deal with those types of situations.

CHAPTER 5

The Global Vulnerability

GUSTAVO WILCHES-CHAUX
SENA, Popayán, Colombia

Introduction

This paper is a summary of a chapter of my book *Desastres, Ecologismo y Formación Professional* (Disasters, Ecology and Training) published in 1989 by SENA, a Colombian Government training agency for which I worked for twelve years as Regional Manager in the Departamento del Cauca, a region in the south-west of Colombia. The book is part of a 'Tools for Crisis' project which I have been involved with since the earthquake that destroyed my native town, Popayán, the capital city of Cauca, in March 1983. The purpose of the project is to develop a 'tool box' of environmental, education, and community training and development concepts, which will help individuals or communities facing crises to cope better and produce positive answers to these situations. We based the project on the Chinese approach towards crisis, which can be simultaneously or alternatively Danger *and* Opportunity, depending on the human ability to react to the hazard. The 'tools' are to be developed and tested in four crisis 'territories':

- natural disasters
- death by terminal disease (like AIDS or cancer)
- violence
- drug addiction.

Three factors allow us to compare the four given 'territories' in this project:

- they are all present in our daily life, not only in Colombia, but also in our local region: they are all symptoms and results of our vulnerability as a society;

- they are all the product of our social incapacity to transform our cultural patterns in a suitable way as an answer to changing situations;
- when there is a crisis in one of those 'territories', the 'solution' has normally been brought from outside the 'system' (individual or community) instead of reinforcing the system's own tools for coping.

It is possible to find similarities between, for example, the 'processing of information' by a person suffering cancer, and by a community living in a disaster-prone area.

Stewart Alsop wrote that a terminal cancer patient has the right to receive *all* the information that he asks for, but *only* the information that he asks for, meaning that each person has the ability to process in a given time a certain amount and quality of information but no more. The responsibility of the 'outer agent' is to interpret this ability of the patient and to deliver the information in such a way that he can make constructive use of it. Working with communities near active volcanoes in Colombia, we have seen on several occasions how the same information, given using different words and metaphors, produces different reactions. We have worked with journalists, authorities and with the people themselves, to analyse those reactions and the communication patterns that provoke them.

Language – including the metaphors used to describe the crisis and our own position in it – is a major factor in selecting the route of danger or the route of opportunity. There is a well-known story about a shoemaker who sent two of his sellers to find new markets for his products in an isolated Third World region. One day he received a telegram from one of the sellers saying: 'Nothing to do. Nobody uses shoes.' The next day he received the following telegram from the other seller: 'Excellent possibilities. Everybody is barefoot.'

The role of external intervention in any of the four 'territories' could either help people suffering crisis to cope independently or make them more dependent and hence weaker: foreign agencies' agents in a natural disaster scenario may work to reinforce the local coping mechanisms, as a doctor may work to reinforce his patient's own immune system. Or both of them can use their knowledge and technology to replace the community's or the patient's own ability to recover by themselves, observing their own priorities and according to their own (and not the foreigners') world view.

This 'Tools for Crisis' project was born out of our need as mere citizens, Government officers, NGOs, workers and educators, to face the current Colombian crisis of which we are all participants. We have expanded the project in our work with former guerrilleros who signed peace agreements with the Government and are now in a process of readapting to 'civil' life, and with victims of drug addiction or violence in its multiple forms, which is the worst disaster striking Colombia today.

The approach to 'The Global Vulnerability' that we summarize in this paper shows a pattern of work that we use with communities in disaster prone

31

regions. This is a 'tool' of particular – but not exclusive – importance in the 'territory' of natural disasters. We motivate local leaders, local authorities, students and teachers, workers and housewives, to make their own global vulnerability analysis and to understand it as a complex and dynamic system of which they themselves and their cultural and social patterns are active elements. And we invite them to find in their own social and cultural living heritage, most of the tools that they need to cope in a crisis situation or to mitigate their vulnerability.

As far as we are part of the same global crisis, our principal and permanent challenge is to test those tools in our own ability to keep on going despite the situation of violence surrounding us.

Where Do Disasters Come From?

Disasters can be seen as the product of two factors: risk and vulnerability

Although there are almost as many definitions as authors, for the purpose of this paper we will consider that a *risk* is any natural or man-made event which affects a community which is then not able to adapt itself to the new environment, modified by this event, or which is not able to cope with its consequences without suffering major traumas in its physical, social or economical structures, or in the life, health and property of its inhabitants. That is: a vulnerable community.

In many cases events which are apparently caused by nature – and so may be regarded as 'natural' risks – are the result of human activities. For example, floods or droughts are usually caused by deforestation, poor soil management, human caused erosion, etc. Forest fires can be both natural or man-made.

As *vulnerability* we will consider the fact that a community is not able to modify itself in order to absorb the changes in the outer environment or in its own internal structure. Vulnerability will then be synonymous with weakness, lack of flexibility or failure in adaptation.

The concepts of risk and vulnerability cannot be considered in isolation from one another. An event will be a risk only if it happens in a community which is vulnerable to this particular event, and vulnerabilities always occur where particular risks are present. For example, a community in the Colombian Pacific Coast can be vulnerable to the risk of fire because its buildings are made of wood, but not to the risk of earthquakes, which are common in the region, because wood structures happen to be light and flexible. When people start building their houses in brick and cement (heavy and rigid materials) in order to reduce their vulnerability to fires, they become more vulnerable to earthquakes.

Even light rain can be a risk for some low-income communities in Lima (Peru), whose houses are not designed to withstand rain, but heavy rain will just be a normal, natural event for Indian communities in the Amazon Basin, adapted to live under this particular condition.

The Global Vulnerability

Vulnerability must be seen as a complex and dynamic system. I am proposing eleven different points of view to approach this system in each particular community. It is important to underline that those *are not* different kinds of vulnerability, but different points of view, different approaches to a single but complex system in which all the elements are strongly inter-related.

Natural vulnerability

All living beings, including human beings, are vulnerable by the very fact of being alive. Most life can exist only in a relatively narrow spectrum of temperature, humidity, atmospheric density and composition, environmental radiations, etc. Day-by-day natural ecosystems are growing weaker in terms of their loss of genetic diversity: the more variety, the more ability of adaptation and hence the less vulnerability to environmental changes. And the less vulnerable the ecosystem, the stronger the community which depends on it.

Physical vulnerability

This refers to the location of human settlements in disaster prone areas such as in the vicinity of active volcanoes, on top of active seismic faults, on the slope of landslide prone mountains or in the vicinity of flooding rivers.

It refers as well to the lack of adequate physical structures to withstand tremors or earthquakes. This fact is linked to the lack of building knowledge (technical vulnerability), lack of awareness (educative vulnerability) or lack of money to invest in proper structures (economic vulnerability).

For better or worse, vulnerability by location is always linked to economic reasons: people live in the vicinity of active volcanoes because it is a guarantee of fertile soil, and hence high income; or they live on landslide prone slopes or in flood prone areas because that is the cheapest land they can afford.

Economic vulnerability

This is the base of all vulnerability. It is well known that there is a relation between low income and vulnerability.

It has already been mentioned how physical vulnerability is linked with economy. Another example is drought: it will be a disaster only if the community which suffers it depends on rain to obtain its income. Each summer drought is a major disaster for single-crop peasants in the South-West of Colombia for which corn is their only source of income, while drought is the normal condition for oil barons in Texas or Arabia.

Social vulnerability

This makes reference to the fact that the stronger the social web within a society, the less vulnerable and the more able to recover is that society after a disaster. If social organizations in a community are root-based and representative, and if there are solid leadership patterns, it will be more able to evolve successfully in the face of internal or external hazards.

Political vulnerability

This refers to the autonomy of a community to participate in the process of decision-making which affects its own interests. Highly centralized Governments are surrounded by vulnerable communities.

Being a bit cynical, we can say that political vulnerability is also the incapability of a community to become a problem for others or for the central Government.

Technical vulnerability

We have already mentioned that it is the lack of technical knowledge or appliances which allow a community to avoid a risk. Seismic resisting structures (earthquakes), irrigation (floods) and early-warning systems (volcanic eruptions) are ways of mitigating those risks.

Ideologic vulnerability

The predominant world view among community members may do them weaker or stronger in front of certain given risks. If people believe that disasters are the will of God and nothing can be done to avoid them, their community will be more vulnerable than that in which members are well aware of the real causes of disasters. Ideologies can do a lot to prevent or make disasters worse.

Cultural vulnerability

Strongly linked with the former approaches, cultural vulnerability refers to the ruling values, social patterns and authority structures within a given society. The response to a risk or a disaster will be different in a community where solidarity is a shared value than in one where it is unknown: as it will be different in a community ruled by 'machismo', than in one where women and children have a choice.

Educative vulnerability

There is an incapability in the formal education systems to prepare community members for the real world. This is extremely grave in the Third World where education materials are often modelled – or even produced – to mirror industrial world patterns. The loss of traditional community knowledge, which is being replaced by foreign concepts, is a cause of identity crisis and growing vulnerability.

Ecological vulnerability

Highly vulnerable ecosystems are synonymous with highly risky ecosystems for the communities which directly harm them or, indirectly, for other communities. Floods in low lands are mostly caused by forest destruction in high lands. Mangroves destruction in coastal areas increases vulnerability to surges and tsunamis. Loss of biodiversity in tropical forests increases the risk of plagues. Deforestation, atmospheric pollution and the ozone layer destruction, increases the greenhouse effect and makes the whole human race more vulnerable to harmful radiations.

Institutional vulnerability

There is the case of the very exclusive social club that burned yet firemen were not allowed in . . . because they were not affiliated.

In many communities, laws, bureaucracy and formal procedures are so strong and rigid that they impede any flexibility and a fast and adequate response to new, unexpected – and even expected – situations. This is common wherever the external form is considered more important than the content.

CHAPTER 6

Materials and Construction Techniques for Disaster Protection

ROBIN SPENCE

The Martin Centre for Architectural and Urban Studies
University of Cambridge, UK

Introduction

I have been asked to assess the progress over the last twelve years in the field of materials and construction techniques for disaster protection for the small dwelling, and also to make some suggestions as to what needs to be tackled over the next ten years of the IDNDR.

Having spent the last twelve years surveying the disaster protection activity of others mostly from a secure academic base in the UK, I feel singularly poorly qualified to do either of these things. Before the 1978 conference I had not worked at all in disaster protection or relief, but primarily in development work on small-scale building materials in Africa and India, which makes it a little difficult to make an adequate assessment of progress.

Indeed, it seemed to me at the time that given the need in rural communities worldwide for improved techniques, the extraordinarily high level of interest on the part of development agencies and academics on the special situation of natural disasters, which I became aware of that time, was difficult to justify. And after a decade of working in the disaster field, I still believe there is a serious imbalance.

There is a natural tendency for those of us who see the Third World primarily through the news media to see it in terms of the dramatic events which catch the headlines rather than the slow creeping disaster of poverty. Voluntary development agencies get caught up in this because it is those same events which evoke the biggest response in the donating public. And academics tend to study problems for which research funding is available.

But every serious study of disaster vulnerability of the last ten years has been forced to the obvious conclusion that vulnerability is an adjunct of poverty, and that disaster-protection programmes which do not acknowledge this will be futile. It is generally true that the poorest are the most vulnerable: it is also true that in most cases they are quite well aware of their vulnerability – to cyclones, floods or earthquakes – and know at least some of the things that they could do to reduce their vulnerability. Usually they take the risks they do because economically it is their only option, or perhaps, like those who farm on the fertile slopes of active volcanoes, it is their best option.

We would probably all agree by now that what is most needed to make any significant impact on natural disasters is a general reduction in poverty leading to an increase in people's *options* to reduce their vulnerability – either to build improved dwellings and community defences or to relocate away from the vulnerable location. And there is growing evidence that the general development process is not always assisted by highlighting certain disaster areas (actual or potential) as targets for special development assistance. Indeed as Eric Dudley's paper (in this volume) has shown, it may easily be retarded by such activities. In this sense there is a concern that the whole objective of the IDNDR – which is to target resources specifically into disaster areas and disaster protection programmes – may be misdirected, if it merely diverts resources into this area rather than generating extra resources.

But the IDNDR is a fact and the aim of this conference should certainly not be to condemn it, but rather to suggest ways to make constructive use of the energies and resources which it can release. In this paper I want to look at some of the general trends of the last decade as they affect disaster vulnerability and try to suggest some ways in which we can go from here. Primarily the observations are drawn from looking at earthquake vulnerability and protection programmes, but the conclusions may be relevant to other types of disasters as well. I shall be concerned with long-term reconstruction or disaster protection rather than short-term relief.

General Trends

The last decade has been one of great activity at a theoretical and organisational development level, but unhappily one of comparatively little progress or increased security for potential disaster victims. Three broad general trends which can be identified over the period are:

- for the vast majority of the rural poor in the developing countries housing conditions are deteriorating rather than improving;
- intermediate technology has had little impact on building technology;
- urbanisation and modernisation have created new types and concentrations of disaster vulnerability.

Improvement of rural housing depends on the availability of cash income to purchase materials. There are some rural parts of the world where cash incomes have been increasing, notably in Asia, but in most developing countries they have been static or in decline for much of the last decade. Moreover pressure on the land from increasing population and deforestation are rapidly depleting the availability of the trees, plants and animal products which formerly provided free building materials. Timber for roofing, doors, furniture; grass or palm leaves for thatch; animal dung for flooring and plastering – these are in short supply because of growing demand, shrinking woodlands and competing other uses such as industrial demand or for use as fuel. Cash is now needed to obtain these materials or the manufactured alternatives such as cement, CGI roof sheets, burnt bricks and concrete blocks. And these materials have been rapidly escalating in price because of their energy and foreign exchange costs.

In terms of disaster resistance, the loss of the vegetable materials, particularly timber, has the further damaging consequence that it is these materials which help provide structural continuity and integrity to otherwise brittle mud and stone construction, and their loss increases the vulnerability of already vulnerable forms of construction. There is an urgent need to look for alternatives to these traditional energy absorbers.

In these circumstances it would be expected that *intermediate technologies* for building materials production would begin to be adopted – technologies which make little use of factory equipment or imported materials, but are based on local resources and skills, and have the potential to be self-replicating in relatively poor communities. In practice, although there are some exceptions which I will mention later, these intermediate technology materials have not yet made a significant impact. Technologies like fibre-concrete roofing, stabilised soil blocks, lime-pozzolana cements are well-established and have been shown to be successful and economically viable on a pilot-project level. Yet they do not seem to have begun to be used on a large scale away from the protective environment of the development project. New efforts to discover and define what is appropriate are needed. For the most part the gap in technological options between the traditional labour-intensive techniques and the modern factory-based materials remains as wide as ever.

It would be expected that the processes of urbanisation and modernisation would begin to lead a reduction in vulnerability, at least for those involved. Unfortunately this does not seem to be the case. New building technologies offer the potential for greater structural resistance – against earthquakes, high winds – but the evidence from many recent disasters – the Mexico City, Armenia and Iran earthquakes and the Jamaica hurricanes, for example – is that when these techniques are applied without a comparable understanding of the nature of the material, they can be lethal. Reinforced concrete frames with inadequate reinforcement or badly made concrete collapse quickly and catastrophically, high rise blocks of precast panel construction disintegrate, inadequately tied steel sheet roofs blow dangerously about. The skills needed to design and build safely with these materials are often missing. Likewise the processes of urbanisation force people to occupy land which is highly unsuitable for settlement because of its vulnerability to landslides, liquefaction or flooding; and to use cheap impermanent materials which are highly vulnerable to hazards such as fire, flooding or high winds. Over the last decade, urbanisation has dramatically changed both the nature of vulnerability and the scale of potential disasters.

Signs of Progress

Within this generally bleak overall picture there are some encouraging signs. Ten years is a short period of time in relation to the overall processes of economic and social development, so it is good to note that:

- there has been some progress in the development of viable low-cost alternative building materials;
- there is now a better understanding of the causes of the vulnerability of small dwellings and the means to counter it;
- there has been a significant shift from the view of housing as an entity to be provided towards seeing it as a process to be facilitated;
- there has been a substantial growth of international – and especially "south-south" – networking and technological dialogue.

Small-scale building materials

Two important new technologies have become firmly established over the last ten years – fibre concrete roofing and mini-cement. In 1978, fibre-concrete roofing was still at an early experimental stage. The successful use of natural fibres of local materials to replace the imported glass fibre originally used, and the shift from fragile sheets to more robust tiles, along with the development of locally manufactured forming and vibrating equipment has enabled this material to take off in a big way in one country – Kenya – and other countries are following.

Following years of development work starting in the 1960s, Indian industrialists have perfected a technology for producing Portland cement at scales down to 25 tonnes per day. The plants are cheap to build, simple to run, and can be established quickly on relatively small reserves of raw materials. The technology is rapidly gaining ground in India, with approaching 100 mini-plants in operation in 1988, and plants are now being established in other countries.

The progress of other materials has been less spectacular, but through the work of UNCHS, ITDG, Craterre, SKAT, Action-Aid and others technologies such as small-scale lime-burning, lime-pozzolana cement production, stabilised soil blockmaking, small-scale brick and tile-making, gypsum production have been further developed, tested, and many descriptive 'how-to' guides prepared.

The significance of all this work for disaster protection is that it is now possible to use the process of disaster reconstruction as an opportunity to introduce new or upgraded small-scale building materials manufacture to the damaged area rather than flooding it with imports. This happened to some extent in the Bangladesh and in Armenia, and is the approach recommended by the UN mission to Iran.

Understanding vulnerability and disaster resistance

Before 1978 there had been almost no systematic study of the vulnerability of small dwellings and how to reduce it. Razani's (1978) remarkable contribution to the conference was almost alone in the field. Compared with the immense amount of work on the more high-technology aspects of disaster protection – over 1000 papers at the 1988 Ninth World Conference on Earthquake Engineering, in Tokyo, for instance – the effort directed to the small dwelling is still pathetically small. But serious research has begun. Field missions to all the major damaging earthquakes of the last ten years have defined vulnerability in statistical terms, identified precise mechanisms of disintegration and collapse, and suggested remedies. Shaking table studies of alternative strengthening concepts have been carried out in India, Peru, Mexico, California, Turkey and China. Risk mitigation studies have been carried out in a number of high-risk areas. Cost benefit studies have shown that strengthening can be cost-effective in terms of saving future relief and reconstruction costs in addition to saving lives. And manuals or guides on how to strengthen existing buildings as well as how to build disaster-resistance into new small dwellings have been produced in many languages. In several municipalities in California regulations requiring the upgrading of particularly vulnerable buildings are in place and are being implemented, and other parts of the world are following.

There has also been progress in the recognition of the need for multi-disciplinary studies of housing in disaster areas. The 1980 Karakoram Project established a model for the simultaneous study of the technical, socio-economic and cultural dimensions of housing in high-risk areas, in which the conclusions of the individual teams within the study were profoundly influenced by the other disciplines involved. Similar studies were conducted in Southern Italy after the 1980 earthquake and in Eastern Turkey.

There is a growing awareness of the central importance of the protection of lifelines – roads, power and water-supply networks in particular – if small communities are to be able to recover rapidly from the effects of a disaster.

But the task is immense. Modern materials and forms of construction are international, and those building high-rise buildings with steel and reinforced concrete in Peru can assume that specifications developed in Europe are adequate. For the small dwelling and the small community each region has its own very distinct technology and often materials, the performance of which cannot be assumed to be the same as similar materials elsewhere. Cultural and socio-economic factors constrain the options for protection. There is an urgent need for more regionally based research on the types of dwelling lived in by the majority of the population to the exclusion of the more esoteric problems which are more likely to win international recognition. There is also a need for greatly expanded cross-disciplinary involvement in the planning of settlements and housing programmes.

Process versus product

Until the 1970s there was still an assumption that it was the function of the relief and reconstruction programmes to provide houses to replace those lost. The 1978 conference and many other studies since have shown the futility of this approach. It is now widely (but not yet universally) acknowledged that the most valuable role that relief agencies can play is to facilitate reconstruction – not so as to recreate the pre-existing situation, but in such a way as to improve the disaster resistance of the housing stock without changing its essential nature. Thus the training of builders has become a key activity of the relief agencies. This was the model presented at the 1978 conference by the Oxfam-World Neighbours programme in Guatemala, but the process has been further elaborated in more recent events. Two examples are worth looking at in some detail.

The Ecuador earthquakes of 5 March 1987 severely damaged rural housing over a wide area in the remote and sparsely populated Andean highlands. The predominant form of construction in the area is to use rammed earth walls, with a clay tile roof. The principal structural weakness of these dwellings was that the corners of the walls were inadequately bonded and fell out under the earthquake shaking, leaving the rest of the wall unrestrained; this resulted from the vertical joints being inadequately staggered, and being too close to the corners. An additional weakness is the lack of rigidity of the roof structure and a poor junction between roof and wall. A local voluntary agency devised a training programme for reconstruction based on a technology essentially the same as is traditionally used, but with simple modifications to eliminate the perceived weaknesses (Dudley 1988). The proposed solution to the corner problem was the introduction of an 'L'-shaped mould to cast the corners as a single monolithic unit (see Dudley, Figure 2, in this volume). One leg of the mould is twice the length of the other, so by flipping the mould on alternate layers a good well-staggered bond is created. The corner was chamfered on the inside to reduce the stress concentration arising from bending forces. Builders from the affected communities were trained in the construction and use of the

41

mould, and also shown how a roof can be built so that it is stronger, and how a ring beam can be provided set in a channel cut in the top of the earth wall. Using these techniques thousands of strengthened houses were rebuilt after the earthquake, with limited financial and technical assistance from voluntary agencies.

The earthquake which occurred in Dhamar Province of the Yemen Arab Republic on 13 December 1982 caused widespread damage and destruction in an area where the traditional form of construction is of stone masonry. Rural as well as urban houses are often two or more storeys high, with walls of rubble or dressed stone and timber floors and heavy flat timber roofs. OXFAM established a training programme for reconstruction, which, like that in Ecuador, was aimed at local builders, with the intention of introducing some simple techniques for strengthening houses, using locally available materials and skills (Leslie 1984). The principal causes of weakness in traditionally constructed dwellings were found to be at the wall-to-wall junctions where separation occurred, at the junctions of walls and roofs, where the timber joists separated from their supporting walls, and in the separation and disintegration of the masonry walls themselves, due to inadequate bonding. The training programme emphasised single storey building, and demonstrated techniques (such as better mortar, stone dressing and through bonding) for constructing a wall with better integrity and earthquake resistance. It also offered a range of techniques for both strengthening the corners and providing a ring beam to connect the tops of the walls and the roof. Over a period of two and a half years over 800 builders were trained, about 25% of the total number of builders in the area, and most were found to have changed their practices as a result of the course (Coburn and Leslie 1985).

As well as builder training several of the disaster reconstruction programmes over the last ten years have had the effect of developing a cadre of trained professionals and field workers in several countries who understand the issues and will be in a position to take quick and effective action in the event of future disasters.

International cooperation

Improved international cooperation must be a good sign for the future, even if the results are not immediately apparent. The establishment of networks such as the International Network on Earthen and Low-Strength Masonry Buildings in Seismic areas, and the connections fostered through the conferences in Albuquerque, Delhi, Lima and Ankara has brought the experience of field-workers and the perspective of academics into contact with each other to mutual benefit. There has been a similar growth of international networking in the field of building materials through the work of SKAT, GATE and ITDG.

Although grossly underfunded, the establishment of UNCHS in Nairobi has had a catalytic effect on the development of new knowledge and experience and on the international transfer of information which must be expanded.

And there is evidence that as a result of all this information exchange, ideas developed in one place are beginning to be adopted elsewhere. The Indian success with small-scale cement technology referred to was partly stimulated by the well-publicised though probably over-estimated Chinese successes with mini-cement in the 1960s and 1970s. The approach adopted in the Ecuador reconstruction programme described above drew heavily on the OXFAM Yemen builder training programme. And the pace of interchange is growing.

Conclusion: An Agenda for the IDNDR

A crucial test for any proposed programme of action should be whether or not it contributes to long-term development, and whether the resources used could alternatively have been used to provide more distributed benefits. A short list of such programmes might include:

- programmes to strengthen the local building and building materials industries so that they can better respond to both normal needs and the occasional large reconstruction programme. The proposals of Charles Cockburn at this conference described in more detail what might be involved. There is an enormous amount that could be done in many countries to make the building industry less dependent on imported materials and technologies;
- programmes to investigate options for upgrading traditional building systems in ways which are cost-effective, vulnerability reducing and culturally appropriate, and to promote the best options through joint action of Government and NGOs;
- programmes to investigate the options for urban migrants to reduce their vulnerability through low-cost modifications to existing forms of construction, improved siting and improved infrastructure – particularly in areas with a frequent recurrence of disasters;
- studies to assess the cost effectiveness of a range of options for reducing risk and simultaneously meeting other development criteria, as a stimulus for both political and financial support.

The support and intercommunication of such national and local activities requires a strengthened role for the UN. The impact of the UN in the field of disaster reduction is seriously hampered by the multitude of UN agencies involved – UNCHS, UNDRO, UNESCO, UNIDO, UNDP and others. The international community should seek a restructuring of the UN role so that all activities related to disaster protection are the responsibility of one (existing) UN body – and part of the task of the IDNDR should then be to see that that body is properly funded to carry out the task.

REFERENCES

COBURN, A.W. and LESLIE, J.D.L. (1985) *Dhamar Building Education Project: Project Assessment*, OXFAM Oxford, UK.

DUDLÈY, E. (1988) 'Disaster Mitigation: Strong Houses or Strong Institutions', *Disasters* 12.2.

LESLIE, J.D.L. (1984) 'Think Before You Build: an Earthquake Reconstruction Project in Yemen', *International Symposium on Earthquake Relief in Less-Industrialized Areas*, Zurich, Switzerland.

RAZANI, R. (1978) 'Seismic Protection of Unreinforced Masonry and Adobe Housing in Less-Developed Countries', *Disasters and the Small Dwelling*, Pergamon, Oxford, UK.

CHAPTER 7

Disaster Prevention and Mitigation in Latin America and the Caribbean: Notes on the Decade of the 1990s

STEPHEN BENDER
Department of Regional Development and Environment
Organization of American States[1]
Washington DC, USA

Introduction

There have been various discussions since the last conference on disasters and the small dwelling in 1978 to examine the linkages between disasters and development. One outcome of those discussions has been growing awareness on the part of international development assistance agencies and national Governments of the vulnerability of all types of development activities, particularly capital investment projects, to natural disasters.

The issue is how to better integrate natural hazard management concerns into the development planning process. This is particularly critical for those segments of the population who are less able to protect themselves against the hazards that natural events pose, and the vulnerability of their settlements.

How well we are able to manage the complex interaction between the environment, development and disasters will determine the future success of the common mission of our institutions. The prime objective of the natural hazards-related technical cooperation work of the General Secretariat of the OAS (GS/OAS) is to reduce disaster vulnerability in the context of integrated development planning. Through three principal and interrelated activities – technical cooperation, training and technology transfer – the GS/OAS has worked at the countries' request, often in coordination with several other institutions to identify hazards, propose mitigation measures, train mid-level professionals from various disciplines, and introduce effective and cost efficient methods for hazard assessment and mitigation in more than 25 OAS member states.

The primary support for the activities has come from USAID's Office of Foreign Disaster Assistance. This office, like its sister offices in other international agencies, dedicates its resources primarily to emergency pre-paredness and response, but it has seen fit to provide funds for longer term prevention activities. Support from such agencies is presently far too scarce, and it often comes from humanitarian assistance offices, while mainstream development assistance offices in the agencies provide funding only after the occurrence of a disaster.

Natural hazard management activities carried out by the GS/OAS have covered geographical areas as large as the Paraguayan Chaco and as small as individual villages in the Caribbean island countries. They have included subject matter as diverse as the evaluation of flooding, landslides and desertification, the use of geographic and geo-referenced information systems for planning and emergency management, satellite remote sensing technology, videos and printed manuals for use by local officials, lifeline mapping of critical facilities, and the systematic compilation of information on natural hazards, natural resources, population and infrastructure in the form of data sets, technical reports and computer-generated maps for inclusion in development planning studies.

From this perspective, there are five points to be made as we look at the 1990s, natural hazard management, and the small building:

- Disasters create constituencies. Natural hazard management seldom creates similar constituencies.
- Natural hazard management must be more closely tied to other environ-mental issues which are gaining so much global attention.
- Who is vulnerable, to what hazard and why, must be examined in regional, national and local terms if appropriate vulnerability reduction strategies are to be drawn up and implemented.
- Reducing vulnerability must be seen in a shifting context of not only the public use of private interest, but also the private use of public interest. Economic efficiency, incentives, and free market forces must be combined with society's responsibility assumed by Government, for the health, safety and welfare of its population.
- We can and must change the way development takes place by empowering through knowledge, experience, and resources those who are vulnerable to natural hazards.

The Issue of Constituencies

First of all, let it be said that of the three major groups related to disaster management that function nationally and internationally – natural phenomena and engineering research entities, emergency preparedness and response agencies, and development planning and financing institutions – the last named has also been the last to begin to deal on a non-crisis basis with hazard management issues. At the same time, it is the planning community which is in the best position to act as a catalyst to bring these three groups together. Planners are both users and producers of natural hazard information. While not often formally charged with the task, planners produce hazard evaluations, particularly in the areas of atmospheric and hydrologic hazards. They should take the lead in setting research priorities. They are best placed to identify those elements of the existing and proposed production and service infrastructure which are at risk and for which political, economic and social decisions dictate that a substantial reduction in vulnerability is either impossible or improbable. Responding to repeated calls from the emergency management group for hazard maps, planners should increase their activities in hazard assessment as part of development planning studies.

Second, during the remaining years of this century and beyond, development theory and practice will be shaped to an ever increasing degree by response to natural hazards. This is in contrast to the forces that have shaped past growth, such as the availability of broad expanses of uninhabited or little developed forests, valleys and plains, or the creation of entire new cities built around the extraction or transformation of a single resource, or the single purpose extension of infrastructure networks to colonize remaining large tracts of land. These natural events will dictate the location, beneficiaries, affected sectors and providers of financial support often without the availability of alternatives in the traditional context of development.

For the region, we must avoid a situation where disaster relief is the principal form of development assistance; where post-disaster reconstruction depletes scarce resources otherwise destined for new investments; and where institutional divisions between disaster management and development assistance create a void in policies, programmes and projects which address the utilization of resources in the face of ever increasing demands and vulnerability, particularly of the poor.

Third, the International Decade for Natural Disaster Reduction (IDNDR) gives all of us a mandate to affect the way development will take place, particularly in lessening disaster vulnerability through development planning.

We must use the time available to our best advantage. A decade can be a short time. Mid-level professionals in public and private service will mature during the decade and by its end, many will have assumed leadership positions in their respective sectors. Sectoral programmes and projects, recently identified and those yet to come, can be shaped by a planning process that includes hazard analysis and a selection of appropriate mitigation measures.

Single focus development mandates, so prevalent during the past two decades, are giving way to multisectoral, interdisciplinary approaches which concentrate on the competition inherent in assuring resource use on a continuing basis and on the need for conflict resolution.

This is of particular relevance to disaster reduction. The attractiveness of creating an area of specialization out of each new development focus can and should give way to a better understanding on the part of all involved disciplines of the importance of considering the consequences of natural events.

An Environmental Issue

There is a direct, if not much discussed, relationship between disasters, the environment and development.

In Latin America and the Caribbean, growing population pressures and the demands made on the region's ecosystems have long outstripped their capacity to provide sufficient goods and services in a non-value added condition, particularly in urban environments. Safe building sites, together with food, fuel and building materials, are all naturally occurring goods and services in great demand, particularly by the urban poor. As their immediate availability has become scarce, they must be brought from distant sources. Value must be added in the form of energy, transportation, transformation, commercialization, and profit, to name the most common components. These components are often the substance of development plans and investments.

Building sites safe from natural hazards, pollution and accidents for homes, offices, businesses and public infrastructure must often be engineered. But far too often, disaster mitigation is limited to on-site design which at best allows for the passing on of the hazard. In the worst case, the inhabitants have neither the technical nor the financial means to reduce the vulnerability of even their own endeavours.

If sustainability includes the continuing provision of safe building sites, then environments, whether rural or urban, must be managed in an integrated way, including the recognition of the impact natural events have on those environments, both in terms of positive attributes and hazards.

More so than the decade of disaster reduction, which is a chosen subject matter, the 1990s is the 'decade of the environment', a subject matter that has been thrust upon us.

Natural events and the hazards they pose are part of the systems that make up our environments. On the benefit side, natural events shape the topography, deposit volcanic soils, flush estuaries, water the land, expose buried resources, dispose of combustible material, and continually reset regenerating cycles into motion.

Natural hazards are part of 'environmental problems' in every sense of the word. They affect the endangered species habitat or fauna, make manifest the alteration of natural systems, heighten the impact of those systems' degradation and spread in an uncontrollable way the results of humans spoiling their environments.

Natural hazards are a global issue in the same vein as other issues which hold our attention because of their power to affect major portions of the Earth's population. There should be more of a sense of immediacy in preventing natural disasters, particularly by the international development assistance community, because they generate the demand for significant amounts of capital to repair and replace what is destroyed and damaged. There should also be an increasing adoption of this issue by the development community as its own because it affords, among all the issues, perhaps the most manageable of situations. The risks are amenable to study, mitigation measures are available, and populations benefiting from vulnerability reduction actions can sense the results.

But natural disasters, even with their frequent occurrence and high cost, appear to generate little constituency for their prevention. On the other hand, less is known about the risks posed by other environmental problems, yet constituencies abound, particularly for wildlife and wildlands:

- the threat of nuclear war appears to be greatly diminished;
- global warming is still to be confirmed, and yet conjecture as to its impact is bringing about changes in policy that affects long-term economic activity;
- the depletion of the ozone layer is confirmed to be variable in its extent and duration with the debate continuing as to its impact;
- sea-level rise is possible, but its impacts in time and space, though the subject of intense debate, remain uncertain;
- tropical deforestation is being monitored in ever increasing detail but political resolution of its causes, as well as estimates of the costs and benefits to the human population, are not yet available;
- although bio-diversity depletion is documented, calls for slowing the process are built on theoretical arguments rather than on what we know and understand.

The forgotten issue is the increasing vulnerability of the human population to natural hazards which often occur because of human activity, and often in the name of development, which is the goal of nations.

Natural hazards will have most impact on the populations of the world during the present decade. At the same time, natural hazards have been consistently omitted from discussions on the environment. Yet they can most readily be specified in terms of location, severity, time and even the probability of occurrence. Therefore of all of the environmental issues, it is natural hazards whose impacts can most effectively be mitigated and with certainty. Likewise, of the issues, natural disaster mitigation is most dependent on changing the way development takes place, and there already exist methods for its reduction which permit the identification of the vulnerable human population, allow for capital investment and for the definition and implementation of mitigation measures.

STEPHEN BENDER

The Who, What and Why of Vulnerability

The world's poor are increasing at a rate higher than the overall population growth of the planet, and are, proportionately, the most vulnerable to natural disasters. This vulnerability is due primarily to the characteristics of the physical space – the ground sites and the buildings they occupy.

Over 80% of international grant funds for developing countries for disaster mitigation, and over 90% of all funds spent on disaster mitigation go to disaster relief and replacing lost investment. Most of these actions are in direct response to the needs of the poor.

The remaining disaster mitigation funds go to reducing the vulnerability to loss of life and property through prevention in a development planning and implementation context on a non-specific event basis.

Saving lives and reducing economic impact can be dealt with on three levels: 1, immediately after an event, as an emergency situation, attending to the injured and to damaged property; 2, as vulnerability reduction of basic, service and production infrastructure (all non-residential construction); 3, as vulnerability reduction of human shelter and immediate settlement surroundings.

In developing countries, it is primarily the public sector, with the collaboration of the private sector, each acting through local, national and international mechanisms, which attends to the first two levels on a priority basis.

The inhabitants of developing countries, particularly the poor, must first and foremost attend to vulnerability reduction of their own shelter setting. Those inhabitants often take for granted, and at no direct monetary cost to themselves, the copious quantities of naturally occurring high quality goods and services from their environments, which they consume. The ecosystems that provide air to breathe, water to drink, food to eat, fuels to burn, clays to make bricks, and wood to raise roofs also provide safe building sites. They are among the goods and services most sought after and most needed.

The poor, in existing families and in new families to come in this decade (often more than 50% of a developing country's population are under the age of 16), will continue to seek the 'free' natural goods and services as long as they are available. These families will continue to change their environments to satisfy their basic needs.

The poor, particularly in a region where the majority of them live in urban areas, continue to deplete their immediate surroundings of the desired goods and services, and move into the hinterland to acquire the same, usually in insufficient quantities and of poorer quality. And they seek to acquire these goods and services in the most non-value added (non-cash outlay) manner possible.

The many manifestations of acquisition of food, fuel, building materials, and building sites in a non-value added manner, for example pollution, erosion, deforestation are often at odds with management practices which provide for sustainable yields. In addition, they are often at odds with social, legal and economic norms and policies.

Unfortunately comparatively safe building sites, in terms of vulnerability to natural disasters, are fewer than the demand, and there is no available system to increase the natural supply. There is, however, evidence that human activities, particularly in the name of development, decrease the number of less vulnerable sites.

While the poor use their own labour to acquire food, fuel and building materials, use of their own labour to transform a more vulnerable building site to a less vulnerable one even at zero opportunity cost is almost impossible given the characteristics of these naturally hazardous events.

Reducing Vulnerability in a Changing Context

Other than issues directly related to the manner in which the shelter and its immediate surroundings are designed and constructed, reduction of vulnerability to natural disasters is generally beyond the efforts of the individual shelter inhabitant. Actions are best taken collectively, and most effectively, through society's institutions. Lessening the loss of life and reducing the economic impact of natural disasters in something other than post-disaster emergency situations is part of environmental management. It begins with public sector policy and includes both the public and private sector actions to protect productive natural systems and basic, service and production infrastructure.

Managing natural hazards to reduce the impact of disasters caused by hurricanes, floods, drought, landslides, earthquakes and tsunami must be addressed by focusing on actions that lessen vulnerability where it counts: decisions to build new structures, to rebuild after disasters and to mitigate vulnerability of existing structures – all in relation to the building site.

Given the vulnerability reduction resources available and the characteristics of the development activities in Latin America and the Caribbean that result in capital investments in production facilities, infrastructure and settlements, a primary way to lessen the economic impact of disasters is through influencing development decisions early on in the planning process. Site vulnerability issues, whether at a large or small scale, must be examined before mitigation measures for individual structures, whether existing or programmed, are selected and implemented. This applies to activities in the private and public sectors alike.

When a disaster strikes, commercial facilities, human settlements and supporting infrastructure are damaged or destroyed, investments in capital expenditures are lost, and the poor, whether poor Governments or poor citizens, usually bear the greatest losses because their vulnerability is the greatest.

Lessening economic impact takes time because a capital investment project, whether a house, business or road, takes time to plan and build. Whether a sufficient measure of vulnerability reduction has been included in the project may not be known until enough time passes for the next event to occur, making 'field tested' case studies difficult to come by in the short term. And knowledge of the results of certain events, such as tsunami, landslides and floods, dictate that staying out of harm's way is the best policy; structurally withstanding the event is an improbable if not inefficient use of resources.

Strategies for lessening the impact on what exists are strikingly similar to those for lessening the impact on what is to be built. First and foremost, there are similarities in the type of information needed to make the most effective use of available resources applied to mitigation. There exists a private use of public interest: the use of free information to make the best decisions possible concerning the investment of capital. Selection of a site for an investment or the understanding of the nature of the vulnerability that affects an existing investment is critical to compete in a marketplace where the consequences are borne if all risks are not properly addressed. There is interest on the part of the public sector both in the health, safety and welfare of the country's citizens, and in the preparation and dissemination of pertinent information about what is vulnerable to natural hazards and why.

There are pointed arguments for more effectively changing social behaviour, such as dealing with natural hazard vulnerability, by changing the incentives of the marketplace (Natsios 1990). The public sector uses the interest of the private sector in maximizing its resources by giving it incentives, rather than regulations, to reduce vulnerability to natural hazards. Market-like incentives will not work in all cases and are reserved for protecting economic assets. At the same time, the private sector can use, free of charge, information generated by public sector interest in vulnerability reduction because of the latter's legitimate mandate and concern to act on behalf of the entire population.

Lessening the vulnerability of what exists, whether a house, factory or road, is the most difficult. To begin with, 90% of all investments expected to be in place at the end of the century already exist. Because of this, the point of departure on the long road to lessening economic impact is to identify the hazards that threaten what is built and what is vulnerable.

Vulnerability reduction usually entails retrofitting (reinforcing) structures, if such an action is economically and physically, as well as socially, feasible. It also requires sufficient hazard information about the site, which seldom exists, to specify the type and quantity of retrofitting action needed, or to indicate that relocation measures are necessary.

Lessening the vulnerability of what is to be built is the easier task. This is true, not because it will amount to no more than ten per cent of the total in place capital investment in the region at the end of the century, but because it is much more efficient, when the vulnerability posed by natural hazards is known, to move the project to an alternative site (since there are almost always alternatives), selecting the site with full acceptance of the mitigation measures necessary to achieve a desired level of risk.

There is ample technical knowledge available about how to build once the vulnerability is known for the chosen building site. For the poor country or the poor individual, the issue is the public and public sectors using that knowledge to design and implement construction projects. As an example, there is more than enough technical information available – free of charge to the public and private sectors alike – concerning safe housing construction for any number of natural hazards if it would only be used by international and national development assistance agencies and NGOs, national and local lending institutions, and local professionals and tradespeople. The problem is that quite often this building construction information is never used because these same organizations or individuals seldom pay any attention to the hazards that threaten the site, which means, logically, they perceive little need for acquiring and using knowledge concerning safe building practices.

The lessons learned from three decades of disasters and development in the region, including recent insights into the damage caused by earthquakes in Mexico City, Armero and Loma Prieta, point to the fact that serious efforts to lessen the economic impact of natural disasters for what exists or what is to be built, and particularly lessening the economic impact of disasters in poor countries and for poor people, must begin with site vulnerability analysis and its incorporation into development planning.

Changing the Way Development Takes Place

Vulnerability reduction for populations in terms of their shelter and immediate surroundings must be accompanied by vulnerability reduction to infrastructure, while we continue to provide appropriate humanitarian assistance in emergency situations. This longer term prevention of disasters in the context of development planning and implementation must be given a higher environmental management priority. Technical cooperation is a necessary component. Vulnerability reduction depends heavily on development assistance and financing entities, and their role in development cooperation.

Collaboration and communication must take place between the development community who plan and fund development projects, the scientific and engineering research community who query and publish, and those who prepare for and respond to natural disasters – the emergency preparedness and response community.

This important task of technical cooperation must contain three elements: technical assistance, training and technology transfer. At the regional, national and local levels, these activities should be carried out with the increased participation of the private sector and a more focused direction with continuity of support from the public sector.

Technical assistance must accompany development project preparation processes and focus on these areas:

53

- An overview of natural hazards and development planning should be prepared for each developing country which describes the natural hazards, their relation to existing natural resource and environmental management issues, disaster histories, basic technical documentation available, key national institutions and professionals to be consulted in country, and related population, infrastructure and natural resource information. Much of the information needed to compile these documents is available and there are processes in place to prepare them for Latin America and the Caribbean.
- The preparation of sector vulnerability assessments to natural hazards at a national level. These assessments would include the preparation of investment projects for mitigating losses according to defined mitigation strategies as well as indications to the emergency preparedness and response community of which sector components are vulnerable without possibility, at least in the short to medium term, of significant vulnerability reduction. Assessment models for priority sectors exist or are in preparation. Sector vulnerability assessments would both use and add to the information in the country overviews.
- The preparation, at the outset of all capital investment projects, of a brief to be included in initial project documentation on the natural hazards context of the investment project. This action will use, in part, the resources of the country overviews. The processes are in place to begin this activity and much of the information is available.
- Each subsequent phase of the investment project preparation cycle will address vulnerability and vulnerability reduction issues until the final loan document defines and approves a specified vulnerability level and mitigation measures.
- The above activities of technical cooperation should be a mandatory part of post-disaster reconstruction programmes in order to take advantage of the improved receptiveness to disaster prevention actions during such a period.

Training, the acquisition of skills, knowledge and attitudes, must accompany the technical assistance:

- Technicians of developing countries should be trained in the preparation and updating of the above mentioned natural hazards and development planning overview documents. They would participate in regional workshops, followed by national workshops as each country progresses through a series of activities. Training approaches and experience in this activity exist in Latin America and the Caribbean.
- Professionals from selected sectors should be trained in techniques of assessing vulnerability to natural hazards as part of national programmes for disaster mitigation. Regional workshops would be followed by national assessments as countries complete a series of activities aimed at preparation and implementation of investment projects as part of the overall sector

development strategy. Training approaches and experience in this activity exist in Latin America. As applicable, regional sectoral agencies will also be trained in the techniques to continue development of the programme.

- Professionals involved in investment project formulation for different sectors should be trained in the use of natural hazard information. Basic training course materials and instructors are available.
- Professionals involved in sectoral planning and project identification should be trained in specific natural hazard assessment and sectoral planning to fortify their understanding and use of natural hazard information in sector policy, programmes and projects. Courses will be offered in:

  – integrated planning of large river basins with emphasis on basic infrastructure (energy, transportation and water resources) in international border regions;
  – integrated management of urban watersheds with emphasis on natural hazard vulnerability reduction and natural resource use for meeting the food, fuel, building material and building site needs of the poor;
  – assessment of landslide hazards with emphasis on urban settlement areas and energy, transportation and production infrastructure networks;
  – assessment of desertification processes with emphasis on integrated river basin development, food production, forest management and settlement expansion.

Technology transfer should be part of technical assistance activities as well as an activity that generates the subject matter of formal training activities:

- natural hazards information management techniques, including manual and computer-based approaches, should be made available to national planning and project formulation processes. Relevant technology, selection and installation experience is available.
- mapping techniques, including manual and computer-based approaches, for dealing with natural hazard, natural resource, population and infrastructure information should be made available to national planning and project formulation processes. Relevant technology selection and installation experience is available, particularly as related to match needs with existing country experience and equipment.
- in coordination with emergency preparedness and response entities, emergency information management systems should be made available to appropriate national agencies, including those responsible for the infrastructure that forms part of the critical facilities (health, energy, transportation, public safety, communications, etc.) for use immediately before, during and after a natural disaster.

We must recognize that the next decade presents an opportunity to continue important work already begun. Mechanisms exist for the creation and distribution of basic hazard information briefs to be incorporated into country development strategies, environmental profiles, natural resource atlases, preliminary mission reports, project programming documents, and other similar items.

Training focus areas, course content, and institutional support mechanisms have been identified to offer programmes in hazard analysis, mitigation measure selection, and hazard assessment and mapping as part of multi-sectoral, interdisciplinary development planning studies.

Professionals from the region with academic preparation and disaster-related experience are available to continue their work in planning development and in training.

Likewise, research and engineering institutions exist which have long dealt with hazard assessment, particularly in the area of geologic hazards. It is time to initiate new activities as well as support existing endeavours as these institutions set out priorities in terms of training, technology transfer, and information sharing.

For the planning community, the challenge of the decade is particularly important because there are already in place planning mechanisms at the national, sub-national and local levels in most countries. The best opportunity to lessen disaster vulnerability in the region is assuring that hazard assessment and mitigation are part of the policy, programme and, most importantly, the project preparation processes from the earliest stages.

Through Government mandates, funding agency requirements and development assistance offerings, all this can be done. Without separating out hazards as a sector or an impact analysis operation, all involved disciplines must be prepared to present and discuss disaster vulnerability and participate in the decision-making process which weighs vulnerability with competing social, economic, political and financial claims for resource use.

For the Latin American and Caribbean region, we should use ongoing planning and development projects, beginning at the sub-national and national levels, to reinforce the use of the personnel and information that is available and that will become available through the actions described above. The planning community, which must take an increasing role in disaster prevention, should seek out opportunities to work with the emergency management, and research and engineering communities.

REFERENCE

NATSIOS, A. (1990) 'Disaster Mitigation and Economic Incentives', *Colloquium on the Environmental and Natural Disaster Management*, The World Bank, Washington DC, USA.

NOTE

1. The views expressed are those of the author and do not necessarily reflect those of the General Secretariat of the Organization of American States (OAS) nor of its member states.

CHAPTER 8

Problems in Post-Disaster Resettlement: Cross Cultural Perspectives[1]

ANTHONY OLIVER-SMITH

*Department of Anthropology, Turlington Hall 1350,
University of Florida, Gainesville, Florida, USA*

Introduction

After falling once to an attack by Indians, weathering a series of eight serious earthquakes and suffering a huge landslide between the sixteenth and eighteenth centuries, the Spanish Captain General of Santiago de Guatemala gave the order in 1773 for the site to be abandoned and the city to be relocated for the third time to safer terrain. The citizenry objected to the decision, but the relocation began nonetheless in 1775 and a new capital, Nueva Guatemala de la Asuncion, was founded. Many people, however, still refused to abandon the old site, now known as Antigua, whereupon the authorities forcibly closed the city's remaining stores in 1779. All these efforts notwithstanding, the old site was almost immediately repopulated and continues to exist today as one of Guatemala's major tourist attractions (Tobriner 1980: 14–15).

The case of Antigua is but one of many in the historical record in which a population devastated by a natural disaster refuses to leave their homesite or is relocated in a new site which fails to thrive resulting in its abandonment and/or the repopulation of the original site. The insistence of disaster victims on remaining in environments which are either totally devastated or overtly dangerous has occasionally been interpreted as an example of the non-rational in human behaviour, referring to such metaphorical expressions of the human-land relationship as 'the maternal roots' or the 'native soil' (Zwingmann 1973). Others have stressed material concerns in the reluctance of people to relocate after disasters (Oliver-Smith 1977; Coburn et al. 1984). Indeed, there is no necessary contradiction between the two positions since both sets of variables clearly play important roles in conditioning people's perceptions of and reactions to post-disaster resettlement. In addition, we can also look to resettlement projects themselves as the causes of their own success or failure. The frequent failure of resettlement projects is understandable, since such dislocation often constitutes another disaster in which the entire community is affected, the economy disrupted, and the group becomes temporarily or permanently dependent on outside aid, as has been pointed out by Torry (1978), Davis (1978) and others. Given the complex and problematic nature of uprooting and resettlement in general (Scudder and Colson 1982), it is worth asking why authorities deem it necessary so often to resettle people.

The reason most often cited for resettlement after disaster is continued or expanded vulnerability to natural hazard. Natural or technological protective features may be destroyed or new hazards created by disaster impact making continued habitation in the site extremely dangerous. However, often issues other than geologic safety enter into the decision to relocate earthquake stricken populations. Earthquakes and other disasters may provide convenient pretexts for population concentration (and control), the conglomeration of population groups for national or regional development plans for the national integration of minorities, all of which may be issues of less than immediate local concern in the choice of sites for resettlement.

Factors in Post-Earthquake Resettlement

In this paper I would like to consider the factors in post-earthquake resettlement which have proved crucial in determining successful or unsuccessful outcomes in examples of projects from different cultures. In my discussion of resettlement projects after earthquakes which failed, I draw on cases from the Middle East, mainly Turkey after the 1970, 1971 and 1976 earthquakes (Aysan and Oliver 1987; Kronenberger 1984; Coburn et al. 1984; Mitchell 1981; Lamping 1984; Ulubas 1980; Selman and Selman 1980), and Iran after the 1972 earthquake (Razani 1984). I have occasionally drawn as well on my own work in the Peruvian Andes. The fact that I have chosen the Middle Eastern data for examples of failures should not be taken as an indication that there have been no successes there. However, as Selman and Selman (1980) point out, successes are the exception to the rule. Aysan and Oliver, while highlighting the successes in New Gediz in Turkey, also state that, despite being declared unsafe by geologists, old Gediz has been completely repopulated (1987: 29). Coburn et al., in discussing the successes and failures of resettlement in Bingol Province in Turkey have suggested that three factors, the physical environment of the new settlement, the relationship to the old village and the capability of the community to develop itself, are crucial in determining the success or failure of a resettlement project (1984: 52). After searching the literature, I, in effect, subsume these factors in finding that the factors behind the rejection and/or failure of resettlement projects after earthquakes can be grouped into four major categories: site, layout, housing and popular input.

Before discussing the causes of failure, it might be well to define what constitutes a failed resettlement project. At one level, outright rejection and abandonment of the site can be safely interpreted as failure. However, not all cases are as clear cut. Coburn et al., regarding the uneven development performance of resettled villages in Turkey, suggest that the success or failure of a settlement should be judged by the extent to which the village has become self-reliant in its own right or a viable partner to its original village (1984: 52). This condition can be best assessed by six factors: 1) the number of houses still occupied, 2) the modification of the form and internal layout of the provided housing, 3) the degree of maintenance and state of repair, 4) the development of gardens, tree planting and enclosures thereof, 5) the extension of buildings and investment in them, and 6) the construction of private buildings (Coburn et al. 1984: 52).

I will now attempt to summarize briefly the problems attributed to the factors of site, layout, housing and popular input in the failure or rejection of resettlement projects after the earthquakes previously cited. Poor choice of site for resettlement is one of the most frequently mentioned factors for resettlement failure. It is often the case that sites for resettlement after disaster are chosen with factors other than the welfare and development of the population in mind. Land may be designated for a resettlement project because of ease of acquisition, particularly in the case of Government owned or controlled property (Coburn et al. 1984). Accessibility and topography favouring rapid construction for authorities seeking to maximize efficiency in the use of resources and 'speedy solutions' are also cited as reasons for poor site choices (Coburn et al. 1984; Razani 1984). Poor sites are also chosen out of ignorance or lack of concern with ecological and economic concerns. Resettlement sites, particularly those chosen for flat terrain for ease of construction, have failed because they afforded little shelter from the elements, particularly wind and snow (Lamping 1984; Coburn et al. 1984; Ulubas 1980). Distance from resources such as water or pasture (Lamping 1984) or labour and commodity markets (Oliver-Smith 1986) are also factors which contribute to the rejection or failure of resettlement sites. Social factors such as distance from kin or from the old village, in cases where partial resettlement is attempted, are also cited as major factors in the failure of new villages (Kronenberger 1984; Lamping 1984; UNDRO 1982; Razani 1984).

The layout or design of the settlement is frequently cited as a source of sufficient dissatisfaction with resettlement to result in the abandonment of the site. Again ease of construction and the imposition of urban middle-class values on rural populations seem to lie at the root of problems of monotonous, uniform, camp-like designs for resettled populations. Such resettled village layouts lack the variety as well as the culturally constructed ritual spaces required by people in their environments (Razani 1984; Kronenberger 1984).

Village designs which do not permit the clustering of kin and old neighbourhood groups are faulted for bringing about failure also (Coburn et al. 1984). Failure in the layout to provide for sufficient space around dwellings in the settlement for tool sheds, animal pens and other agricultural needs often leads to the abandonment of resettlement sites (Lamping 1984; Razani 1984; Kronenberger 1984; Oliver-Smith 1986).

Housing design and construction are often blamed for the rejection or failure of post-disaster resettlement projects. Faulty construction and inferior materials in houses soon become evident with use and create difficult living conditions, particularly regarding thermal protection in different seasons (Razani 1984; Coburn et al. 1984; Lamping 1984; Ulubas 1980). Houses are cited as being too small for large rural extended families (Ulubas 1980; Lamping 1984). The loss of privacy is another frequent complaint leading to the abandonment of settlements (Ulubas 1980). Traditional houses have evolved over time as functional to the needs of the household unit. The design of resettlement houses is often inappropriate for domestic activities which require different kinds of spaces for different uses according to seasons (Coburn et al. 1984: 53).

Projects which suffer failure or at best are only partially successful are often characterized by policies which depend very little on consultation with the population to be resettled (Oliver-Smith 1988; Lamping 1984; Razani 1984). Many of the issues mentioned regarding poor site selection, inappropriate settlement design and unsatisfactory housing derive from a lack of consultation with the people and the consequent lack of understanding of their socially and culturally derived needs and values, not to mention the benefit of their intimate knowledge and long experience in the local environment. Compounding this lack of understanding of local needs and values is the frequent importation of outside labour to construct the settlement itself, not only robbing people of a sense of participation in their new village, but also depriving them of the opportunity to gain new and relevant skills for jobs in a developing economy. Such lack of participation also produces little sense of ownership or personal responsibility for either home or the village, as well as a prolonged period of dependency on outside resources, all features common to failed post-disaster resettlement projects.

Before considering some post-earthquake resettlement projects which succeeded, let me first define success. I am inclined to follow guidelines suggested by Michael Cernea which approach resettlement as 'a multisided opportunity for the reconstruction of systems of production and human settlements that . . . represent a development in the standard of life of those affected, as well as in the regional economy of which they are a part' (1988: 19). Writing of policies developed by the World Bank, Cernea recommends that 'the major objective is to ensure that settlers are afforded opportunities to become established and economically self-sustaining in the shortest possible period . . .' (1988: 19), while recognizing that new settlements are expanding socio-cultural systems whose collective needs will increase over time (1988: 20). Therefore, resettlement must also be development oriented and planning must take into account that the social and physical infrastructure, school and health services, access to employment opportunities, and housing plot allotments and dwellings will meet expanded needs (1988: 20). Further, to be successful resettlement schemes should effect a '. . . transfer of responsibility from settlement agencies to the settlers themselves' (Cernea 1988: 28). In assessing success, I would suggest that similar criteria to those suggested by Coburn et al. (1984) and myself noted earlier in this paper might be employed.

With these general criteria in mind, I would like to discuss briefly several examples of post-disaster resettlement which have followed an implicit development orientation. Glittenberg, as part of a global study of the 1976 Guatemalan earthquake (Bates 1982), studied reconstruction in four urban settlements, two of which I would like to examine here. The earthquake left homeless and bereft of most personal possessions thousands of people living in substandard housing in both outlying and internal neighbourhoods of Guatemala City. In the immediate aftermath people constructed shelters of scrap materials, cardboard, sheet metal and in the rain and cold which followed the earthquake endured much hardship. For the people of the working-class neighbourhoods of La Florida, San Francisco, el Milagro and Mixco on the rim of the capital remaining in their original settlement was made impossible by the instability of the terrain. The leaders of the neighbourhoods in cooperation with missionaries of the Calvary Church and a group of students from San Carlos University organized a land invasion of over 1,000 families. Faced with such a fait accompli, BANVI, the National Housing Bank, agreed to buy the land and CEMEC, the Emergency Committee of the Calvary Church, agreed to build 1500 houses (26 sq m), a health station, a ten-room primary school, a market, a church, a park, a slaughterhouse, and a first aid station. BANVI agreed to urbanize each lot, lay out and gravel streets, help provide electricity, potable water and drainage. The obligation of the participants was to participate in all decision-making, commit three weeks' labour to house construction and pay a mortgage of $8–10 per month. The title to the house was transferred after a year of proper care and use as the owner's family residence. The settlement became known as Carolingia in honour of the students who helped organize the invasion.

Carolingia is now known as one of the most aggressive and highly organized communities in the country. The high level of organization, the result of dynamic internal leaders and outside assistance, is based on the participation of all community members and has been a key factor in the success of the project. Despite the major technical, organizational, and material inputs by BANVI and CEMEC, the high degree of participation in decision making has conferred a sense of both competence and proprietorship to the people. When they have met with bureaucratic resistance in their attempts to acquire needs for the settlement, they have been able effectively to pressure, sometimes through demonstrations, the authorities to respond to their demands. In effect, the disaster and the experience of the resettlement has increased the level of expectations of the people and encouraged higher levels of personal and political empowerment (Glittenberg 1982: 666–676).

A second example of successful resettlement contrasts with the first in the lack of formal planning that was employed. After the disaster thousands of survivors from the unstable ravines of the city took refuge on the flat land along the sides of a freeway that crosses the city. There was little plan as the refugees set up their shacks of cardboard, tin and discarded wood. There was no organized sanitation for as many as 30,000 refugees. Open ditches of raw sewage flowed throughout the settlement, creating a continual threat to the health of residents. Property lines were marked by footpaths and soon natural features such as hills, streams or trees became accepted as boundary markers between settlements.

One such settlement soon became known as the Fourth of February, named after the day of the earthquake. By September there were 2000 shacks of wood and cardboard in the Fourth of February, which with the passing of time, displayed improvements, but there was still little plan to the settlement. Initially, BANVI attempted to remove the squatters, but then relented and began to address settlement needs in an ad hoc, patchwork fashion, first bringing in tanks of water and then putting in pipes. Subsequently, a public school, a clinic and a police station were added in 1978 and the settlement began to take on the appearance of a somewhat haphazard suburb. The settlement was led by two committees, each with its following of approximately 800 families among the 10,000–15,000 residents. These committees were highly organized, dividing the settlement into sections with elected representatives from each section to bring issues and problems before the general committees. For example, they managed to steal electricity for the settlement by tapping into power lines that ran along the freeway. The Government took no action against them. In addition, the committees organized volunteer action to clean streets, make cement blocks for houses and build houses. The committee boards of directors acted as volunteer fire departments, burial organizations, ambulance services, and an informal judicial system. An active internal economic life also emerged as numerous small businesses arose within the settlement, including food sellers, retail merchandise and services.

In April 1979 BANVI announced a further resettlement plan, participation in which was to be decided by plebiscite. Approximately one half of the residents chose to be resettled elsewhere in the city on land bought by BANVI and houses to be purchased through BANDESA for a cost of $4000 to be paid over 10 to 15 years. In January 1980 the houses of those who chose to stay in the Fourth of February were dismantled in preparation for the construction of a new settlement and in July land was cleared, water and sewer systems were installed, and houses began to be built, for which the residents were to pay

$10–15 a month. Despite the fact that it took major Government support to improve the standard of housing and other aspects of the settlement, the Fourth of February stands as an example of the natural process of coping with disaster and dislocation without formal organizations. The internal organization that arose in the community was very effective at dealing with problems of the aftermath even under poverty stricken conditions, but major improvements in urbanization and housing and community services needed considerable outside assistance (Glittenberg 1982: 677–688).

Conclusion

Post-disaster reconstruction success or failure is much more than delivering and constructing houses and towns. It is as much a question of how it is done as it is of what or how much is done. It is clear from the material we have explored in this paper that earthquake-stricken peoples need material assistance of major kinds, but where the problems are conceptualized as largely economic and technological, that is, in terms of efficiency in building dwellings that get people minimally sheltered as quickly as possible, the chances of success are reduced. On the other hand, where post-disaster reconstruction and resettlement are approached as socio-cultural as well as material problems, in which the victim population participates in both planning and implementation, the chances for success are enhanced. The two Guatemalan cases cited illustrate the importance of balancing questions of efficiency and speed with the social and psychological benefits to individual and community to be gained by regaining some control over one's life and the life of one's community by participation in the planning and construction of the settlement where one is to live. Indeed, the capacity of a community to develop itself, cited by Coburn et al (1984) as one of the crucial factors which affect the way a settlement develops, can be engendered or enhanced by just such participation.

Acknowledgement

The author is grateful to the National Center for Earthquake Engineering Research and to its Assistant Director, Dr Jelena Pantelic, for invaluable assistance in both searching for and obtaining bibliographic materials on post-disaster resettlement projects.

REFERENCES

AYSAN, Y. and OLIVER, P. (1987) *Housing and Culture After Earthquakes*, Oxford Polytechnic, Oxford, UK.

BATES, F.L. (1982) *Recovery, Change and Development: A Longitudinal Study of the 1976 Guatemalan Earthquake*, University of Georgia, Athens, USA.

CERNEA, M. (1988) *Involuntary Resettlement in Development Projects*, The World Bank, Washington DC, USA.

COBURN, A.W., LESLIE, J.D.L. and TABBAN, A. (1984) 'Reconstruction and Resettlement 11 Years Later: A Case Study of Bingol Province, Eastern Turkey', in S. Schupisser and J. Studer (eds) *Earthquake Relief in Less Industrialized Areas*, A.A. Balkema, Rotterdam, Netherlands.

DAVIS, I. (1978) *Shelter After Disaster*, Oxford Polytechnic Press, Oxford, UK.

GLITTENBERG, J.K. (1982) 'Reconstruction in Four Urban Post Disaster Settlements', in F.L. Bates (ed.) *Recovery, Change and Development: A Longitudinal Study of the 1976 Guatemalan Earthquake, Vol 2*, the University of Georgia, Athens, USA.

KRONENBERGER, J. (1984) 'The German Red Cross in the Earthquake Zone of Turkey – Regions of Van and Erzurum', in S. Schupisser and J. Studer (eds) *Earthquake Relief in Less Industrialized Areas*, A.A. Balkema, Rotterdam, Netherlands.

LAMPING, H. (1984) 'The Use of Indigenous Sources for Post-Disaster Housing-Some Geographical Aspects', in S. Schupisser and J. Studer (eds) *Earthquake Relief in Less Industrialized Areas*, A.A. Balkema, Rotterdam, Netherlands.

MITCHELL, W. (1981) 'Earthquakes in Turkey: Reconstruction Problems, Damage Prediction and Recovery Forecasting for Earthen Structures', in *International Workshop on Earthen Buildings in Seismic Areas, Conference Proceedings Vol. 2*, University of New Mexico, Albuquerque, USA.

OLIVER-SMITH, A. (1986) *The Martyred City: Death and Rebirth in the Andes*, University of New Mexico Press, Albuquerque, USA.

OLIVER-SMITH, A. (1977) 'Traditional Agriculture, Central Places and Post-Disaster Urban Relocation in Peru', *American Ethnologist* 4(1):102–116.

RAZANI, R. (1984) 'Earthquake Disaster Reconstruction Experience in Iran', in S. Schupisser and J. Studer (eds) *Earthquake Relief in Less Industrialized Areas*, A.A. Balkema, Rotterdam, Netherlands.

SCUDDER, T. and COLSON, E. (1982) 'From Welfare to Development: A Conceptual Framework for the Analysis of Dislocated People', in A. Hansen and A. Oliver-Smith (eds) *Involuntary Migration and Resettlement: The Problems and Responses of Dislocated People*, Westview Press, Boulder, Col., USA.

SELMAN, G. and SELMAN, M. (1980) 'An Innovative Case of Local Participation in Disaster Housing: Resettlement Following the 1957 Abant and 1967 Mudurnu Earthquakes', in *Proceedings of the Seventh World Conference on Earthquake Engineering: Socio-Economic Aspects and Studies of Specific Earthquakes*, Istanbul, Turkey.

TOBRINER, S. (1980) 'Earthquakes and Planning in the 17th and 18th Centuries', *Journal of Architectural Education* 33(4):11–15.

TORRY, W.I. (1978) 'Natural Disasters, Social Structure and Change in Traditional Societies', *Journal of African and Asian Studies*, XIII(3–4):167–183.

ULUBUS, A. (1980) 'Post-Earthquake Housing in the Villages of Gediz', in *Proceedings of the Seventh World Conference on Earthquake Engineering: Socio-Economic Aspects and Studies of Specific Earthquakes*, Istanbul, Turkey.

UNDRO (UNITED NATIONS DISASTER RELIEF OFFICE) (1982) *Shelter After Disaster*, United Nations, New York, USA.

ZWINGMANN, C. (1973) 'The Nostalgic Phenomenon and its Exploitation', in Charles Zwingmann and Maria Pfister-Ammende (eds) *Uprooting and After*, Springer-Verlag, New York, USA.

Note

1. A version of this paper was published in *Disasters*, 15(1): 12–23.

CHAPTER 9

The Socio-Cultural and Behavioural Context of Disasters and Small Dwellings

RUSSELL R. DYNES

Disaster Research Center, Department of Sociology,
University of Delaware, Newark, USA

Introduction

Social scientists are often at a disadvantage at interdisciplinary conferences for several reasons. Some of these disadvantages relate to the role which others perceive they should play and others relate to the style of presentation. First, in reference to style, social scientists, in general, do not use slides and other visual imagery in their presentations. The reasons for this are not clear. I have observed, however, that ineptitude with slide projectors is rather universal and not discipline related. But slides do provide a sense of 'hard' reality to audiences when words seldom do. Therefore, slides give the audience a sense of apparent truth which perhaps is not deserved. I am not suggesting that pictures distort truth, although they can, but I am suggesting that they can capture well physical reality but reveal little of social reality. Certainly, here, attention to construction details, to aesthetics, to physical layout are important but there needs to be a reminder that a small dwelling is not just a structure, a house, but that it is also a home. Being a home makes it in the location of family relationships, of generational ties, of socialization of children and of the construction of meaning. These aspects are seldom seen on slides but that does not mean they are not important. They are, and perhaps those dimensions are more critical to restore after disasters than are broken roofs. Furthermore, slides of small dwellings often do not convey the linkages to the social reality of the large human community. This often can be inferred by examining the background of the slide. But the human community is more than incidental background. The fact that such social reality is not easily portrayed does not mean that it is not critically important.

Other misunderstandings can arise concerning the appropriate role of social scientists in understanding disaster related issues. It is often assumed that social scientists are defenders of 'people'. In most discussions, people are 'problematic' to disaster mitigation, preparedness, response and recovery. Given that assumption, there is the underlying premise that if social scientists could only solve the 'people' problem, all else would be right with the world. Innovative technological schemes could now be implemented with considerable ease and these schemes, in the long run, would benefit the 'people' even if they do not know it.

These rather persistent images underplay the contributions that social sciences can play in understanding disasters. While disaster can be studied in a number of ways, at its core, disaster means 'social' disruption. That social disruption is only partial and somewhat incidentally related to damage to physical structures. Today, of course, we have a number of measures of physical agents and impacts. We can measure wind speed and direction. We can measure storm surges and flood stages. We have Richter and Mercalli scales to measure earth movements. We can do body counts and catalogue injuries as well as delineate 'injuries' to building structures and other environments. When we measure all of these dimensions, none of them captures the most important impacts on social life. We have no good measures of broken social relationships, created by death, injury or relocation. We have few clues as to the costs of disrupted work patterns and their accompanying economic losses. We have no good measures of the consequences of the segmentation and disorganization of community life, nor do we even attempt to measure the costs of delayed and disrupted futures. In effect, all disasters are failures on the part of human systems where the physical infrastructure fails to protect people from conditions which threaten their well being.

On the Importance of Understanding the Socio-Cultural Context

By suggesting that 'disaster' is, in effect, social disruption, this does not imply that if we could adequately measure that social disruption, there would be simple and effective solutions to 'disaster problems', including that of post impact housing. But it does imply that the social sciences can provide one kind of understanding of disaster and of housing issues. Some of this understanding will, in fact, raise complicated questions about the implementation of certain 'technological' and engineering solutions. For example, certain disciplines may ask: 'How do we construct dams to make them stronger to protect flood plains?' while, again, social scientists may ask: 'What are socially useful ways to use flood plains?' Obviously, these questions lead to quite different answers. At times, social scientists might contribute to changing the question to get more productive answers. For many years, agencies which monitor hazards have expressed puzzlement as to why people do not heed their warnings. But in recent years certain agencies have made considerable progress when they reframed the questions in the following way: 'How can we, as an agency, issue warnings that people will heed?' Such agencies, then, have expanded their role to be concerned with risk communication, public understanding and message content, as well as increasing the accuracy of their monitoring through better technology.

In certain instances, the importance of the socio-cultural context is obvious but the solutions to problems of less developed societies is often assumed to be 'development' and in particular the diffusion of appropriate technology. For example, disaster mitigation efforts in many developed societies have often focused on zoning restrictions and on the development of building codes. But in most less developed societies, the most disaster vulnerable areas are squatter communities, surrounding urban areas, populated by rural migrants drawn to marginal employment opportunities in the city. Given that situation, should rural reconstruction and land reform be seen as the major disaster mitigation strategy? Should building codes be enforced only among land owners and landlords? Or should conventional Western efforts of disaster mitigation be given low priority in the development schemes of others? After all, in areas where there is major flooding on a 50 year cycle, what mitigation strategies should be implemented for a population where the life expectancy is 40 years? These are difficult value questions which can be solved neither by the infusion of technology nor by the conceptualizations of social scientists.

On the other hand, the social sciences can contribute to understanding why 'good ideas' often do not turn out so well when introduced in other societies. Disaster impact is often used as a rationale for the relocation of towns and villages to safer ground. Therefore, aims of disaster mitigation can be achieved combined with improvements in housing. Such projects are seen by their donors as contributing to 'development' and to disaster mitigation, since they utilize construction techniques which make housing more disaster proof. Unfortunately, many such projects are less than successful in creating new communities. We know much about building houses but we know much less about building viable communities. What donors see as new communities are usually only collections of new houses, populated by people torn from their previous social networks. Donors are willing to repair structures but not to repair social networks. It is true that, in certain instances, communities develop from collections of new housing but generally only after the planned community is replanned by the residents. Donor generosity, in fact, can delay 'recovery' since disaster recovery, in the final analysis, means that the social networks have been repaired. Speeding the repair of those social networks might be given the first priority in disaster recovery, although most donors would not consider such an option concrete enough.

In the long run, social sciences will not be able to provide pat answers to problems such as these but often can provide insight into why technically adequate solutions 'fail' and how failures might be changed into 'successes'. In addition, the social sciences can point out how technological solutions to disaster vulnerability can also disrupt socio-cultural systems. Development projects, such as dam construction intended to increase energy and decrease floods, have resulted in extensive social costs, destroying established communities with little effort to maintain their social viability.

Ultimately, the contributions of the social sciences may be greatest in sharpening the debate on political solutions and on the direction of public policy. This does not imply an automatic rejection of technological solutions to disaster related issues, but points to the fact that the implementation of any solution takes place within a specific, political, economic and socio-cultural situation. Understanding that situation requires the contributions which the social sciences can make.

On the Limits of Cultural Variability

One of the areas where the social sciences has contributed to important public understanding is the notion of cultural variability. This is an important insight to overcome the Eurocentric view which claimed 'civilization' to be the central expression of 'developed' societies compared with the rest of the 'primitives'. Certainly the understanding is important that there are many possible patterns of behaviour and these had to be understood and valued within their own system of evaluation, collectively called culture. On the other hand, that understanding has often been pushed to the conclusion that there are no similarities, or perhaps no universals between and among societies. Given that view, it is impossible to generalize about behaviour across societies and thus the social sciences are only valuable in identifying the diversity of behaviour but have nothing to contribute to understanding processes across societies.

Dealing specifically with disaster behaviour, there has developed, within the last forty years, a considerable volume of social science research, most of it, of course, in industrialized countries and much of it in the United States. (For a useful summary, see Drabek 1986.) In examining that research, one is struck with the similarity of behavioural response to risk, to warning, to the emergency itself and to recovery. At the level of individual and family response in all societies, there is striking continuity. On the other hand, cultural differences are most frequently revealed in terms of the organizational structure and the political structure. Some societies are rich with community organizations which can deal with disaster; others are not. Some societies assume a helplessness and dependence on the Government; others do not. Some societies expect a diffuse and decentralized decision-making system; others reflect a centralized and direct governance. For some societies, a disaster is a problem to be solved; for others, it is an opportunity to replace the problem-solving structure in the society. In some societies, disaster response and recovery is an individual and private affair; in others, it is a corporate and Governmental task.

The reason for raising these issues here is that, in thinking trans-societally about disaster behaviour and response, there is often a tendency to see the major contributions of the social sciences as having the intellectual tools and concepts to explicate cultural differences. It is argued here that there are great similarities in the social processes centring on the reaction of societies to disaster. The primary variations rest at the difference in social structure. These differences can provide considerable understanding as to improving social adaptability in all social systems.

On the International Decade

The critical importance of understanding the socio-cultural context of disaster is especially important for the near future. The decade of the 1990s has been identified by the United Nations as the International Decade for Natural Disaster Reduction (IDNDR). This calls for a worldwide effort to mitigate the effects of natural disasters and to reduce the vulnerability of human communities to destructive environmental forces. Such an effort internationally will have its counterpart in various national states to provide a focus on efforts to reduce the negative consequences of disasters. To reach that important goal, it will be necessary to utilize all branches of knowledge, including the social sciences. In many places, much of the initial effort has been directed toward the development of new technologies which it is claimed will contribute to greater social and economic development. Development efforts carried out without regard to environmental consequences can expose human systems to even greater disaster vulnerability. Resources spent on costly technological solutions can draw scarce resources away from equally effective and less costly solutions. For example, investment in warning systems may be directed toward the purchase of advanced electronic equipment rather than on the development of messages which can be understood and heeded. In any event, the International Decade does have the potential for focusing both Governmental and scientific attention on the reduction of the effects of natural disaster. It can lead to technological innovation and to social invention. But social invention is likely to have greater and longer lasting consequences.

REFERENCE

DRABEK, T.E. (1986) *Human Systems Responses to Disaster: An Inventory of Sociological Findings*, Springer-Verlag, New York, USA.

CHAPTER 10

A View of the Role of NGOs in Natural Disaster Work

REINHARD SKINNER

Intermediate Technology Development Group
Rugby, UK

Introduction

In this conference, as elsewhere, much has been made of the distinction between natural disaster work based on relief efforts and that which is concerned more with prevention and mitigation. The latter 'school' is particularly vocal: it is keen to establish that the relief approach is not only partial and merely reactive, but also may actually be incompatible with development as a whole. The main reason given for this is that while the focus is on relief, development efforts tend to be forgotten and the latter can actually help reduce the impact of disasters.

Similarly, it has in this forum been clear that some friction exists between those representing the natural sciences and others from the social disciplines. This seems to be a purely artificial problem brought about by misunderstanding; one would hope it has less to do with professional jealousies or territorialism. What appears to be the cause is the injection into the disaster debate, which has often been dominated by considerations of quantitative prediction and logistics, of a social and behavioural dimension. What should be seen as an additional tool in coping with disasters is too often regarded as a rival approach.

The following notes present a view of the role which can be fruitfully adopted by NGOs. It is a straightforward view but one which allows natural and social sciences to be treated as complementary. If the reader concludes that what has been said is almost too obvious to have been worth recording, the author's purpose will have been achieved.

Process and Event

The main difference between the 'relief' and 'development' approaches to disasters is that the former is concerned with coping with the situation, or event, while the latter aims to mitigate its effects through development efforts carried out over a period of time – a 'process' view of the disaster environment. I will concentrate on the latter, while by no means denying the importance of relief work when a disaster occurs. Indeed, it is clear that part of the 'process' will be this event, though it can be only a part.

In the context of human settlements, development takes both physical and social forms. Layouts have to be made and house designs drawn, while educational, health and recreational needs will make demands on behaviour and attitudes as much as on the skills of the architect and engineer to provide structures.

The siting of dwellings and settlements as a whole in hazard-prone areas will require the skills of the geologist, the hydrologist and, perhaps, other physical scientists. The intended beneficiaries, however, will need to be convinced of the suitability of the sites, the acceptability of layouts and designs, and the advantages of building materials to be used. Without this, as has been found in numerous settlement development projects, residents will justifiably employ the range of subverting strategies they invariably possess. Where there is local agreement, however, the project becomes a more amicable activity and may bring forth local resources, in the form of cooperation, which make it easier to implement.

To reach such a position requires discussion between officials and beneficiaries. This in turn assumes a degree of exchange of opinions and the willingness on both sides to consider the possibility that the other may have some ideas which are more appropriate to the situation than its own. In other words, it is a collaborative and participatory process.

The Technical and the Social

It has been said before, but is worth repeating, that to involve the people in housing cannot be limited to any one stage of the process. If they are involved in planning, they are more likely than otherwise to be prepared to offer their efforts in implementation, and if they are included in implementation they are more likely to be willing to assist in maintenance. One is usually more disposed to caring for what one has had a part in designing and constructing than something which has been imposed. To ask for participation in one of these stages without a corresponding involvement in the others is to ignore this interconnection of behavioural traits. The same is true of any development activity which relies on local cooperation for sustainability rather than being one-off events.

This being the case, one is now working in the realm of local organisational actions, including leadership, mutual aid, group solidarity and group pressures to conform. Indeed, we are in the realm in which the social sciences thrive. If we want to locate a settlement on a site relatively safe from landslips, making use of community labour in building with unfamiliar but relatively earthquake resistant materials, it is essential to have a strong natural scientific, architectural and engineering input. But no less important will be the extent to which the sociologist or anthropologist may be able to link the intended beneficiary to an acceptable introduction of these changes.

An important example here which frequently manifests itself in the shelter field is the rejection of new technologies. While a technique, or new and improved materials may have been developed, these are not always acceptable to the intended beneficiaries. ITDG has found this in more than one instance in Peru. In Lima, residents of a squatter settlement refused to use stabilised 'adobe' (mud block) and preferred to save to buy far more expensive concrete blocks since the latter were identified with 'modern, urban' life and the former with the type of construction which had, albeit in a more primitive form, been employed for centuries in the 'backward' rural areas which they had left behind.

In rural areas there have been similar responses. In sites prone to floods much research has been carried out by state and non-Governmental institutions into more durable building materials. Residents, however, have frequently rejected their use, resorting instead to the materials which have failed them in the past but whose advantages and limitations they do at least understand.

Intervention, Popular Response and NGOs

The above examples point again to the need for the technical to be complemented by the social. It is only by understanding why people accept or reject technical innovation that the latter can be of practical use. In Peru, ITDG has undertaken a study which attempts to do this, and the results have recently been published (Monzón and Olíden 1990). One of the questions raised during the research was that of optimal timing of technology introduction for the mitigation of disasters.

It was considered whether directly after a major disaster, victims might be more amenable to change. In a disaster situation people may be so desperate that they are willing to accept almost anything, at least in the short term, and may thereafter come to realise that there were indeed advantages to the new technology. Whatever the answer, a moral question is raised: however sound the new technology concerned, is it justifiable to capitalise upon the poor's misfortune in a manner which is also implicitly paternalistic?

In the urban situation an attempt was made to overcome rejection by assisting in the construction of a communal building which, it was hoped, would serve to demonstrate the technical value of the material which would then lead to residents adopting it for their own dwellings. In fact, the resistance has continued; it would appear that the striving for conspicuous 'urban' status is overriding. The next question might be whether the rapidly inflating conventional building materials costs and falling real incomes in Peru would make the new technology more acceptable. The outcome is yet to be seen.

The Peruvian examples referred to show how an NGO has seen the way in which technical and social issues are melded in the disaster and human settlement situation. It is also likely that NGOs are best suited to recognising when this type of problem arises and what alternative possibilities exist for their solution. State bodies tend to be too compartmentalised in their own specialisms, such as research into structures and building materials, to take on such a role. Their mandates are usually limited not to include what is essentially community development work. State agencies charged with community work are not renowned for their technical abilities in the field under discussion. NGOs, on the other hand, are more likely to work at community level and to rely upon the cooperation of residents. This means that they are, in principle at least, able to link their particular technical expertise to community aspirations and expressed needs. Though this has not always been the 'modus operandi' NGOs have adopted, at least the potential is there to be exploited.

This makes it possible to suggest that NGOs, such as ITDG, have a number of roles in the area of disasters and the small dwelling:

- they can stimulate community involvement in the design, implementation and maintenance of disaster mitigation and prevention activities in a way in which agencies with more distant geographical and social relationships and narrower professional concerns are unable to do;
- by the same token, they can link communities to relevant state and other outside bodies. The latter will benefit from the liaison role of the NGO which facilitate their technical contributions being integrated into the community in a participatory manner. For the community, the NGO is able to identify available institutional and financial resources which can be integrated into mitigation work;
- the NGO can undertake long-term activities, such as research, training and assistance in local organizations, which larger bodies at national and international levels are not, at present, apparently willing to do (though this may well change during the course of the International Decade for Natural Disaster Reduction). For the time being they prefer to involve themselves in discreet and short-term disaster work rather than the longer development activities which are specially geared to disaster reduction.

Conclusion

In the preceding pages it has been mentioned that disaster work is not just about relief but involves a broader range of development activities. These were shown to bring out the need for collaboration between official agencies and beneficiary communities as well as the place which both natural and social sciences hold.

None of the above strikes the author as contentious. However, certain issues are raised which are ripe for a more profound examination than is possible here. The first of these is that relief and development agencies need to be brought together to formulate ways in which their respective talents can be dovetailed into one another. If the Decade arrives at a partial answer to this it will have achieved a great deal. A question which will arise when considering this will be how locally specific, or 'customised', programmes can be established which are also replicable, at least in part.

Secondly, the specific ways in which different participants in disaster work, natural and social scientists, communities and NGOs, can pool their resources need to be explored. Following from this, training programmes will need to be established at national and local level for the participants who are about to engage in this largely new cooperative venture.

Thirdly, since disaster reduction exercises will depend upon community support, it will be vital to acquire a better understanding of the variables which affect behaviour, attitudes and motivation. The work undertaken by ITDG and mentioned above is a possible starting point here.

Are these areas in which other NGOs have a special role to play?

REFERENCE

MONZÓN, F.M. and OLÍDEN, J.C. (1990) *Tecnología y Vivienda Popular*, ITDG and CIDAP, Lima, Peru.

CHAPTER 11

Cross Cultural Disaster Planning: The Alice Springs Flood

JOHN HANDMER

Centre for Resource and Environmental Studies
National University, Canberra, Australia

Introduction

The settlement of Alice Springs is subject to occasional flooding by the Todd River. The river bed is dry most of the time, sandy and lightly timbered. Along with its central location, these factors make the river bed an attractive place for Aboriginal campers. In addition, a number of Aboriginal 'town camps' are located in flood prone areas. Despite its benign appearance the short warning time of between one and five hours makes camping in or adjacent to the river bed particularly hazardous. People living in these situations constitute the groups most at risk from flooding in Alice Springs.

The question arises as to how well they are served by the flood warning and emergency response system. This paper examines these issues through a study of a major flood which occurred over Easter 1988. Flood damages, the warning system and emergency response are reviewed with emphasis on the Aboriginal community.

Floods in Alice Springs

Alice Springs is a city of some 24,000 people located in Central Australia, where it is the only sizeable settlement. By most standards it is a remote place being about 1500 km from any major urban area. The city is subject to occasional flooding from the Todd River, which rises on rocky country some five hours' river travel time north of Alice and vanishes in the desert sands south-east of the city. The river bed is sandy, lightly timbered and dry, except during flooding. Four creeks (drains) feed into the river as it passes through the built-up area. The area suffered serious flooding over Easter 1988; comparable floods had last occurred in 1983. The official warning system can provide between one and five hours' notice of flooding; however no official warnings were provided to the public before the Easter 1988 flood.

The Study

Following the flood, a team from the Centre for Resource and Environmental Studies (CRES) was commissioned by the Northern Territory Power and Water Authority (PAWA), to assess flood damages and to study the operation of the flood warning system. The study brief specified that special attention was to be paid to the Aboriginal community, which appeared to have been particularly severely affected by the flood. The brief also limited the study to the urban area of Alice Springs. Results are reported in full in Handmer et al (1989).

Information for the study came from documentary sources and from interviews. The material was collected during two visits to Alice Springs, 30 May –7 June and 11–18 August 1988. Documentary sources included reports on the flood, material on file and a number of organisations and newspapers.

Interviews were administered in four distinct groups: (i) a questionnaire survey of a sample of 28 flooded households, 25 flooded businesses, and 8 flooded Government organisations; (ii) 7 interviews with officials and organisations involved in the flood forecasting, warning and emergency response system; (iii) interviews with 4 members of the broadcast media; and (iv) interviews with members of the Aboriginal community, and with organisations dealing with Aboriginal concerns.

Damages were assessed for the residential sector using the ANUFLOOD procedure, while estimates for other sectors came directly from interviews. ANUFLOOD is a commercially available computer package for the assessment of tangible direct flood damages and flood mitigation options. Use of the procedure is becoming standard practice throughout much of Australia and New Zealand.

The study team included members experienced in working with Aboriginal people in Alice Springs and elsewhere. Aboriginal people were approached through the Tangentyere Council, an Aboriginal organisation which represents and provides services to the Alice Springs town camp communities. Tangentyere staff, the staff of the Aboriginal media (the Central Australian Aboriginal Media Association, known as CAAMA radio, and Imparja television), Aboriginal Congress (a medical organisation), the Sacred Sites Authority, and the Central Land Council, were interviewed. Camp communities and river bed campers were visited and some members interviewed with the guidance of Tangentyere staff.

This paper concentrates on the Aboriginal Community.

Aboriginal 'Town Camps' and River Bed Campers

Aboriginal people comprise some 10 per cent of the Alice Springs urban population. They live in conventional housing distributed throughout the town, and in some 19 town camps both within and on the outskirts of Alice Springs. 'Town camp' is a term given to an Aboriginal housing or camping site in or near a town. Many of the 'town camps' have housing units suitable for extended family occupation.

The Todd River bed is used as a camping area by people who do not have an established place to stay. This includes: Aboriginal people visiting the town who have no kin in Alice Springs; visitors whose kin have no room for their relatives; and groups who are between town camps. The last group would include those who have moved because of a death in their camp, but who have yet to find space in another town camp. (Moving to another area because of the death of a relative is common in Aboriginal culture.)

Importantly for this case study, the river bed is also home to some people who have houses in town camps but have left them to avoid heavy drinking or offensive behaviour by other camp members or visitors. Disturbing behaviour is a common problem for campers in Alice Springs and elsewhere (Collman 1988; Ross 1990). The river bed camps are made up predominantly of older people who keep all their personal belongings (blankets, pots, and clothes) with them. It is estimated that at any one time there are approximately 200 river bed campers.

Flooding and Aborigines

Traditional Aboriginal lifestyle demands close observation and intimate knowledge of environmental indicators. So it is quite logical that flooding along the Todd River has rarely taken Aborigines by surprise. This is despite the partial destruction of Aboriginal culture and the negative impact of alcohol. The 1988 floods appear to be an exception. However, water from the Todd is by no means the only way that town camps can be flooded. They may be flooded by creeks, overflowing drains and overland flow due to heavy local rain. Some camps, although not flooded, may be isolated by flood waters (Figure 1).

There is no doubt that Aborigines in and near Alice Springs are particularly severely affected by flooding. Many camping areas and some dwellings are inundated, and the accompanying bad weather forces people to crowd into the

79

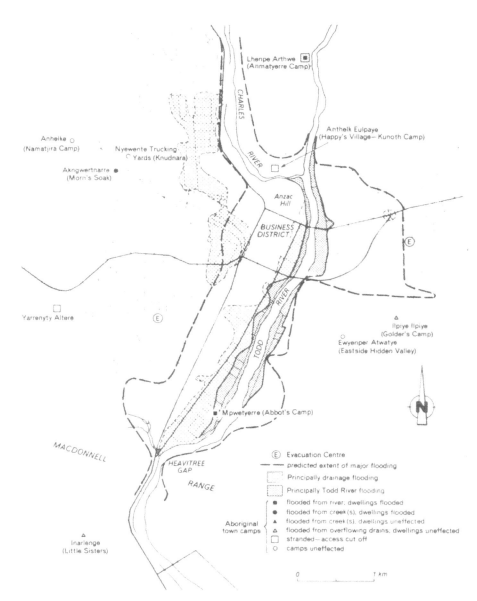

FIGURE 1   *Map of Alice Springs showing areas flooded in 1988 (stippled), location of some Aboriginal town camps (others are beyond the borders of the map) and predicted extent of major flooding*

remaining dwellings. Clearly, flash flooding poses safety problems for those camping in river beds, who may also lose their possessions.

Severe natural events, such as major flooding, may be seen as retribution for some transgression of Aboriginal values. Violation of a sacred area could constitute such a transgression. Nevertheless, traditional Aborigines were not passive in the face of flood threat. For example, Aboriginals of the Clarence and Richmond rivers of north coast New South Wales maintained special reserves for use during floods. In these reserves game and other foods were left untouched except during major flooding (Pratos 1972; Sabhe 1970). 'Hunter/ collectors are not impervious to the tyranny of floods . . . but their way of life affords more security than that enjoyed by food-producing people' (Torry 1979:522). Traditionally, Aborigines in Central Australia were nomadic and did not have permanent camps. It appears they may have avoided camping in the Todd, preferring rock shelters and other sites adjacent to the river. Now, none are nomadic and circumstances such as restricted access to adjacent sites have virtually forced some Aborigines to stay in the river bed.

Flood Damages

Aboriginal losses

Direct damage to property managed by Aboriginal organisations within Alice Springs is estimated at $68,000. (All values are in 1988 Australian dollars.) This includes damage from flood waters other than the Todd River. In addition, about 75 river bed campers lost all their possessions, and many people had to seek alternative accommodation.

However, the greatest losses in the Aboriginal community were the intangibles of death, racial tension, and stress and potential health effects. Three Aboriginal river bed campers drowned in the Todd. Racial tension may have increased for two reasons: a *perception* in some quarters that the emergency procedures were racist in that the Aboriginal community received a lower level of service; and comments by some politicians suggesting that the flood would have been controlled by a dam if it had not been for Aboriginal opposition. Aboriginal opposition to the proposed dam resulted from concern over a sacred site lying within the reservoir limits. It also reflected scepticism about the Government's real motives. There was concern that once the dam was built it could easily be converted from a temporary storage for flood waters, into a recreation facility permanently inundating the sacred site.

It is particularly difficult to assess the impact of the flood on Aboriginal health as their health status is generally poor, which tends to mask the impact of a single event. The poor health is another indicator of the marginalised status of Aborigines within Australian society, and of their consequent increased vulnerability to hazards. In the past, it appears that flooding and heavy rain have been associated with an increased incidence of pneumonia among town campers. This is probably a result of people crowding into the remaining dry houses.

Overall losses

These damages to the Aboriginal community should be seen in the context of overall losses to Alice Springs (apart from those to town camp and river bed campers). Over 200 dwellings and some 35 commercial enterprises experienced overfloor flooding or major damage from overground inundation. In addition, many roads and other infrastructure were damaged. The residential tangible damage is estimated at $1,730,000 and that for the commercial sector at $960,000. Including additional damage to infrastructure within the area of the study, the best estimate for combined damage is $3,461,000. These values do not include flood damage to property and facilities caused by the same event outside the city. Alice Springs also experienced extensive damage from wind and rain and losses due to the surcharge of the urban drainage system. These have not generally been included except where such losses were within the limits of flood water from the Todd. Of the households interviewed which had experienced overfloor flooding, 60 per cent reported stress induced emotional or health problems as a result of the flood. In some instances there were direct links to physical health, eg heart conditions and asthma. In others the flood experience resulted in stress during subsequent periods of heavy rain.

Warnings and Emergency Response

Those responsible for flood warning in Alice Springs face two major problems: limited time and limited coverage. The main gauge at Wigley George on the Todd River provides about one hour's accurate warning of flooding in the city. Several additional hours general warning may be received from a catchment rainfall gauge. However, the city may also be inundated by local runoff or storm-water drain surcharge for which there is no warning. In this respect the system is typical of those in Australian urban areas, where serious flooding may occur without activation of the warning system. Ignoring drainage problems may also reduce the credibility of the warning system and related public information. Clearly, there is little time available for those in or near the river bed.

The system is fairly complex and has been characterised by equipment failure at the flood detection end. A number of additional problems have limited its effectiveness in the past, many of which are common to most warning systems. One unusual aspect was an apparent need to convene the

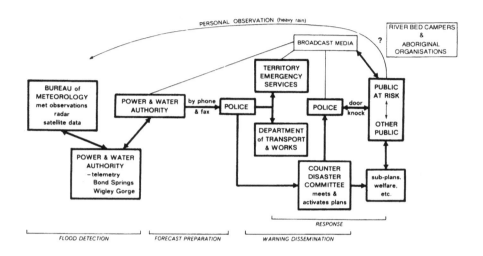

FIGURE 2 *The Alice Springs flood warning system, Easter 1988. The official system is shown in heavy type. Note that Aboriginal groups and all media were not part of this system*

Counter Disaster Committee, a police responsibility, before the disaster plan could be activated. By the time the Committee met at 9am on 31 March, the flood was approaching its peak.

Notifying the Aboriginal community

No one had formal responsibility for ensuring that the warning was passed on to Aboriginal groups including river bed campers – clearly the group most at risk (Figure 2). In the past they have left the danger area well before flooding, but the 1988 flood showed that a warning procedure is needed. The Aboriginal community is not well networked with the non-Aboriginal community and must therefore be specifically targeted.

Curiously, the broadcast media, essential for rapid warning dissemination, were not part of the system. This included the local Aboriginal radio and television, an important source of information for town camp and river bed dwellers.

Once the water authority detects a flood, they pass the information on to only one organisation, the police. It is up to the police to notify all other groups. This represented a serious weakness in the information chain. Apart from the likelihood of delays, the police may lack credibility in the eyes of some Aborigines. Aboriginal organisations and all broadcast media should be among those notified by the water authority.

Pre-flood publicity

The authorities had compiled a pre-flood information brochure – a concept which received wide endorsement. The brochure contains a map of Alice Springs showing the extent of the 1:20, 1:50 and 1:100 floods, descriptions of the flood risk and warning system, and advice on appropriate action before and during a flood. (A 1:100 flood is that flood with a 1 in 100 chance of being equalled or exceeded in any given year.) It did not say how people could expect to receive their initial warning.

Unfortunately, although the brochure had been widely distributed, it had not reached the various Aboriginal organisations, town camps or river bed campers. In any case, it is probably too technical in nature to be of much value to the public at risk (the modern consumer does not generally have to work hard for information), and especially for Aborigines many of whom use English as a second language. In the Alice Springs town camps of the early 1980s nine Aboriginal languages were spoken (Ross 1981). Brochures are not usually seen as effective vehicles for public information, but the recall level of over 50 per cent among non-Aboriginals is probably slightly better than average for this type of programme. The useful map of Alice Springs may have helped to ensure that people retained the brochure for longer than would otherwise have been the case.

Those responsible for public flood information programmes, such as the brochure, should clearly specify the target audiences, and what impact they would like to have on the targets. Effective ways of reaching the different target groups could then be developed.

Warning System Performance

Those flooded did not receive official warnings before inundation started. These were virtually non-existent and were belatedly broadcast over only one of the three local radio stations. It is perhaps a paradox that despite this there were few complaints. People seemed reasonably satisfied with the system, although some would have liked a warning and more information on urban drainage overflow. This satisfaction probably results from very low expectations (see also Parker and Neal 1990).

There is little reliance on official flood warnings and the provision of warnings in Alice Springs was seen as a difficult task by those interviewed.

Many people, including members of Aboriginal organisations, realised that flooding was likely because of the sustained heavy rain. Personal observation of environmental indicators warned these people. Aborigines in low lying town camps and most of those camped in the river bed were warned by the bad weather and by officials from their organisations.

Nevertheless, some were slow to move to safer areas. Many had nowhere acceptable to move to, as the few options were also seen as risky. For those who moved to the river bed to avoid town-camp conflict, the most obvious alternative was to return to their camps. However, the problems resulting from alcohol abuse and violence in some camps, compounded by pressures to share food and cash in accordance with kinship norms, make some river bed campers reluctant to return before flood water appeared. Ross (1990) points out that household heads, and others with financial resources, may 'be severely put upon in terms of food, funds, housework and noise' without any rights to demand reciprocal contributions or different behaviour. River bed campers concerned about this may wait hoping that an evacuation centre or other option would emerge. In the 1988 flood the evacuation centres were not opened early enough to be available for those leaving the river bed. By the time the centres were opened the river was flowing.

When evacuation centres are available there are still cultural barriers to their use. In Aboriginal society relationships between individuals and clans are carefully defined and observed. There are widespread avoidance relationships, such as between women and any men classified socially as their sons-in-law. Members of different language groups also avoid close contact. Equally, Aboriginal people feel uncomfortable in the presence of non-Aboriginal people, and may hesitate to use evacuation centres for this reason; the feeling is reciprocated by many non-Aborigines (Keen et al 1988).

Conclusion

Much of the Australian Aboriginal community occupies a marginal position in socio-economic terms. As with other marginalised groups they are therefore likely to be especially vulnerable to natural (and other) hazards (Handmer, 1984). This is certainly the case in Alice Springs for those Aborigines living in town camps or camping in the bed of the Todd River, who constitute the group most at risk from flooding. In dollar terms their losses are not great, but they suffer very substantial intangible losses.

The Aboriginal and non-Aboriginal communities are not well linked, and the pre-flood publicity and warning system largely missed the town camps, river bed campers and their organisations. To overcome this the authorities need to work with the Aboriginal organisations and media, who indicated that they would like to be more involved in all aspects of flood hazard management. For their part, the authorities need to appreciate the pressures on Aborigines attempting to cope with European style housing and traditional kinship responsibilities. The flood warning plan should assign specific responsibility for notifying the high risk groups of potential flooding. Reduction in the hazard facing town and river bed campers is most likely to follow activity directed at improving their socio-economic condition.

Acknowledgement

This paper is based on work funded by the Northern Territory Power and Water Authority. Special thanks are due to Ruth Birgin and Meg Keen who participated in the field work, Helen Ross who provided guidance on Aboriginal matters, and to Dingle Smith and Mark Greenaway who calculated the tangible flood damage.

REFERENCES

COLLMAN, G. (1988) *Fringe Campers and Welfare*, University of Queensland Press, Brisbane, Australia.

HANDMER, J.W. (1984) *Property Acquisition for Flood Damage Reduction*, Australian Water Resources Council, Final Report for Project 80/125, (also available as CRES Working Paper 1986/26) Canberra, Australia.

HANDMER, J.W., SMITH, D.I. and GREENAWAY, M. (1989) *Flood Warning and Damages in Alice Springs*, in three parts, prepared for the Northern Territory Power and Water Authority, Darwin, Australia.

KEEN, M., ROSS, H. and HANDMER, J.W. (1988) 'The Cultural Dimension of Hazard Management: Flooding in Alice Springs', *Newsletter of the International Panel for Risk Reduction in Hazard Prone Areas*, FHRC, Middlesex Polytechnic. No. 3, November: 23–27.

PARKER, D.J. and NEAL, J. (1990) 'Evaluating the Performance of Flood Warning Systems', in J.W. Handmer and E.C. Penning-Rowsell (eds) *Hazards and the Communication of Risk*, Gower, Aldershot, UK.

PRATOS, M.D. (1972) *Aborigines and Europeans on the Northern Rivers of NSW 1823–1881*, unpublished MA thesis, Macquarie University, Sydney, Australia.

ROSS, H. (1981) *Submission to House of Representatives Standing Committee on Aboriginal Affairs: Inquiry into Fringe-Dwelling Aboriginal Communities*, Australian Institute of Aboriginal Studies, Canberra, Australia.

ROSS, H. (1987) *Just for Living: Aboriginal Perceptions of Housing in Northwest Australia*, Aboriginal Studies Press, Canberra, Australia.

ROSS, H. (1990) 'Household Compositions and Use of Space', Paper for *Organizing for an Ecologically Sustainable Australia*, Centre for Resource and

Environmental Studies, Australian National University, Canberra, 8–19 May 1990.

SABHE, N. (1970) *An Ethnohistory of the Clarence Valley*, unpublished MA thesis, University of New England, Armidale, NSW, Australia.

TORRY, W.I. (1979) 'Anthropological Studies in Hazardous Environments: Past Trends and New Horizons', *Current Anthropology* 20(3): 517–541.

CHAPTER 12

Disasters and Housing Policy for Rural Bangladesh

DAVID OAKLEY

Consultant,
United Nations Disaster Relief Organisation (UNDRO)
Geneva, Switzerland

Introduction

This paper considers rural housing policy formulation in the context of settlement pattern and development strategies. It proposes four types of programmes to be identified at the national Government level. A case is made for the establishment of a unit of Government to be responsible for the formulation of rural housing improvement: an enabling rather than an executive agency.

Settlement and Society

Many studies have shown (Ali 1986; Jansen 1987; BUET 1981; BRAC Prokashana 1986) that the rural society of Bangladesh is a society of very active social and economic transactions by which elites maintain their position and the poor lose assets to the elites. Flood disasters accelerate the number of transactions in which the poor lose control of assets. Even if a poor household's dwelling survives the flood, their economic position may be so imperilled that they have to pass over ownership to a member of the rural elite in return for a loan or a share in cropping.

Rural house clusters or village settlements are artifacts which can be seen. The visitor from the urban world can be forgiven for not looking beyond that which is seen, but to do no more is to misunderstand the nature of the buildings we can see clustered in bari and para. The villager knows them to stand at the intersection of a number of forces that determine size, shape, quality and their relationship one to the other.

Each household is in its own particular balance within the net of influences and the house – damaged or not by the flood – itself forms an element in the balancing net. The perception of need as seen by a household in the net will not be the same as the perception of need as seen from assisting agencies of GOB and the NGOs.

Destruction of the family house or its severe damage by flood puts the owner or renter into a newly unstable relationship within the net of village money lending, job opportunities and status within faction group: or as a fringe member of a group. Some very poor households are tipped over into destitution by the house loss. But a house represents only a part of their need.

Recognition of Housing Need

How the need is recognised is all important. It will structure the design of a programme to meet the (perceived) need. One way of getting at need technically is by way of recognising location (in relation to flood experience) and by homestead form of tenure.

(1) Those with title to a homestead site:

- those who have an earth walled house whose walls and plinth need reconstruction and a new roof structure and roof covering provided;
- those who have a totally destroyed earth walled house but who have dropped down the status and income scale to a point where their only option is to demolish the earth walls to make a higher plinth, and then erect or have erected a bamboo-framed, jute stick or bamboo mat, walled and roofed house;
- those who have a bamboo and jute stick house which has rotted through the flood.

(2) Those who live in a settlement but who are without title to a homestead site.

- those on rented or rent-free land provided by kin group or faction. Their need for a new house may be great, (the danger of a ground landowner pushing them out of the house once it is built is perhaps just as great);
- those for whom GOB makes Khas land available on lease or by gifting.

(3) Those who squat on marginal lands, river char and around beel areas.

- land ownership is a difficulty in relation to these households. It is perhaps more useful to see them as semi-nomads who cultivate for part of the year. The lands they work are greatly at risk from flooding and drought. At times of flood the people move up on to high embankments, taking their shelters with them.

Locations

Each village (mouza), para and bari will be set in a particular context of flood hazard which requires recognition. Design and specification of replacement dwellings will be changed by different site circumstances. The characteristic building situations of Bangladesh are:

- within a flood protected scheme area that did not fail (was neither broken or overtopped) in 1987 or 1988;
- within a flood protected area but where protective embankments were not completed in 1987 or 1988; but are expected to be before commencement of following flood seasons;
- within flood protected area but where flood broke through or overtopped embankments;
- in completed river flood protected areas but where internal floods originated from heavy rainfalls and overland flooding from an unexpected quarter;
- within a drainage scheme but not one that is flood protected.

The complexity of the definition of need becomes apparent even when making a reconnaissance of the terrain (Figure 1). The social and economic perception can be only by the rural inhabitants themselves. The assessment of the engineering and planning aspects of need is a question of bringing local perceptions and knowledge into conjunction with professional expert assessment of location risk and dwelling type risk.

Shelter Design and Construction

This topic, when conventionally studied, is with a focus on 'the buildings'. In rural Bangladesh, this is not a useful approach since house design and construction and settlement layout are so intimately interconnected with the rural culture, polity and economy.

A three-eyed vision is required to gain insight, an insight that is required if appropriate programmes of housing intervention are to be devised. The three eyes must be for:

- the forms, structure, materials and site situation of the dwellings;
- the organizational, contracting and self-help systems through which they come into being;
- the cultural and social meaning of the dwellings for the local community.

Floods of an expected character, depth and length of stay are an annual event in Bangladesh. Such floods are part of the conception of 'everyday

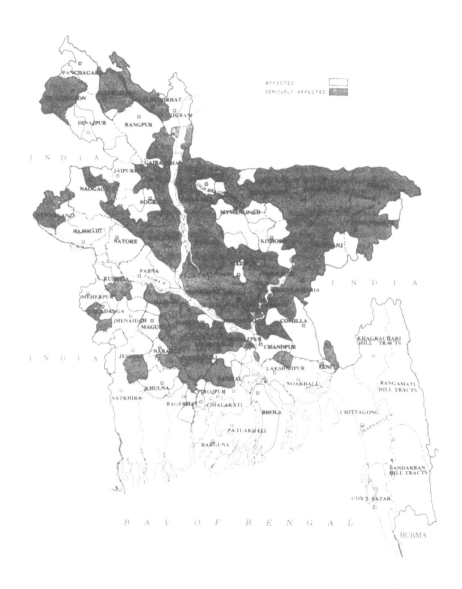

FIGURE 1   *Bangladesh floods: regional and global environmental perspectives*
[Source: Oakley Report, UNDP, Dhaka, 1988]

occurrence'. It is the flood that is exceptionally deep and long staying; or which takes place in areas unaccustomed to floods, which is felt as 'disaster'.

A disaster is an interruption in the previously normal sequence and pattern of human habitation. That is in the location of dwellings in a community of homesteads and villages connected by paths, roads and railway, ferry and river boat. Dwelling renovation and reconstruction may have to exhibit some design elements which are new. But continuity is also important. Respect has to be paid to traditional solutions which have worked in the past; even where changed perception of risks now leads to the need to review and perhaps modify the tradition. This assertion is relevant both to the design of transitional rehabilitation shelters and to the permanent shelter reconstruction programmes.

Technical Intervention

As understanding develops in the minds of those who wish to help improve rural shelter in the face of flood risk, so the complexity of the process in which intervention is proposed becomes more evident. Supply of finished or semi-finished structures appears as an option that may relate to relatively few households (dwellers on char lands for example or homeless widows with large families). Changes in design, material purchase may be a better option for many. Skill training may be needed where transformation of building process seems indicated (Oakley 1987).

Policy Search

As the relief-dominated period after the floods shades away into that of rehabilitation and reconstruction, so the declared general policies of Government in settlement developments and housing begin to shape project proposals precipitated by recognition of needs and identified scenarios of future disasters.

Institutional framework of Government

There is no lead agency for housing in Bangladesh: no Ministry of Housing or Settlements or Rural Housing Bureau. This has made the progression of any Government policy drive to stimulate private initiatives in housing and shelter provision difficult to both mount or sustain.

A number of Government agencies have roles in housing action but they operate in separate contexts and lack coordination, or any common approach, to rural housing as might be defined by:

- income group recognition;
- affordability assessment.

Private institutions

Many international and national Non-Government Organizations and Voluntary Bodies are active in rural development. Representatives are present here today. Some have included building material development and house construction in their integrated rural programmes. Some have developed 'design-and-implement' house type supply programmes to the needy after flood disasters. There has been some success but also many implementation difficulties. There will be much to learn from an analysis of the NGO experiences.

Institutional efficiency

Currently, for the rural housing sector this efficiency is very low. A base agency or bureau is a necessity. This should act as GOB 'client' for rural housing improvement and:

- set policy;
- identify technical/social objectives;
- define technical standards;
- approve operating delivery programmes;
- stimulate financing ideas and prime agreed action;
- encourage Research and Development;
- enable private commercial bodies and NGOs to contribute in all the above through providing a GOB enabling institutional setting.

Since this is a policy area in which GOB has decided to limit itself to the client function, the implementing and executive agencies (voluntary bodies and active NGOs) need to form a negotiating board to deal as a group with the GOB client Bureau (when formed).

Programme and Project Design

Project is used here to mean a proposal to carry out work within an identified rural shelter programme, for example:

- Emergency Shelter;
- Char Lands Shelter;

- House Improvement Programme;
- Refuge House Types.

Policy Framework

The policy framework forms (together with the recognition of types of households under impact of flood disaster) one of the defining elements of the problem that is to be solved by the project design. As a result of declared intention, study and research, it is then possible to determine why the pattern of housing is as it is. This is then viewed in relation to national policy and standards, in the light of the scale of technical and financial inputs likely to be available, to create a policy. From the policy integration of analysis and synthesis, some viable goals can be defined, which can give a housing programme and plan, presented in relation to household and house condition, and specific income groups. This then leads to technical development and financial planning; resource assembly; the design of delivery systems; and the identification of agencies of delivery in the field.

Unless such a policy/planning/delivery system is in place at the national level, then all urban and rural housing project designers have to re-rehearse all the issues and set standards anew each time.

Project Style

The basic elements in shelter project formulation are recognition of need; policy and programming; the production and delivery process; and 'the product' and its evaluation. Some project designs focus intensely on interventions in the building and delivery process. Others are more product-oriented, seeing process merely as a means to an end, and not as an essential developmental or training device.

Type 1: *Relief and Welfare* oriented and focusing on the destitute; by-passing village factions and any local priorities based on non-disaster-affected criteria. The project can be either process-oriented, for example, giving away building materials; or product-oriented, the giving away of a constructed core house or a completed dwelling. *Social reverberations that may stem from the gifting are not considered in a Type 1 project.* Emergency housing along the top of river embankments: housing for char lands dwellers tends to fall into this type.

Type 2: *Encouragement of Self-Reliant, Self-Help, Shelter-Making Activity.* This is primarily process-oriented where managing the process is 'the project'. Standards are set for the product, but these are generally restricted to health and safety.

Type 3: *A Safe House* in developing rural economy protected by disaster preparedness action. This is achieved through national level and Upazila level policy unification; disaster vulnerability mapping; pilot projects that test elements of evolving policy; and continuous monitoring and feed-back. This style is the full programme aspiration. Today it is achievable only in those areas where flood risks are minimal. As more control is exerted over river confinement and water conveyance, more areas can be brought into this style of project. Action on flood control will bring more land into this category.

Type 4: *The Dwelling as a Refuge.* This style is adopted because over much of Bangladesh Type 3 cannot be aspired to for many years to come. Process can be as for Type 2 and may be accompanied by associate programmes of building material production, component production (for example precast concrete columns, prefabricated ceiling/sleeping floors, etc.), skill training.

Project Development

Within a framework of institutionalised policy and appreciation of project styles/types, particular projects can be developed that relate to people in certain conditions and locations.

Identification of groups in need

These can be defined in numerous ways and in many combinations. The need to be flood affected would be parameter number one. After that, income group category and whether landholder – large, medium, small or landless – is revealing of economic plight. NGOs will have developed indicators of local relevance and will also know who is both poor and flood destitute.

In time, a nationally agreed means of identification/description needs to be evolved as a project formulation guide.

REFERENCES

ALI, A.M.M. SHAWKA (1986) *Politics and Land System in Bangladesh*, National Institute of Local Government, Dhaka, Bangladesh.

BRAC Prokashana, (1986) *Who Gets What And Why: Resource Allocation in a Bangladesh Village*, 2nd edn, Dhaka, Bangladesh.

BUET (1981) *Rural Housing in Bangladesh*, Housing and Environmental Research Cell, BUET and the Housing and Building Research Institute, GOB, Dhaka, Bangladesh.

GOB/UNCHS/UNDP (1989) Rural Housing Project Proposal.

JANSEN, E.G. (1987) *Rural Bangladesh: Competition for Scarce Resources*, University Press, Dhaka, Bangladesh.

OAKLEY, D. (1987) *Infrastructure Damage and Rehabilitation: Bangladesh Floods.*

CHAPTER 13

Choice of Technique: Housing Provision by NGOs Following the 1988 Floods in Bangladesh[1]

JOHN BORTON and TONY BECK
with
JANE PRYER, NAUSHAD FAIZ,
NURUL ALAM and MIKE CHAUHAN[2]

Introduction

This paper draws on material gathered during an evaluation of NGO post-flood rehabilitation activities in Bangladesh during 1988–89 to discuss some of the issues involved in selecting the design of housing to provide in a post-flood rehabilitation programme. Of the agencies included in the evaluation all but one selected designs intended to be resistant to future floods. These were found to be significantly more expensive, took longer to provide than designs not intended to be flood resistant, and also created the potential for the 'rehabilitation' houses provided on a grant basis to undermine development programmes providing housing to poor groups on a loan basis. The paper concludes that the selection of flood resistant designs was inappropriate considering the unprecedented need for new houses following the 1988 floods, but that more research is needed on appropriate, low-cost designs for highly flood-prone environments.

The 1988 floods in Bangladesh are generally acknowledged to have been one of the most prolonged, extensive and damaging inundations in Bangladesh this century (e.g. Rogers, Lydon and Seckler 1989). The natural causes were intensive rainfall over the northern part of the country and in the neighbouring states of India, Nepal and Bhutan and the extremely rare event of the peak flows of the Brahmaputra and the Ganges occurring simultaneously. At their greatest extent in the first week of September 1988, the floodwaters covered approximately 46% of the surface area of the country (Figure 1). This

FIGURE 1 *Approximate area of Bangladesh flooded on 24 September 1988 –*
bar = 70 km
[Source: Tracing from NOAA satellite image]

compares with the 'normal' annual floods which cover approximately 20–30% of the country to a lesser depth.

During the floods many millions of people temporarily abandoned their homes to shelter on higher ground or in buildings above the water level. All forms of public and private infrastructure in the affected areas, i.e. roads, railways, water control works, housing, education and health facilities were damaged or destroyed. The disruption to economic and social life was extensive. Millions of households were forced to sell assets, take on debt or, in the case of poorer families, increase their debt burden. Many families were rendered completely destitute. The extent of human suffering is likely to have been increased by the fact that the floods occurred so soon after the severe floods of 1987.

As part of its response, the UK Overseas Development Administration (ODA) provided £5 million in grants to UK-based NGOs and their Bangladeshi partner agencies. Half of this amount was provided for immediate relief, whilst the other half, disbursed to ten NGOs between November 1988 and March 1989, was provided for rehabilitation purposes. ODA commissioned an evaluation of the grants provided for rehabilitation purposes and this was carried out between August 1989 and February 1990 by a multi-disciplinary team of British and Bangladeshi researchers, including a civil engineer.[3] This was the first evaluation of grants by ODA to British NGOs for post-disaster rehabilitation and it also represented the first evaluation that considered the recipients of assistance provided.

The evaluation found that house construction was the most significant activity, accounting for an estimated 30% of the expenditures under the ODA rehabilitation grants and forming part of the rehabilitation programmes of eight out of the twelve recipient agencies.[4] By comparison, the expenditures on the other main activities were: employment creation 15%; dry ration provision 14%; bridge repair/construction 12%; and agricultural rehabilitation 9%.

This paper is not intended to be a comprehensive study of post-flood rehabilitation housing in Bangladesh.[5] Instead it is merely intended to share with a wider audience some of the findings of the evaluation in regard to the housing activities of the NGOs studied and to suggest issues which we see as requiring further study.

Housing as an NGO Post-Flood Rehabilitation Activity

Millions of houses were destroyed and damaged in rural areas by the 1988 floods. The Bangladesh Bureau of Statistics estimates that 5.1 million were completely destroyed and 6.9 million partially destroyed (BBS 1989). If these estimates are accurate then the housing of over one quarter of the total population was completely destroyed and over one third partially destroyed.

The greater height of the 1988 floods led to the inundation of a large area of the country and damaged raised homesteads, which had not been affected by either the severe floods of 1984 or 1987.

Whilst the need for rural house construction was undoubtedly greater following the 1988 floods than previous floods, it does appear that awareness of rural housing needs generally had increased between 1984 and 1988, so that housing was accorded higher priority as an NGO rehabilitation activity after the 1988 flood. A study of the role of 12 NGOs in the response to the 1984 floods found that employment creation and agricultural rehabilitation were the main activities in terms of expenditure whilst house repairs and construction hardly featured (Gallagher 1985).

Factors likely to have contributed to the greater awareness of housing needs in rural areas generally were the Government's 'Cluster Village' programme (Operation Thikana) and the Grameen Bank's 'Basic House' loan programme (see below). It is also possible that for some agencies their perception that increased resources would be available after the 1988 floods led them to take on an activity which previously had been considered to be inappropriate by virtue of its higher cost per family assisted than any other rehabilitation inputs. But an important consequence of this shift in priorities is that several agencies were planning and implementing sizeable house construction programmes for the first time and consequently they were not able to draw on their experience of rehabilitation work after the 1984 and 1987 floods.

Types of Housing

Between them the eight NGOs which included housing components within their rehabilitation programmes constructed a total of 13,250 houses and approximately 1,900 low-cost urban temporary houses. Two agencies (Agencies B and C) accounted for over 90% of the total number of houses constructed.[6] Apart from two of the smaller agencies which provided houses on a loan basis (unaware that this was contrary to the intentions of ODA), the vast majority of houses were provided free of charge to the selected recipients.

There was considerable variation in the design and cost of houses constructed (see Table 1), perhaps reflecting the novelty of housing as a rehabilitation activity for some NGOs. Only one agency provided housing in urban slum settlements and these were very low-cost structures of bamboo matting and polythene sheets costing Taka 1,400 (£27). These houses were an attempt by the agency to respond to the housing needs in areas where the land was rented and security of tenure notoriously poor.

In peri-urban and rural areas, most houses had roofs of corrugated galvanised iron (CGI) sheeting, though one agency used clay tiles. These were supported by posts of either bamboo, wood, pre-cast concrete or galvanised iron pipe. The unit costs of the structures varied from Taka 5,200

TABLE 1 *House design, costs and numbers constructed of agencies studied*

Agency	Cost (£)	Number constructed	Materials
A	£160	188	Concrete pillars, double pitch CGI sheet roof.
B	£28	1900	Bamboo matting, polythene sheet.
	£170	3450	Single pitched CGI sheet roof, galvanised iron poles.
C ·	£100	approx 9000	Double pitched CGI roof, bamboo poles.
D	£260	100	Double pitched CGI sheet roof, galvanised iron poles.
E	£160	N/A	Concrete pillars, double pitched CGI sheet roof.
F	£110	62	CGI sheet, wooden poles.
	£165	20	CGI sheet, wooden poles.
	£250	19	Cluster village houses.
G	£220	150	CGI sheet concrete pillars.
	£300	100	'Ideal Village'. CGI sheet/clay tile roofs. Concrete pillars.
H	£150	160	CGI sheet roof.
Total rural/peri-urban houses		13,249	
Total urban temporary houses		1900	

(approximately £100) in the case of Agency C, to Taka 15,000 (£300) in the case of Agency G.

The methods by which the houses were erected also varied. The agency providing the lowest cost house (Agency C) actively involved the recipients in the programme by distributing the materials (bamboo poles, CGI sheeting, ridge tiles and nails) at central points within their project areas, so that the selected beneficiaries had to transport the materials back to their village and erect the houses. In some cases this agency provided a small cash contribution towards the possible costs of hired labour during construction. In most cases, however, the houses were constructed by contractors (agencies B and D) or locally hired labour (agencies A, E, F, G, H) and then handed over to the beneficiaries. In their housing programmes therefore, only one of the agencies directly utilised the abilities of most recipients to assist themselves.

Choice of Design

As would be expected, the design of house selected reflected the objectives of the agency. Thus, Agency C gave high priority to speed of construction and maximising the numbers assisted and this is reflected in the low cost, less durable design. However, this agency managed to provide 9,000 carefully selected beneficiaries in five different project areas of the country with their housing materials before the end of December 1988. The majority of houses were constructed within a few days of the receipt of the materials. This agency had intentionally planned a relief and rehabilitation programme of three months duration to enable the staff diverted to the programme to return to their regular activities and also to avoid some of the problems encountered during a relief and rehabilitation programme implemented over a longer period in the Pabna area following the 1987 floods.

In contrast, all the other agencies appear to have attached higher priority to durability in selecting a design. An important consideration by these other agencies was the desire to construct houses which would be capable of resisting future floods. An important influence for some agencies was their experience of having provided houses not designed to resist floods as part of their rehabilitation activities following the 1987 floods, only to see many of them destroyed again the following year.

Ensuring that low-cost rural houses have a greater measure of resistance to floods requires that roofs be supported by concrete or iron posts which are stuck into the ground, or plinth, upon which the house is constructed. The theory underlying this design is that though the flood waters will sweep away the mud/bamboo matting walls, the posts and roof will be left standing when the flood recedes and the family will be able to reinhabit the house quickly and at minimal additional cost.

Apart from Agency C all the ODA-funded houses were intended to be 'flood resistant'. This had a number of important implications in terms of, for instance, the cost per house and the length of time before families were provided with a house. In considering the appropriateness of the decision to provide houses which were 'flood resistant', we would offer the following points for consideration.

Cost of construction: replacement or improvement?

The 'flood resistant' houses were more expensive than the CGI sheet/bamboo pole houses provided by agency C which in turn were more expensive than the traditional structures typically being replaced. The unit costs of the 'flood resistant' designs ranged from Taka 8,850 to Taka 15,600 (£170 to £300), whereas the average cost for the design selected by agency C was Taka 5,200 (£100). The cost of constructing a traditional bamboo and thatch structure during 'normal' times varies depending on whether family or hired labour is used and on spatial and seasonal variations in the cost of materials. However, for the sake of comparison, on average such a structure would cost approximately Taka 1,500 (£29).

As a result of the floods, bamboo and thatch became unavailable in some areas and increased in price in other areas. For some of the agencies the prospect of procurement difficulties for traditional materials was a consideration in their decision to select designs using non-traditional materials such as CGI sheet and iron and concrete pillars. Information on the availability and price of such materials was not collected by members of the evaluation team during the visits to the project sites due to the limited time available and the need to also investigate the other, non-housing components of the rehabilitation programmes. It is therefore not possible to give a picture of the extent to which traditional housing materials were unavailable or the degree to which their prices were inflated in the months immediately following the flood.

As the vast majority of houses being replaced had been constructed from traditional materials and as none of the agencies studied selected designs involving thatch roofs, none can be considered to have provided houses which directly 'replaced' the houses that had been destroyed. By using CGI sheet (or clay tiles) as the roofing material all the designs represented an 'improvement' over the houses they were designed to replace. As noted above it is not possible to state whether the provision of designs involving thatch roofs was a realistic option in some areas, so in these areas the bamboo pole and CGI sheet design used by Agency C might be regarded as a 'replacement' design even though it represented a distinct 'improvement' in terms of roofing material. However, the 'flood resistant' designs set out to alter and, from the perspective of the agencies, improve upon a crucial design characteristic. In terms of design and cost therefore they clearly represented an 'improvement' upon the houses being replaced.

The significant difference in cost between the design selected by Agency C and the 'flood resistant' designs meant that in opting for the latter an agency automatically halved the number of families it could assist with new housing. In the context of the unprecedented scale of the need for housing following the flood and the limited resources available for responding to it, the decision by all but one of the agencies studied to opt for the 'flood resistant' design was highly questionable.

Length of time for construction

Given the immediate need of the beneficiaries for shelter and the cold spells that occur during the winter months (December to February), speed of construction should have been an important consideration. The overall picture on the length of time for the houses to be provided is that the 'flood resistant' houses took longer to construct than the design used by Agency C.

This picture is confused by the fact that many of the agencies experienced delays in obtaining the approval of the Government of Bangladesh for their rehabilitation programmes. However, the programmes of Agencies B and C are comparable as neither agency awaited full approval before commencing their housing programmes. Whereas Agency C completed the distribution of materials for 9,000 houses by the end of December 1988, Agency B did not complete the construction of its 3,450 houses until June 1989, with April 1989 apparently being the month of peak construction. For those agencies which awaited full approval the bulk of construction appears to have taken place during June and July 1989. Thus, whilst Agency C was able to complete the provision of its new houses within three months of the flood waters receding from many parts of the country, the other agencies using the 'flood resistant' design generally took eight or nine months to complete the provision of their houses. Whereas Agency C was able to meet the immediate housing needs and enable households to get through the next cold season with a roof over their heads, the other agencies were unable to do so.

Overlap with development programmes in the rural housing sector

The use of a more durable design raises the potential of the houses provided free, overlapping with, and possibly undermining, housing provided on a loan basis by development programmes. The largest such programme to date in the rural areas of Bangladesh has been that of the Grameen Bank, originally a local NGO but now incorporated within the Bangladesh Bank and well known for its approach of supplying credit without collateral to poorer sections of the population (Chowdhury 1989, Hossain 1988).

Since 1987 the Grameen Bank, with a much wider geographical coverage than the NGOs studied, has provided loans for the construction of a standard 'basic house' design of concrete pillars with CGI roofs and sanitary water seal latrines. By the end of 1988 the loan ceiling was Taka 10,000 (£200) and the annual rate of interest charged 5%. Applicants have to have been members of the Grameen Bank for at least two years and to have had a successful record of repayments on previous loans. By April 1989 over 54,000 loans had been approved (Islam, Chowdhury and Ali 1989).

Due to the widespread coverage of the Grameen Bank scheme, the similarity in design to most of the ODA-funded houses (except the design used by Agency C) and the fact that many of the ODA-funded houses were not constructed until around eight months after the flood, it is possible that the ODA-funded 'flood resistant' houses might be perceived as undermining what appears to be a viable long-term development programme. Were it the case that the ODA-funded houses were targeted on a poorer group than those able to take on the commitments of a Grameen Bank house this would not be a problem. In the absence of a detailed study of the socio-economic background of the recipients of the ODA-funded houses and the Grameen Bank housing loans, it is not possible to assess precisely who the two sets of beneficiaries were. However, there are reasons to believe that there was some overlap between the groups reached by the two programmes.

One reason for this is that most of the ODA-funded houses were allocated to those who owned their own homestead land (i.e. the plot of land upon which the house is constructed).[7] This automatically excluded those households not owning homestead land, generally acknowledged to be the poorest group in rural Bangladesh (e.g. UNRISD 1987). Another reason is that despite claims by the agencies in their funding proposals that the assistance would be targeted on the 'poorest' groups among the flood-affected population, this was not always the case. Some agencies did not carry out careful surveys before selecting beneficiaries with the result that some houses were found to have been allocated to households who could not be considered to have been the poorest of those with homestead land.

Maintenance costs

In selecting 'flood resistant' designs, a major consideration of the agencies was that once assisted, a household would not require housing assistance after subsequent floods. Intuitively, it would appear to be more cost effective to provide a household *once* with a flood resistant house rather than every three or four years with a cheaper design. However, this would need to be tested by a detailed study over a period of several years. It remains to be seen how durable the 'flood resistant' designs actually are, not only at withstanding severe floods that may occur in the future, but also in terms of their quality of construction. The civil engineer on the team noted exposed reinforcing rods in some of the houses using concrete pillars and the likelihood of rust on welds fixing roofs to galvanised iron poles. If for the sake of argument the effective life of a flood resistant design is as short as seven or eight years and severe floods occur every five years, then it may well be the case that designs costing half as much as the flood resistant ones represent a more cost-effective solution.

Another factor which led some agencies to favour costly pillar materials is that bamboo or wooden posts need to be frequently replaced. An untreated bamboo pole will probably rot where it enters the soil after 12–18 months. The average cost of bamboo poles in the design used by Agency C was approximately Taka 250 (i.e. £5). But, at this cost, large numbers of houses can be constructed and the replacement cost is within the means of most families.

Lack of consultation with beneficiaries

The fact that many agencies did not directly utilise the abilities of most recipients to assist themselves has been noted above. A related characteristic noted by the team in relation to all the rehabilitation programmes was the lack of consultation with beneficiaries during the selection of the design. So far as we know none of the agencies consulted potential beneficiaries before adopting a particular design. Given that 'flood resistant' housing was a new and, for all the NGOs studied, an untested component and given the high unit costs of the houses and the length of time that elapsed before they were actually constructed, the lack of consultation is remarkable.

During interviews with beneficiaries at selected project sites, members of the team informed them of the approximate cost of their house and asked if the money could have been better spent. The almost universal response by the beneficiaries was that they would have preferred a lower cost house with the rest of the money being spent on an income generating item or activity, such as a cow. It would, of course, be unrealistic to think that a house *and* a cow were potentially available. In the context of the scale of needs after the 1988 floods, if an agency had selected a lower cost house it would probably have used the funds to increase the number of beneficiaries rather than offer the selected beneficiaries a house and another comparatively high value asset. However, it would seem to be the case that most beneficiaries would not have been significantly less satisfied with a lower cost house rather than a 'flood resistant' design.

The appropriateness of 'flood resistant' houses in flood-prone areas

Whereas the above points relate directly to the appropriateness of 'flood resistant' houses within the post-flood rehabilitation programmes funded by ODA, there are also broader issues concerning their appropriateness in the flood-prone areas of Bangladesh.

A significant proportion of flood-prone land in Bangladesh is also prone to changing river courses and riverbank erosion (Haque and Zaman 1989). In such areas houses which are constructed of low cost, easily replaceable materials or where the high value items are removable may be a more appropriate design. When the floods came in 1988, many families are reported to have taken high value building materials, such as CGI sheeting, with them when seeking a refuge. Members of the evaluation team witnessed this phenomenon with houses that had been provided by Agency C in Khaliajuri Upazila. Erosion which had occurred since the 1988 floods had removed a spit of land on which 40 of the houses had been constructed. The houses had been dismantled and moved to safe ground in Khaliajuri town, where the families were living under the double-pitched CGI sheet roofs, while waiting to be allocated *khas* (Government owned) land.

Even in flood-prone areas which are not prone to riverbank erosion it might be the case that 'flood resistant' designs are inappropriate. For centuries the traditional house types on land prone to flooding in Bangladesh have been low cost, rapidly replaceable structures using the locally available materials of thatch and bamboo. For instance survey reports by representatives of the East India Company in the early 1800s (e.g. Buchanan 1928) comment on the almost total absence of *pukka* dwellings in flood-prone areas and the fact that even rich people lived in mud, bamboo, reed and straw structures. More recently researchers working in the Kosi floodplain in Bihar in the early 1970s noted that large landowners, often with holdings of 50–150 acres, continued to use traditional designs of low cost materials obtained from renewable natural resources, even within recently embanked areas (Clay – personal communication 1990, see also Joy and Everitt 1976). Thus, low cost, easily replaceable structures may be seen as a form of adaptation to a particularly flood-prone environment. Against this background, interventions by external agencies to provide 'flood resistant' designs in flood-prone areas need very careful scrutiny.

Conclusion and Further Research

On the basis of the above considerations, the conclusion reached by the evaluation team was that it was inappropriate for agencies to select 'flood resistant' designs in the provision of housing after the 1988 floods. In summary, the selection of such designs by all but one of the agencies studied:

- significantly reduced the number of households that could be assisted;
- delayed by several months the provision of shelter to beneficiaries;
- may possibly undermine what appears to be a viable long-term development programme implemented by the Grameen Bank;
- introduced untested designs whose appropriateness in a highly flood-prone environment is open to question.

Following the 1978 Conference on 'Disasters and the Small Dwelling' Ian Davis identified a key issue as being:

For the intervenors to recognise the complexity and subtlety of housing; to educate their field staff to the need to listen and learn prior to decision-making; in major disasters to locate and hire expertise (preferably local) prior to embarking on housing programmes (Davis 1981:733).

From the above experiences it might appear that relief agencies have absorbed little of the sensible advice offered a decade ago. Why this might be the case is not the subject of this paper. The judgement of those agencies selecting untested, 'flood resistant' designs at a time of unprecedented housing need and a massive emergency programme deserves, in our opinion, to be criticised. That NGOs which espouse the virtues of the participatory approach should have selected non-traditional designs without consulting the potential beneficiaries is remarkable. However, we would suggest that not all the blame should be placed at the door of the agencies themselves. Most of the academic literature on housing in East and South Asia continues to be focused on urban housing and settlement rather than rural housing, despite the importance of housing as a major item of expenditure for the rural poor (Drakakis-Smith 1988). Had more studies been undertaken of rural housing in Bangladesh prior to the 1988 floods, it is conceivable that NGOs would have had a clearer indication of the problems of selecting 'flood resistant' designs.

As has been suggested by this paper, serious questions remain to be answered as to the appropriate design of housing for use by the rural poor in the Ganges-Brahmaputra floodplain. These can only be answered by detailed studies conducted over a period of years. Such studies ought not to confine themselves to housing designs alone, as it might be the case that a more cost effective form of flood resistance is not the introduction of new designs but such measures as the raising of earth platforms.

REFERENCES

BBS (BANGLADESH BUREAU OF STATISTICS) (1989) *Statistical Pocket Book of Bangladesh 1989*, Ministry of Planning, Dhaka, Bangladesh.

BUCHANAN, F. (1928) *An Account of the District of Burnea in 1809–1810*, edited by V.H. Jackson, Bihar and Orissa Research Society, Patna, India.

CHOWDHURY, A.N. (1989) *Let Grassroots Speak: People's Participation, Self-Help Groups and NGOs in Bangladesh*, University Press, Dhaka, Bangladesh.

DAVIS, I. (1981) 'Disasters and Settlements – Towards an Understanding of the Key Issues', *Habitat International 5.5/6*.

DRAKAKIS-SMITH, D. (1988) 'Housing', in M. Pacione (ed.) *Geography of the Third World: Progress and Prospects*, Routledge, London, UK.

GALLAGHER, R. (1985) 'Flood Monitoring in Bangladesh: A Study of Responses to the 1984 Crisis', War on Want, London, UK.

HAQUE, C.E. and ZAMAN M.Q. (1989) 'Coping With Riverbank Erosion Hazard and Displacement in Bangladesh: Survival Strategies and Adjustments', *Disasters 13.4*.

HOSSAIN, M. (1988) 'Credit For Alleviation of Rural Poverty: The Grammen Bank in Bangladesh', Research Report 65, IFPRI, Washington DC, USA.

ISLAM, N., CHOWDHURY, A.I. and ALI, K. (1989) 'Evaluation of the Grammen Bank's Rural Housing Programme with UNDP Funding', Centre for Urban Studies, University of Dhaka, Bangladesh.

JOY, J.L. and EVERITT, E. (eds) (1976) *The Kosi Symposium. The Rural Problem in North East Bihar: An Analysis, Policy and Planning*, Institute of Development Studies, Brighton, UK.

ROGERS, P., LYDON, P. and SECKLER D. (1989) 'Eastern Waters Study: Strategies to Manage Flood and Drought in the Ganges-Brahmaputra Basin', Prepared for USAID by the Irrigation Support Project for Asia and Near East (ISPAN) Washington DC, USA.

UNRISD (1987) *The Assault That Failed: Six Villages of Bangladesh*, Geneva, Switzerland.

NOTES

1. The authors would like to thank Edward Clay, Director of RDI, for his helpful suggestions during the preparation of this paper.
2. The authors were members of the Relief and Development Institute team which carried out the evaluation for the UK Overseas Development Administration. J. Borton is an agricultural economist currently employed as a Research Fellow, heading the Relief and Disaster Policy Programme at the Overseas Development Institute, London; Dr T. Beck is a social welfare specialist currently attached to the Institute of Asian Research at the University of British Columbia, Canada; Dr J. Pryer is a nutritionist currently working at the Environmental Epidemiology Unit, Department of Health and Policy, the London School of Hygiene and Tropical Medicine, London. Dr N. Faiz is a freelance economist based in Dhaka; Dr N. Alam is Associate Professor and Chairperson at the Department of Anthropology at Jahangirnagar University, Bangladesh; and M. Chauhan is a civil engineer with Mott MacDonald Ltd, Cambridge.
3. 'Evaluation of ODA Support for NGO Post-Flood Rehabilitation Activities in Bangladesh 1988–89', Relief and Development Institute, London, 1990.
4. Whilst ten grants were made, twelve agencies received the grants as a result of one of the UK agencies passing on the funds to Bangladeshi partner agencies.
5. It should be noted that other international and Bangladeshi NGOs (e.g. the Bangladesh Red Crescent Society/League of Red Cross and Red Crescent Societies and the Bangladesh Rural Advancement Committee) also carried out substantial house construction programmes after the 1988 floods, but these were not included in the evaluation study and are not discussed here.
6. The agencies are not named in this paper for reasons of confidentiality and to ensure that attention is focused on the issues involved rather than on the characteristics and merits of particular agencies.
7. Two of the smaller agencies (Agencies G and H) attempted to provide land as part of their housing programme – one by using *khas* land provided by the Government and the other by purchasing the land using project funds.

CHAPTER 14

Floods in Bangladesh: Vulnerability and Mitigation Related to Human Settlement

HUGH BRAMMER[1]

Geographer/Consultant, Hove, UK

Introduction

Floods in Bangladesh are a complex phenomenon, with various causes and effects in different places. Traditional settlement patterns and economic activities are well adapted to seasonal flooding. Floodplain settlements are on the highest available ground. Houses are on raised mounds and mainly made of locally available wood, bamboo and jute sticks with straw thatching material. Damage occurs when floods are abnormally high, breaches occur in embankments or land is eroded by shifting river channels. Following severe floods in 1987 and 1988, families raised house plinth levels, and galvanized iron sheets widely supplemented traditional materials in rebuilding and repairs. Some NGOs promoted more costly rigid frame houses. Aid donors supported a $150 million Flood Action Plan mainly comprising studies to identify long-term mitigation measures. Settlement related studies include flood response, flood proofing and resettlement studies.

Geographical Context

At the outset, it is useful, in the context of Bangladesh, to differentiate between flooding and floods. Alluvial floodplains occupy 80% of Bangladesh's area of 145,000 sq km, and much of this land is submerged during the summer monsoon season. Settlements, infrastructure and economic activities are well adapted to this annual flooding. Flooding becomes a hazard – i.e. is liable to cause loss of life, crops or property – when water-levels rise earlier, more

110

rapidly, higher or later than people expected when they made their investment in crops or property. It is flooding which causes damage or loss that is called a 'flood'.

Floods in Bangladesh are a complex phenomenon:

- six kinds of floods are recognized: flash; river; rainwater; tidal; storm surge; and man-made;
- the locations and extent of floods vary considerably from year to year: official records show a range between 3,000 and 82,000 sq km flooded in the years 1954–88;
- there is considerable diversity of relief and soils within the country's floodplains, causing significant regional and local differences in depth of flooding, land use and vulnerability to flood damage;
- for agriculture, the timing of abnormal flooding is often as important as the actual depth of water which occurs.

Bangladesh's physical, socio-economic and demographic environments are also dynamic. That makes it difficult (and perhaps dangerous) to make general statements about floods and flooding in that country. Examples of the dynamic situation include:

- river channels which are, to varying degrees, unstable: both the Brahmaputra and the Ganges have made major shifts in their courses in recent centuries; these and other rivers are constantly eroding their banks and creating new, but ephemeral, land within their channels; and the Brahmaputra shows a preferred tendency to erode its right bank;
- the continued extension of flood embankments (together with new road and railway embankments) which increasingly interfere with overland flood flow and drainage;
- the rapid spread of dry-season irrigation in the last 20 years which has greatly altered traditional cropping patterns, *inter alia* reducing farmers' vulnerability to flood damage;
- the rapid population growth (c.2.5% per annum) which is contributing to the expansion of settlement and cultivation on to flood-prone land, including that within active river channels, as well as to increasing rates of rural-urban migration.

Further details about flood characteristics in Bangladesh and proposed mitigation measures are given in two papers published recently in the *Geographical Journal* (Brammer 1990a, 1990b).

Flood Vulnerability

Traditional floodplain settlements are well adapted to normal seasonal flooding and occasional high floods. They are located on the highest land available,

111

either on river levées or on linear ridges marking the sites of former levées. Individual homesteads and other buildings are constructed on raised earthen mounds, with plinth levels at a height determined by local experience of previous high flood levels. Traditional homestead buildings are simple: single storey, usually arranged around a rectangular compound; generally with a wood or bamboo frame, and with walls of jute sticks or split bamboo matting, but of sun-dried clay or bricks in some regions; thatch (locally tile) roof; outside kitchen; and surrounded by multi-use trees, banana plants, bamboos and a kitchen garden. Increasingly, in recent years, galvanized iron sheets have come into use for roofing and sometimes for walls. Only in the larger towns and cities are multi-storey, brick-built houses or concrete-frame apartment and office blocks found.

Roads and paths between settlements also generally follow the highest land available. Modern roads are made on embankments, and need to be provided with bridges and culverts to allow passage of floodwater, which is expensive. However, there still is considerable movement by boat when the land is flooded in the monsoon season. The main rivers are used by boats throughout the year.

Floodplain settlements are vulnerable to damage by floods under three circumstances: exceptionally high floods; breaching of flood embankments; and river-bank erosion. Damage by tropical cyclones and associated storm surges, to which coastal districts are exposed, is not discussed below; nor is damage by strong winds in line-squalls (nor'-westers) or by hail, though all need to be taken into account in designing improved floodplain housing, discussed in the final section of this paper.

Exceptionally high floods

In many areas along the Brahmaputra and Ganges Rivers in Bangladesh, the floods in 1987 and 1988 were the highest in living memory. Hydrological analyses suggest that they were 1 in 50–100 year events. As such, the plinths of many rural houses were over-topped; substantial parts of Dhaka city and other towns were also flooded; and hundreds of kilometres of road and railway embankments were over-topped or breached. Some flood embankments were also breached, though usually not by over-topping: some were eroded by rivers; but the majority of breaches were man-made, cut by people threatened by high river levels outside embankments or by ponded water within embankments.

Damage to houses by those floods varied with the materials with which they were constructed; the condition of those materials at the time of the flood; the depth and duration of the flooding; and the rate of water flow. Damage was most severe to the flimsy houses of poor people living in settlements within or close to the main river channels where the rapid flow of river water carried away the structures. Elsewhere, the flow of water caused the timber or bamboo frames of some houses to collapse (in part, one suspects, because they were already weakened by decay or insect attack); some clay-built houses also collapsed; and the frames or fabric of other houses were to varying extents damaged by standing in water for up to two weeks and needed replacement after the floods receded. In urban areas, sewage and other wastes carried by the floodwater invaded buildings; sewerage, water and electricity services were also disrupted; and many squatter settlements on low-lying land had to be evacuated.

The extent of damage to household or commercial stock depended on the time available to move stock – depending, in turn, on the rapidity with which water-levels rose and the timeliness of flood warnings – and on the availability of higher places to which stock (including livestock) could be moved. In the 1988 flood, it appears that water levels rose rapidly in parts of the Brahmaputra floodplain in Tangail and Dhaka Districts (including Dhaka city) because of breaching (or cutting) of the river embankments, giving people very little warning of the flood or of the level which it might reach.

On the floodplains adjoining the major rivers, the whole landscape is submerged during a high flood: in 1988, the Brahmaputra was essentially 50–60 km wide, bounded by two tracts of higher land, the Madhupur and Barind Tracts. As in cyclone-prone areas, people in flood-prone areas are loath to leave their homes during times of disaster, mainly for fear of theft of property. As floodwater rises within the homestead, people first move onto beds and other furniture; then, if the water rises higher, they make crude wood or bamboo platforms (*machans*) within the dwelling; eventually they may move onto the roof or into an adjoining tree, if one is available. Only as a last resort do they abandon their dwelling and move by boat or raft to a safer place on the nearest road or flood embankment, in the compound of a more wealthy person or in an institutional building.

Poultry and goats are similarly moved upward in the homestead as far as this may be practicable, and some may be moved to embankments which provide the only available grazing land. Cattle stand in the water and are stall fed as long as possible, but may eventually be swum off to embankments or abandoned. In the high 1987 and 1988 floods, many livestock were swept away when dwellings within and near the main river channels were themselves destroyed or they were sold or abandoned when they could no longer be fed.

Breaching of embankments

The Bangladesh Water Development Board (BWDB) has built about 7,000 km of flood-control embankments. Most of these are in coastal areas to keep out saline water at high tides, but both sides of the Brahmaputra, Ganges and many lesser rivers are embanked for much of their length to keep out river floods, including substantial sections where embankments have been built under local initiative schemes, often with Food-for-Work assistance. Additionally, polders have been created in some floodplain areas that were formerly deeply flooded during the monsoon season, with the enclosed areas drained artificially by pumps, tidal sluices or regulators. Most of these embankments have been built in the last 20–30 years.

Thus, many millions of people now live behind embankments. However, river and polder embankments have frequently been breached, either naturally by bank erosion or more often by so-called public cuts. In general, therefore, people living behind embankments have not altered their traditional settlement patterns in the supposedly protected areas.

There is one important exception to this general statement. In the Dhaka-Narayanganj-Demra (DND) project area, a pump-drained and irrigated area on the eastern margin of Dhaka City, unplanned suburban and industrial sprawl has overwhelmed more than half the polder area, with plinth levels adjusted to the pump-drained hydrological condition, which is 2–4 m below external river levels at high flood stages. In the exceptionally high 1988 flood, the bounding embankment was in danger of being over-topped, and catastrophic flooding within the polder was only averted by action taken by inhabitants of the polder themselves to raise the embankment level by means of sandbags. If this embankment had been breached, property damage within the polder could have amounted to several million pounds.

The DND polder is a relatively small one (5,800 ha) with a relatively enlightened urban population. The local initiative which averted a disaster there in 1988 could not be relied upon to occur in the case of a larger polder with a largely rural population. To the extent that embankments are more successful in future in preventing floods and flooding, so that people feel secure living behind them, there will inevitably be a tendency for people to move onto the protected land and build houses without the traditional high plinths, as happened in the DND area. That implies a need for formal emergency procedures to be worked out to protect lives and property in flood-protected areas. Such procedures do not exist at present. As experience in the DND project area showed, it is almost impossible to impose planning regulations which might prevent the spread of settlement onto protected land or require new buildings to be made with high plinths.

River erosion

The settlements most exposed to damage or loss by floods at present are those on the so-called active floodplains within and adjoining the main rivers. The active floodplain of the Brahmaputra River is 10–20 km wide; that of the Ganges is somewhat less, 5–15 km; but the active floodplains of the Padma and lower Meghna into which these combined rivers flow are 15–25 km across, widening southward into the Meghna estuary. Not only does land within these active floodplains suffer uncontrolled flooding with rapid flow of turbulent river water, but it is also subject to rapid erosion along river banks and those of channels within the floodplain. Lateral erosion rates up to 800 m in a single flood season have been measured in the Brahmaputra (Jamuna) channel. The huge force of the major rivers during floods is also illustrated by scouring depths of 30–50 m measured in their channels and by differences in depth at individual points of as much as 15 m within a 24-hour period due to transport of sediments along their beds.

Concurrently with erosion, new alluvial formations are deposited within and alongside the river channels. This new land is quickly settled and brought under cultivation, despite the risks that the land may be eroded within a few years and that homes, crops and livestock may be lost during severe floods; despite, too, the problems of lack of security and of amenities and public services (including rescue services) on such remote land. The population of such active river floodplains is thought to exceed 1 million; and at least a further 1 million people inhabit similar insecure habitats in the Meghna estuary, where they are also exposed to the hazards of tropical cyclones and storm surges. Clearly, it would be impractical in land-hungry Bangladesh to prevent people from occupying this unstable land, much less to resettle such numbers in less disaster-prone locations. At present, it is not considered technically or economically feasible to stabilize the channels of such mighty rivers, though studies are planned.

Mitigation

A spate of activity followed the 1987 and 1988 flood disasters. The scale of those disasters aroused both national and international determination that such disasters should be considered unacceptable and must be prevented from recurring. Mitigation measures used or proposed are discussed below under three headings: individual; voluntary agencies; and official.

Individual

Flood-affected households rebuilt or repaired their houses to the best of their ability using traditional, low-cost materials. In many cases, this was facilitated by relief or rehabilitation grants from charitable or official sources with which to obtain the required materials. Traditional wood, bamboo, jute-stick and thatching materials have become increasingly scarce and costly, however (as have bricks and tiles), and galvanized iron sheeting was widely used after these floods, both for roofing and for walls. Plastic sheets were also widely used as a temporary measure until more permanent repairs could be made. Established households also took the opportunity to raise homestead plinth levels above the height of the recent floods: one of the author's former servants reported that he had raised the earthen plinth of the bedroom and the cattle shed at his village home by about 1.5 m, an indication of domestic priorities in a resource-poor household.

Another private response was economic. After both the 1987 and 1988 floods, there was a considerable expansion of dry-season irrigation using privately-owned small pumps (a measure facilitated in 1988 by Government liberalizing the import of such pumps). Dry-season rice production increased from c.3 million tons to almost 5 million tons over these two crop years. This expansion reflected both the need for farmers to compensate for lost monsoon-season production (which is mainly rainfed) and for them to switch to more secure production in the relatively disaster-free dry season.

This conversion has not only made farmers' crop production more secure: the greater security provided by irrigation and cultivation in the dry season has also encouraged farmers to switch to the cultivation of high-yielding rice varieties, thus more than doubling the previous production from their land in some flood-prone areas. The benefits of this increased production have, of course, gone mainly to those possessing land and with sufficient assets (or political influence) to obtain irrigation equipment; but the landless have also benefited by increased, and more secure, employment and by more stable prices for the rice they have to purchase.

The additional wealth generated seems to be reflected, in part, by the rapid expansion of 'tin-roofed' houses now seen in rural areas. Whatever one may think about this material aesthetically, its use often does reflect increased wealth. It also provides a saleable asset that can be disposed of if stressed family circumstances should arise in the future. However, roofing sheets need to be firmly attached: detached sheets are a major source of casualties caused by strong winds experienced in nor'-westers, cyclones and tornadoes. This seems to be a subject needing design attention.

Voluntary agencies

There was considerable and widespread relief and rehabilitation activity by voluntary agencies, both national and international, after the 1987 and 1988 floods. *Inter alia*, NGOs provided relief materials or cash grants so that affected families could rebuild or repair their homes. A number of NGOs, including some funded from British sources, supported the provision of houses with concrete or galvanized iron pipe pillars on the grounds that such materials would be more resistant against decay or insect attack than the traditional wood or bamboo, and also more resistant against the force of flood-flow during any future flood; they would also conserve supplies of natural materials already under severe pressure because of the expansion of settlements and the demand for fuel. Although considered 'low-cost', such structures were, in fact, about ten times more costly than those built using traditional materials. The investment and other implications of this type of design are discussed in the paper by Borton and Beck (in this volume).

Official

The scale of the 1987 and 1988 flood disasters stimulated the Government of Bangladesh and its major aid donors to review measures that could be taken to provide a lasting solution to the country's chronic flood problem. UNDP-funded teams reviewed the nature, scale and causes of damage following both these floods. UNDP also funded a study of disaster preparedness needs and a flood policy study after the 1988 flood. French, Japanese and USAID teams simultaneously prepared flood protection proposals. In July 1989, the World Bank was requested to coordinate international efforts to mitigate floods, and prepared a Flood Action Plan based on the earlier Government and international studies. This plan was endorsed at a meeting of donors held in London in December 1989 and implementation began in 1990.

The Flood Action Plan mainly comprises studies required to identify activities for controlling or mitigating the effects of floods. The estimated cost over the period of Bangladesh's current Five Year Plan (1990–95) is c.US $150 million, but it is envisaged that an initial pipeline of projects costing c.$500 million might be identified on which implementation could start within the plan period, and perhaps leading to investments of c.$5 billion over the next 20 years. The Action Plan comprises 26 projects, pilot projects and studies; a special study of economic risk assessment was added later. Both structural and non-structural measures are included: strengthening of some existing flood embankments; works to protect Dhaka City against floods and some riverside towns against bank erosion; five comprehensive regional water development planning studies; flood forecasting, warning and preparedness projects; topographic mapping; various river morphology and training studies; and a number of socio-economic and environment-related studies.

Three plan items are directly relevant to human settlement:

- Item 14, Flood Response Study, will assess the ways in which people living in flood-prone environments have adapted their settlements, economic activities and responses to disasters;
- Item 15, Land Acquisition and Resettlement Study, will deal with the problem of rehabilitating people whose land is purchased compulsorily for the construction of flood embankments. It will also deal with the related problem of resettling people displaced by river-bank erosion, who often 'squat' on adjoining embankments and are difficult to remove;
- Item 23, Flood Proofing Pilot Project, will identify and test structural and non-structural measures which could be taken to improve the resistance of households, communities (urban and rural), infrastructure, commerce and industry to flood damage. This study will run concurrently with Item 14. One possible intervention to be examined is the construction of flood shelters – areas of artificially raised ground – to which people, and possibly their livestock, could move on receipt of a flood warning.

The study components of these projects were due to commence in the second half of 1990. Reports were scheduled for delivery before the end of 1991 so that the information provided can be taken into account in undertaking feasibility studies for water development projects identified by the five regional planning studies.

Other Action Plan activities which touch upon aspects of human settlement are:

- Item 8, Dhaka Town Protection Project, work on which has already commenced;
- Item 9, Other Towns Protection Project, under which technical feasibility studies will be carried out of possible ways of defending a number of towns (probably eight in the first instance) against flooding or bank erosion;
- Item 10, Flood Forecasting and Early Warning Project, and Item 11, Disaster Preparedness Project, to strengthen the existing systems;
- Item 16, Environmental Study, which will include health and sanitation aspects of proposed flood protection interventions;
- Item 20, the Compartmentalization Pilot Project, under which structural and non-structural aspects of water management and development behind flood embankments will be studied and tested, including the impact of water control interventions on the physical, economic and social environments; land use regulation is one aspect needing to be studied under this project.

REFERENCES

BRAMMER, H. (1990a) 'Floods in Bangladesh: I. Geographical Background to the 1987 and 1988 Floods', *Geographical Journal* 156(1):12–22.
BRAMMER, H. (1990b) 'Floods in Bangladesh: II. Flood Mitigation and Environmental Aspects', *Geographical Journal* 156(2):158–65.

NOTE

1. Hugh Brammer is a geographer. He worked with FAO in Bangladesh for 22 years, latterly as Agricultural Development Adviser.

CHAPTER 15

Earthquake Reconstruction for Future Protection

ANDREW COBURN

Cambridge Architectural Research Limited and
The Martin Centre for Architectural and Urban Studies,
University of Cambridge, UK

IGNACIO ARMILLAS

Senior Human Settlements Officer
United Nations Centre for Human Settlements (Habitat)
Nairobi, Kenya

Introduction

Each of the major earthquakes occurring over the past decade has generated a programme of protection planning against future earthquakes. The United Nations, through its technical implementing agencies, has been instrumental in assisting national Governments to develop their protection plans. Specialist United Nations missions have visited each of the major destructive earthquakes and assisted in developing the national protection strategies to be implemented with the reconstruction.

All earthquakes are different, and a wide range of problems are created by earthquakes in the various different parts of the world so there are no standard recipes for turning reconstruction into protection. However, a number of principles have been developed which are outlined here. They are illustrated in the case study of two recent earthquakes, Manjil, Iran, in June 1990 and Luzon, Philippines, July 1991.

ANDREW COBURN and IGNACIO ARMILLAS

Manjil Earthquake, Iran, 21 June 1990

Earthquake Parameters:

Ms: 7.7
Depth: 20–30 km
Local Time: 03:13
UT: 21:13
Surface Fault: approx. 100 km, WNW
Epicentral Intensity: X (MSK)
Strong Motion Records: 19 instruments triggered
Maximum recorded SMI: 65% g Peak Ground Acceleration at Abbar

Casualties:

Death Toll: 36,893 recorded fatalities: probable fatalities over 40,000
Injuries: 36,265 treated injuries 6,000 transferred to Tehran hospitals
Homeless: 500,000

Losses:

Three towns extensively destroyed, 1,600 villages damaged

Residential: 94,813 houses destroyed, 28,822 damaged (83% rural, 17% urban)
Health Facilities: 216 medical buildings, including 2 hospitals, destroyed
Educational: 1,329 schools destroyed
Industrial: 68 factories damaged, $350 million repair cost
Agricultural: 18,000 cattle killed, 58,000 sheep and goats killed, damage to many store buildings: rice, tea and wheat harvest disrupted irrigation channels damaged, reservoir level lowered
Transport: many roads blocked, bridges damaged, landslides and rockfalls
Special: Sefidrud dam damaged, Lowshan power station damaged, electrical networks and communications damaged

Cost:

Damage Repair Cost: US$5 billion
Relief & Emergency: uncalculated
Consequential Costs: uncalculated

Reconstruction technical assistance

After the major earthquake in Iran in June 1990, the United Nations mounted a technical assistance programme to assist the Iranian Government in developing their plans for reconstruction. An international team was sent in to evaluate Government plans and propose a structure for coordinating international aid and development planning. The project that has just been initiated as a result comprises a range of measures including code reviews, code enforcement measures and technical assistance in non-engineered construction to resist earthquakes (Coburn et al. 1990).

Luzon Earthquake, Philippines, 16 July 1990

Earthquake Parameters:
Ms: · 7.8
Depth: 20–30 km
Local Time: 16:26
UT: 07:26
Surface Fault: 100 km, NW, with horizontal displacements < 6 m,
Epicentral Intensity: IX (MSK)
Strong Motion Records: no instruments working at the time in the area

Casualties:
Death Toll: 1,648 killed
Injuries: 2,700 injured
Homeless: 120,000

Losses:
Mountainous areas very badly affected by slope failures, main city of Baguio (pop. 200,000) badly damaged, town of Dagupan extensively affected by liquefaction, many other towns and villages damaged.

Residential: over 50,000 houses damaged

Health Facilities: 69 damaged hospitals, 112 health centres, and 310 local clinics (14% of total health facilities)

Educational: 1,467 schools damaged (24% of region's total), extensive damage to University of Baguio

Industrial: disruption to transportation network affected distribution, mining production badly affected, manufacturing industry badly affected in Baguio City Export Processing Zone. Total foregone revenue in manufacturing estimated at US$8m

Agricultural: major impact on rice production, vegetable growing, fisheries, tobacco and livestock production: total forgone production estimated at approx. US$15 million

Transport: many roads blocked and bridges damaged by massive landslides and slope failures

Cost:
Property Losses: US$500 million
Reconstruction Cost: US$1.5 billion

Relief & Emergency:uncalculated
Consequential Costs: uncalculated

Reconstruction technical assistance

The earthquake in the Philippines in July 1990 destroyed much of the infrastructure and transportation network in the affected area. The main impact of the earthquake was on the economy of the region, affecting businesses, agriculture and tourism. Recovery planning needs to revitalize the economic production of the region as a prerequisite for successful reconstruction and to mitigate the effects of future earthquakes. The United Nations team assembled as technical assistance to the Presidential Reconstruction Task Force focused on regional development issues and economic planning. The four-man team worked on the city master plans and reconstruction strategies of Dagupan and Baguio (Armillas et al. 1990; Booth et al. 1991).

Reconstruction Plans to Reduce Future Earthquake Losses

Reconstruction programmes, developed as a result of these and other earthquakes, and with the assistance of United Nations, can be summarized as a set of six accepted principles. These are as follows:

- use the reconstruction for economic recovery;
- ensure cultural continuity in the reconstruction;
- deconcentrate cities and services;
- instigate safe construction procedures (not just safe design);
- institutionalize safety culture;
- export improvements beyond the reconstruction area.

Use the reconstruction for economic recovery

Economic regeneration is the key to successful reconstruction: restore income as well as buildings. *A strong economy is the best protection against future earthquakes.* A strong economy means more money to spend on stronger buildings and larger financial reserves to cope with future losses.

Identify the weakest members of the economy, those who have lost their economic reserves (house, livestock, livelihood), and ensure that assistance reaches them. Marginal families without reserves can quickly become destitute. Migration of families from rural areas to the towns is accelerated by earthquake losses.

Recovery of agricultural economies: understand the market structure of the region – what is normally produced, how much is sold or consumed by the community itself, where produce is sent to market, the supply and distribution network and how the earthquake has affected the market process. Recovery should ensure both the continued supply of produce to areas outside and to revitalize the livelihoods of farmers within the earthquake affected area. An earthquake often destroys reserves that farmers use to survive poor harvests and bad times: replacement of these reserves is needed for full recovery. Identify the most economically vulnerable members of the community and target aid towards them. Help replace animal losses, tools and seed. Instigate programmes of income supplementing (bee-keeping, dairy processing, craft production).

Revitalizing industrial economies: infrastructure is critical to industry: repair this first. Promote a partnership between private sector and Government. Smaller companies are likely to be under-insured and may be unable to recapitalize and continue in business even if profitable. Look at the Government-imposed restrictions on industry – for example locational zones, pollution controls, labour laws etc. In the emergency is it possible to remove them or relax them during the reconstruction period? Industry is interdependent – look at linkages between factories and where their employees live – is housing damaged as well as their income?

Recovery of commerce and service industries: service industries (shops, small businesses and trades) provide employment and income to a large proportion of the population. Premises are vital to continuity. Provide temporary (lockable) structures for use during the emergency and rehabilitation phase. Loss of customers is the biggest damage caused by earthquakes. Restore communications and information linkages between customers and businesses: newspapers, radio, TV for trade information dissemination.

Central Business Districts (CBDs) tend to be located where they are to take advantage of trade routes and a proximity to markets. Unless the earthquake has changed these basic factors, the CBD will repair itself – damaged buildings form only a small part of the office costs (staff and operating overheads far exceed the structural costs of office buildings). Communications and utilities are vital to the early recovery of CBD.

Recovery of tourism: negative publicity associated with earthquakes can harm short-term tourism returns. An effective and efficient reconstruction programme can be used to counter negative publicity with positive images of recovery and improved facilities. Past examples in other countries (Italy, Greece, Yugoslavia) include making the reconstruction and restoration of earthquake damage into a tourist attraction in its own right. Public relations and tourism marketing should be seriously considered, running promotional campaigns for the region in the main places that tourists come from.

Construction industry and building materials manufacture: the construction industry is often a primary employer and reconstruction operations are a good method of injecting capital into the local economy: local building labourers spend their wages in the local shop – both shop and local labourer benefit. Use an expanded local building industry for rebuilding – use outside contractors as little as possible and in partnership with local companies. A strong local construction industry is a good protection against future earthquakes.

Develop an Integrated Building Materials Plan: use locally manufactured building materials as much as possible, regional materials if necessary and imported materials as little as possible. Examine the materials market and normal production levels. Consider expanding local material production in preference to using materials from elsewhere. Consider substituting materials for local equivalents, even if these are currently poorer quality (provide technical assistance to improve quality). Small-scale manufacturing processes are quicker to set up and expand than large-scale, and distribute investment more rapidly to the local community.

Ensure cultural continuity in the reconstruction

Many examples of reconstruction have failed through assistance being insensitive to local needs and preferences. Relocation and bad reconstruction decisions can cripple the local economic productivity of a settlement and render it more vulnerable in the future.

Relocation of settlements should be avoided wherever possible.

Most settlements are where they are for a reason and it is rare that the threat of future hazard outweighs those reasons. Earthquake damage alone rarely justifies resiting. Major landslide or flooding threats may.

Rehousing in buildings that are different to those normally built by the community for themselves will generate long-term problems: they may quickly become unpopular and investment will be wasted. *Do not provide housing: make housing happen.* Facilitate the normal housing operations and help the local construction industry expand to meet the demand.

Radical agricultural reforms, like farm collectivizations and major land reforms instigated following earthquakes have rarely been successful.

Decisions on reconstruction should be taken at the most local level possible.

Deconcentrate cities and services

An earthquake also presents an opportunity to reappraise physical fabric and urban services. A key strategy for future earthquake protection is to deconcentrate facilities: *Services provided by one central facility are always more at risk than those provided by several smaller facilities.* This principle applies equally to hospitals and campuses, for example, as it does to power stations, telephone exchanges, and water treatment plants. Where damage has been suffered by a facility, rebuild it as a number of smaller units, preferably spread out over an area, rather than as a single unit or in one place.

Similarly, densities or cities may be reappraised in the reconstruction planning. Lower densities can be encouraged by the morphology of urban areas: the area and distance between streets, plots of land made available and in allowable plot ratio developments.

Instigate safe construction procedures

Earthquakes will continue to occur long into the future. It may be a long time before such a destructive earthquake hits the same region again, but it is likely to happen. The region is likely to continue to experience lower intensities fairly frequently.

The next time that Baguio or Dagupan is hit by such a large earthquake may be a century or more away. The steps that are taken to restore the towns and region now must be capable of providing proper protection to the region in that future time, as well as against the frequent tremors it will experience in the meantime.

Some of the buildings built in today's reconstruction will still be around for the next big earthquake, but not many. Buildings that last for 20, 50 or even 100 years will be replaced by others. *The earthquake's reconstruction must be used to instigate safe construction procedures that will continue for the next century.* Just building a set of stronger reconstruction buildings will not be enough if the buildings built later on are as weak as the ones built before the earthquake.

Procedures for a stronger building stock include strong quality control and building code compliance checks. The method of checking and enforcing building standards has to be firmly instigated in a new process that cannot be easily revoked. Quality control needs trained engineers. *Municipal engineers are the front-line troops in future earthquake protection.* Engineering design and training may be reviewed as part of a wider strategy for implementing better construction procedures.

Non-engineered buildings form the highest percentage of the building stock in every region. *Improving the process of producing safer non-engineered buildings involves training the builders that produce them.* Education processes have to be designed specially for them: practical hands-on training is more effective than audio-visual material or books.

Institutionalize safety culture

In a 'Safety Culture', people take account of day-to-day risks they face in their normal decision-making processes: special earthquake-risk programmes are not needed to make it happen.

Public awareness of risk levels is the first step. Public education on risk should be integrated within normal TV programmes, newspaper articles and entertainment rather than as public service announcements. All professional training of engineers, planners, architects, public officials, etc., should include earthquake risk as a module.

Planning decisions, building design, road construction and economic strategies should take earthquake risk into account as a normal part of the factors under consideration. Basic ground rules need proposing for risk minimization in each profession.

Export improvements beyond the reconstruction area

The next earthquake to hit the Philippines is unlikely to happen in the same place. It may occur on another part of the same earthquake fault, further north, or further south, or on another fault system in Luzon, or on another island. To reduce the impact of that event, the full lessons of the Luzon earthquake and the improvements that are instituted in the reconstruction have to be implemented outside the damaged area.

The national institutions responsible for hazard mitigation have to be built up and maintained.

A national risk mitigation plan will identify the areas most at risk from future earthquakes and propose strategies to reduce it. Risk identification involves mapping hazard and future earthquake occurrence, looking at where that hazard threatens major settlements and infrastructure, and how vulnerable the elements are to earthquake occurrence. Public awareness, training, reassessment of investment strategies, deconcentration and safe construction procedures can then be implemented in these areas to ensure that future earthquakes do not pose the same threat to life and economic prosperity as the last one.

REFERENCES

ARMILLAS, I., PETROVSKI, J., COBURN, A.W., CORPUZ, A. and LEWIS, D. (1990) *Technical Report on Luzon Earthquake of 16 July 1990, Republic of Philippines with Recommendations for Reconstruction and Development*, United Nations Centre for Human Settlements (Habitat), Geneva, Switzerland.

BOOTH, E.D., CHANDLER, A.M., WONG, P.K.C. and COBURN, A.W. (1991) *The Luzon, Philippines Earthquake of 16 July 1990, A Field Report by EEFIT*, Institution of Structural Engineers, London, UK.

COBURN, A.W., PETROVSKI, J., RISTIC, D., ARMILLAS I. and BEIRING, N. (1990) *Technical Review of the Impact of the Earthquake of 21 June 1990 in the Provinces of Gilan and Zanjan, Iran*, Office of the United Nations Disaster Relief Coordinator, Geneva, Switzerland.

CHAPTER 16

Hazards Mitigation and Housing Recovery: Watsonville and San Francisco One Year Later

MARY C. COMERIO

University of California
Berkeley, USA

Introduction

The city of Watsonville lost 642 housing units in the 17 October 1989 earthquake. These were primarily small single family dwellings that were knocked off their foundations. In less than one year, 75% have been repaired or replaced. In San Francisco, 500 of the 1482 red-tagged units were demolished and a total of 36,000 units were damaged. To date none of the large brick buildings has been repaired, none of the units torn down has been replaced and only 50% of the wood frame buildings damaged have begun repair work. It is unfair and unrealistic to compare the housing recovery rate of single family dwellings in a small town setting to the replacement of multi-family units in a large city. However, it is valuable to examine what is and is not working in each locale as it pertains to housing issues and hazard mitigation.

On 17 October 1989, at 5:04 pm, an earthquake measuring 7.1 on the Richter scale rocked the Bay Area for 15 seconds. In that brief period a portion of the San Francisco Bay Bridge and a three-quarter mile section of the Nimitz freeway collapsed, and a large number of buildings in Watsonville, Santa Cruz, the Marina and South of Market districts in San Francisco and downtown Oakland sustained significant damage. Perhaps the most important lesson from Loma Prieta was the vulnerability of structures built on fill and soft soils. But with any disaster there are numerous lessons to be drawn on many topics from preparedness, to mitigation, engineering, prediction and response.

This paper will focus specific attention on housing, not only because so many people were directly affected by damage and loss, but also because the problems of recovery and rebuilding are related to the problems of pre-earthquake hazard mitigation. The experience of two cities, San Francisco and Watsonville, represent the spectrum of housing issues affecting large metropolitan areas and small rural towns.

Mitigation

Significant programs for hazards mitigation in existing buildings are relatively new in California. In the last ten years local jurisdictions began the task of identifying potentially hazardous building types, and the engineering community has begun developing techniques for improving building performance for life safety and damage control. During the same period, engineers and emergency preparedness groups have taken steps to develop a public consciousness regarding earthquake hazards, and lobby for building codes which require retroactive repair of unreinforced masonry and tilt-up buildings. In fact, very few cities had mitigation programs in place before 17 October, 1989.

Although the cities of Long Beach and Santa Rosa have had 'active'[1] ordinances since the 1970s, it was the enactment of the Earthquake Hazards Reduction Ordinance (EHRO) in Los Angeles in 1981[2] that helped focus statewide attention on the retrofit of existing unreinforced masonry buildings (known commonly as URMs). The ordinance established a set of priorities for retrofit of the city's 8000 URMs. Emergency facilities, such as hospitals, police and fire stations, were the first to receive citations from the building department. Next in line were buildings defined as high risk (e.g. churches, theaters, offices, and other public assembly buildings). Medium and low risk buildings (housing and industrial uses with relatively low occupancies) were to be cited last. The entire program was designed to be implemented over a period of 15 years.

In 1985, the Mexico City earthquake prompted City Council members to accelerate the program and require completion of all retrofit in 8 years. This happened at the point when the city was just beginning the citation process for medium and low risk buildings which included 1582 residential buildings containing 46,000 housing units. To meet the new schedule established by the Council, all citations were issued by December 1986, all permits should have been secured in 18 months (by June 1988) and all construction should have started within 2 years (by December 1988). The fast-track mitigation program proved to be an unrealistic goal. As of October 1990, only 25% of the buildings cited in 1986 have actually completed construction, approximately 40% are in progress, 25% have made no progress towards construction and 10% have been demolished.[3]

While the implementation problems with the Los Angeles ordinance are the subject of another paper,[4] it is important to note the completion rate for the housing because most California cities look to Los Angeles as a model for engineering requirements as well as for implementation methods. In 1986, at the same time that Los Angeles was 'speeding up' its compliance schedule, the State passed a law requiring all local jurisdictions to inventory their hazardous building stock and develop a 'plan for mitigation'. The law, Senate Bill 547, did not go so far as to provide funding, nor did it require cities to implement retrofit ordinances, but it did put cities on notice that they were responsible for thinking about how to handle this problem.

The 1987 Whittier Narrows earthquake provided the first small test of the Los Angeles retrofit program. Although it was only a moderate earthquake (4.9 on the Richter scale), it did provide the opportunity to review strengthening procedures and renew the political pressure for state and local mitigation programs. Unfortunately, Loma Prieta preceded the adoption of most programs. On the positive side, Loma Prieta did provide a preview of the kind of damage the Bay Area might expect in future earthquakes of similar magnitude. 'Preview' is the appropriate term because it is generally agreed that the short duration of Loma Prieta (15 seconds) and the location of the epicenter (sixty miles south of San Francisco in the Santa Cruz mountains) spared Bay Area cities from more significant damage.

Loma Prieta

The media focused public attention on the collapsed portions of the Bay Bridge and the Nimitz freeway, as well as the damage in San Francisco's Marina district. This was not the whole story. There was extensive damage to older buildings throughout San Francisco and Oakland. In San Francisco, 71% of all buildings damaged were residential. While this residential loss represents only a tiny portion (1.5%) of the city's total housing stock, 60% of the nearly 36,000 units damaged housed low and moderate income people. Nearer to the epicenter, the cities of Santa Cruz and Watsonville each lost 60% of their downtown commercial districts. Further, Watsonville lost 8% of its housing stock, while 76% of the city's total occupied housing was damaged.[5]

For all the cities in the Bay Area affected by Loma Prieta, recovery and mitigation are now two sides of the same coin. For San Francisco and Watsonville, housing (particularly affordable housing) is a critical issue and the experience gained in the year after Loma Prieta should help us to understand the opportunities and the stumbling blocks for both recovery and mitigation.

San Francisco

San Francisco has a population of 720,000 in a 49 square mile area. As a result, San Francisco has a high proportion (75%) of its residential units in multi-family buildings (156,000 of 208,000 not including 19,000 single room occupancy hotels and 28,000 tourist hotels).[6] San Francisco is also a city with large ethnic populations – 90,000 Chinese, 30,000 Southeast Asians, 80,000 Hispanics, 80,000 Blacks – and a significant economic gap between low income minorities and middle class whites.[7]

Thus, who lost housing in the earthquake is equally important as how much was lost. The city reports that there was a total of 360 red-tagged buildings of which one-third were residential. Within one month of the earthquake, more than 500 of the 1482 red-tagged housing units were demolished. Most of these were in multi-family buildings located in the Marina. The remainder are located South of Market and in the Tenderloin. These buildings are empty and fenced to prevent reoccupancy and as protection against further damage. Similarly, the great majority of yellow-tagged buildings outside the Marina were in downtown neighbourhoods. Two-thirds of all the red- and yellow-tagged buildings were low and moderate income housing units.[8]

While many of the wood frame buildings have been repaired for habitability, not all the work is complete. In the Marina and Sunset Districts most of the demolished buildings are being replaced. Fifty per cent of those damaged are in the process of being repaired. By comparison, none of the red- and yellow-tagged single room occupancy hotels and multi-unit brick buildings (over 1300 units) in the Tenderloin and South of Market Street have started repair. Further, it is not clear that the plaster cracks and other minor damage in some 9000 units in these low income neighborhoods has been addressed. The city reports that many landlords are simply ignoring the damage, and tenants are still calling the city about repairs and inspections.[9]

Watsonville

Watsonville is a small town located 150 miles south of San Francisco at the center of one of the world's richest agricultural valleys. Watsonville has a population of 30,000 of which 50% are Hispanic, primarily farmworkers and cannery workers. During the Loma Prieta earthquake, Watsonville lost 642 of its 8100 housing units. These were older wood frame single family houses in the downtown area that were literally knocked off their foundations. The occupants were primarily Hispanic and 40% were owner occupied. In less than one year, more than 75% have been repaired or replaced.[10]

This is an incredible recovery rate. In the news media, Watsonville was portrayed as a poor backwater, and reporters assumed that the loss of housing and three downtown commercial blocks would devastate the city, and that it would never recover. Immediately after the earthquake, Watsonville was compared to Coalingia, where the old downtown was never rebuilt and the economy languished. In fact, Watsonville has approved plans for rebuilding two of the three commercial blocks, and city staff reports that the earthquake has generated new construction in addition to the repair work, as people add second units or additions while they have contractors on site.

How did the housing repair happen so quickly? One critical factor was the Earthquake Relief Fund established by the City to assist with long term recovery. Watsonville received donations from individuals, corporations, foundations, and their sister city in Japan. These donations totaled one million dollars. The city recognized that most emergency aid covered only the first 72 hours. They decided to use the donations to help people who could not qualify for FEMA, SBA or traditional loans. Thus, the city gave away the money in small grants (the largest was $48,000) for housing repair or reconstruction.

The Components of Recovery

In both San Francisco and Watsonville, there was very little business interruption or job loss. A survey of executives by the business-sponsored Bay Area Council said their businesses were only marginally affected by the earthquake. While many Chinatown merchants have argued that the loss of the Embarcadero Freeway has caused a drop in their business, others believe that this was part of a general economic downturn, accentuated by the earthquake. The real damage was in public sector transportation systems and private sector housing.

The obvious question seems to be: how can the little town of Watsonville rebuild or replace the majority of lost housing so quickly, and why has San Francisco been so slow? In part, it is unfair to compare single family wood frame buildings of 1000–2000 square feet to large multi-story, multi-unit buildings. It is valuable, however, to examine what is and is not working in each locale and why. Specific local conditions contributed significantly:

INCENTIVE: in Watsonville 40% of the housing was owner occupied with the remainder owned by the owner-occupant next door or another town resident. In San Francisco, the great majority of the buildings were owned by absentee owners. There is a real difference in incentive for an owner to replace his or her home and that of an investor evaluating the real estate market.

TECHNOLOGY: as stated earlier, there is no comparison between small wood frame single family houses and multi-unit apartment buildings. While building materials were generally available in both areas, the former requires minimal tools and skills while the latter requires engineering and architectural drawings as well as licensed, experienced professional contractors.

FINANCING: in San Francisco the Mayor's Office of Housing estimated a need for $118 million (at $80,000 per unit) to replace red-tagged units. Remembering that 60% of the units lost or damaged were providing affordable housing to low and moderate income tenants, the scale of the public subsidy necessary to retain some of those units for low and moderate income renters is daunting. Further, it is unclear whether buildings in marginal areas such as South of Market and the Tenderloin could obtain private financing for replacement housing. Whereas in Watsonville, the City simply gave away one million dollars in grants of $20,000 to individuals who wanted to repair their house, but could not qualify for conventional financing. Although the grants represent only 5% of the estimated $20 million repair bill, these funds clearly expedited the recovery process.

REGULATION: as in all large cities, construction projects must go through a myriad of planning and building reviews before permits can be issued. Even after an earthquake, there is a limited amount a large city can do to circumvent its own process once the immediate emergency has abated. In a small town like Watsonville, there is an opportunity for City staff to redefine the regulatory process. Watsonville decided to be 'easy on permits and tough on inspections'. In a city where the Planning Director knows most residents by name and the task of repair is relatively straightforward, the city was able to avoid time delays by placing the burden of control on the building inspectors in the field.

AVAILABLE SPACE: in San Francisco there were two very different kinds of tenants and two very different sets of choices. White middle class tenants who lost apartments in the Marina and other outlying districts simply moved to vacant units in other neighborhoods. Landlords offered them breaks on rent and deposits, department stores often offered furniture at cost. For non-English speaking, low income, elderly and transient tenants in the South of Market, there were few opportunities outside the Emergency Shelters and City sponsored homeless shelters. Community groups provided some assistance but could not rehouse those displaced in an already overcrowded undersupplied market. In Watsonville there was also a limited supply of vacant space to accommodate people and business on a temporary basis, and it was clear that even the strong extended family networks could not overcome the need for some temporary housing. Mobile homes were brought in, despite resistance by Federal and local relief agencies, to keep people close to their jobs and the homes they hoped to rebuild.

SELF HELP: in San Francisco, middle class tenants generally accommodated the loss of housing and personal possessions while maintaining their jobs, but low income people had a more difficult time. Displaced tenants South of Market joined the ranks of the homeless, waiting for public assistance. Whereas in Watsonville, cannery workers and farm laborers did not lose their jobs as there was no damage to these industries. These families traditionally rely on themselves and their neighbors, and they simply worked with the local construction labor force to rebuild their homes. Retirees and church groups pitched in and organized volunteer labor and 'house-raising' parties to assist individual families. Such efforts reduced the real costs of construction and built a strong community spirit.

Lessons – One Year Later

On all these points, San Francisco is a victim of scale. The loss of so many affordable units in a city with less than 1% housing vacancy rates is a significant blow, not only to the tenants, but to the City already struggling to maintain an adequate supply of affordable housing. Despite strong public leadership, neither private owners nor the City alone could fund the reconstruction, and state and federal assistance will be too little and too late. Watsonville, by contrast, managed to overcome a potentially devastating loss of affordable housing units and exhibited their own very sensible leadership, targeted critical financing, and was blessed with a strong dose of luck. Other communities cannot guarantee the component of luck, but they can develop the leadership and the creativity to take advantage of local opportunities.

Lesson 1 – Use local resources: human and financial

The recovery program that worked for Watsonville took advantage of local people with a vested interest in restoring their own houses. Had they decided to wait for larger loans or better deals, they might still be waiting. Instead they took what was available and made the best of it, recognizing that each individual house might not reach a level of finish that others would expect, but shelter was more important than community architectural standards.

In San Francisco, the losses from Loma Prieta have made the non-profit community housing organizations recognize the importance of mitigation. These groups have asked the city for training from local engineers so that they can serve as technical inspectors and advisors on their own projects and in their neighborhoods. It is these groups who have begun to include seismic upgrading in their low and moderate income renovation projects before it becomes a city requirement.

Lesson 2 – Balance safety and social needs

San Francisco has been criticized for its slow process in developing a retrofit ordinance and criticized further for opposing a state model code. However, it is clear from the descriptions of conditions in only two cities that it would be impractical to impose a single technical standard on hazardous building types in all locations. This is not an argument for a 'lower' standard for housing than for commercial buildings. Instead it is a recognition that the unique problems facing residents in Chinatown, the Tenderloin and South of Market neighborhoods in San Francisco ought to be dealt with by San Franciscans who can shape a hazards abatement program to local circumstances.

Each community needs to analyse its own inventory and develop specific strategies and methods to abate hazards that meet their own conditions. In

133

some cases, a land use decision to limit building on fill may be more useful than renovating a particular class of building.

Lesson 3 – Integrate technical social and financial analyses into a local program

The main problem with locally based research is that most large-scale aid organizations do not want to accept local solutions; yet all good locally based solutions to specific problems, such as housing production or hazards mitigation, can be understood in terms of a local application of general principles. Watsonville distributed funding quickly, made individuals responsible for their own construction, provided technical assistance, and stayed out of the way. How they did this was quite unique to Watsonville, but what they did would apply to any small-scale community with extensive loss of housing and a minimal loss of jobs.

The arguments that favor local initiative and local control may appear to suggest that disaster assistance and hazards mitigation be taken off the public agenda. That is not the intention. There is a very real need to maintain our building stock over the long term. Natural hazards are one mechanism for reminding us of the need to renovate and extend the useful life of the existing housing stock through mitigation and recovery.

At some level, Watsonville is thankful to the earthquake for giving them the opportunity and the funds to rebuild and improve a large segment of very old and ill maintained housing with donated funds, thus keeping it affordable to moderate income families who will be part of the community for a long time to come.

Conclusion

The final lesson from both Watsonville and San Francisco is that housing is a precious commodity, and both mitigation and recovery are a matter of public choice. In Watsonville, the city chose to spend limited public funds on private property, while the community contributed expertise and labor to assist low income families in rebuilding their homes. With 75% of the housing stock sustaining some damage, city inspectors used the opportunity to advise residents to ensure that houses were bolted to foundations, water heaters strapped, chimneys tied and other obvious hazards mitigated to prevent similar losses in the next earthquake.

In San Francisco, the cost of preventive repair for the undamaged stock could be twice that of the Loma Prieta repair bill, even though the cost per unit for mitigation is about 10% of the cost of a replacement housing unit.[11] The reality for any large city is that it cannot depend on donations, self help, and good neighboring to preserve the existing building stock. Recovery and mitigation will be a slow process involving a significant commitment of public funds and public will. Large cities, however, are not different than small towns in that there is a need to understand the physical conditions of their existing building stock and the social and economic conditions of their inhabitants to develop realistic and implementable programs. If there is any doubt about the importance of that commitment, we have only to look at the numbers of housing units affected in Loma Prieta and multiply that by the probability of the damage in the next earthquake.

NOTES AND REFERENCES

1. Active ordinances target specific buildings, classes of buildings or elements of buildings and require specific action to be taken. By comparison passive abatement programs require hazard reduction only when a predefined action, such as a change of use or major renovation, is taken by the owner.
2. The Earthquake Hazard Reduction Ordinance adopted in Los Angeles in 1981 is commonly known as 'Division 88', its numerical section of the Los Angeles Building Code.
3. Figures on completion of seismic retrofit in Los Angeles were calculated by the Community Development Department based on Building and Safety computer records in October 1990 for a status report to the City Council.
4. Comerio, Mary C. (1990), 'Seismic Safety – At What Price?' *Proceedings of the Fourth National Earthquake Engineering Conference*, Palm Springs, CA, May 1990.
5. Damage figures are based on internal reports from the Cities of Watsonville and San Francisco, and the 1983 City and County Data Book published by the US Department of Commerce, Bureau of the Census.
6. Comerio, Mary C. (1987), *Earthquake Hazards and Housing*, San Francisco Department of City Planning, pp. 21–23.
7. Population data based on 1986 estimates from the San Francisco Department of Public Health, and current estimates from the Center for Southeast Asian Refugee Settlements in San Francisco.
8. 'Earthquake Impact on Low and Moderate Income Housing' Report No. 4, 20 November 1989, from the Mayor's Office of Housing, City and County of San Francisco.
9. Interview with Lawrence Kornfield, Head of Earthquake Statistics, Bureau of Building Inspections, City of San Francisco, 22 August 1990.
10. Interviews with Maurene Owens, Planning Director and Dicksie Allen, Senior Planner, City of Watsonville, August 8, 1990. It should be noted that the remaining 25% of the housing that was not rebuilt is a result of unusual zoning or non-conforming use. The city is working with these owners to find solutions to these sites.
11. The cost of repair is estimated in the Mayor's Office of Housing report cited above as well as in a recent Environmental Impact Report on Earthquake Hazards Reduction in Unreinforced Masonry Buildings, San Francisco Department of City Planning, 8 November 1990.

CHAPTER 17

The Reconstruction of Kalamata City after the 1986 Earthquakes. Some Issues on the Process of Temporary Housing

MIRANDA DANDOULAKI

*National Technical University
of Athens*

Introduction

Kalamata is the capital of the Messinia prefecture and is located about 280km south of Athens. In 1986 it had a population of 41,911 people, 30% of the population of the prefecture (1981 census). Messinia is an agricultural area with Kalamata City serving an additional role as a manufacturing centre. Only 8.3% of the population is employed in the agricultural sector (Urban Plan of Kalamata, 1986).

Kalamata City is a port and this has greatly influenced its development. The city's urban plan was drawn up in 1905. Since then the city has expanded through informal building construction. A few months before the earthquake a new city plan was passed for implementation. The building stock of the city is comparatively new: 41% of the buildings are of reinforced concrete, 15% of mixed reinforced concrete and masonry, while 44% are masonry buildings (Argirakis, 1989).

The 1986 Earthquakes: Physical Parameters and Immediate Effects

Main shock:

Time of occurrence:	13 September 1986, 20.35
Epicentral location:	15km from the city
Magnitude:	Ms=6.20
Strong motion duration:	2.5 seconds

136

Main after shock:

Time of occurrence: 15 September 1986, 14.41
Epicentral location: 11km from the city
Magnitude: Ms=5.40
Strong motion duration: 1 second
(Source: ITSAK, 1986)

The earthquakes caused the deaths of 20 people and injured about 330. These numbers are very low when compared with the effect on buildings. According to the results of an official survey of 10,171 buildings in Kalamata City, 22% had collapsed or were to be demolished and an additional 22% were classified as being heavily damaged. Only 32% of the surveyed buildings were undamaged. Damage was localised in certain areas, such as the 'Old Centre' district of the city which was severely damaged as were the districts of Nisaki and Giannitsanika. Also heavily affected were the areas of informal housing such as Agios Sideris and Agia Paraskevi. However, only minor damage occurred in the bay area of the city. The damage caused by the event totalled about US $700 millions (Pomonis 1990).

Process of Temporary Housing Provision

Because of the fear of possible aftershocks the population was warned not to live in the buildings, even in the undamaged ones, for a few weeks. To cope with the shelter need, tents were distributed. However, the forthcoming winter made the decision on a housing strategy for the homeless a matter of priority. The solution of using prefabricated units was considered within a few days of the earthquake, and it was proposed by the Mayor of Kalamata at a meeting of the municipal council on 24 September. This need was compounded by the public pressure for this type of housing.

Although other alternatives, such as distribution of money to accelerate repair and reconstruction, were considered, the option for prefabricated housing units was selected. This selection was made on the basis of the speed of reconstruction which was aimed to be completed within 4 months, as well as the reusable nature of the units in the event of future earthquakes.

These prefabricated units were intended to shelter people whose houses had collapsed or had to be demolished. This created a demand for 1,000 units. However the demand for housing units increased to 2,870, because of public pressure from people living in houses with heavy but repairable damage, who also claimed housing.

The unit supply procedure

The Greek producers of such prefabricated units were unable to meet the demands for such a large number of housing units. Therefore, international

FIGURE 1 *Examples of prefabricated units constructed in Kalamata City following the 1986 earthquake*

138

FIGURE 1 (contd.)

tenders were sought for the contracts on offer from the Government. Finally, 16 firms were selected to supply and put up 2,870 units of 18 different types due to their size, design, structure, and the technology and materials used. Figure 1 shows four examples of the types and arrangements of these units.

Land appropriation

The land necessary to construct the units was estimated at approximately 140,000m^2. As public and municipal land could not satisfy the demand, private land had to be appropriated. The criteria for land selection were very strict. They included planning, technical and economic considerations. For instance the sites had to be both included within the city's newly defined boundaries and easily accessible. They also had to be flat to limit the cost of infrastructure and services. Avoiding flood-prone areas was yet another of the criteria.

Special care was given to the distribution of the sites, so that, if possible, the homeless could be sheltered in their own neighbourhoods. However, because of difficulties in land acquisition and the non-availability of land in the inner city, not all the selection criteria were fulfilled. Finally, 17 private land sites, some volunteered by their owners, were selected to be acquired.

The procedure for the acquisition of land took longer than expected, mainly because of the inadequacies of the pre-existing legislation for emergency situations. So the municipality had to opt for an alternative solution, which involved leasing land from its owners. Overall, these problems delayed the programme for several months.

Layout plans of the sites

The layout plans of the sites were made by the Ministry of Public Works. The initial intentions of the designers were to create a 'village' type site with open spaces where community activities could take place, and houses that allowed individuals privacy, safety and good sanitation. In larger sites even small shops were provided.

However, this plan kept changing due to the nature of the units, the circumstances, the constraints and the pressures. The final results varied for each site and proved very different from the initial intentions. The linear, concentrated setting of the units meant that privacy for each household was unachievable. Some of the units were not accessible by car and through practical reasons of inconvenience caused further problems in the event of fire. The open spaces were large, but badly set, and so were not used by the local residents. The overall picture of the sites is that of a 'ghetto', and this situation has only been improved by the inhabitants' efforts to make homes of the prefabricated units.

Site development

Several agencies like the Ministry of Public Works, the Municipality of Kalamata and private contractors needed to collaborate and be coordinated both for the site preparation and the construction of the infrastructure. Because of the time pressure and lack of experience of the parties involved, many mistakes were made, especially with regard to the drainage systems, which had to be repaired once the sites were inhabited.

After the infrastructure had been completed, the suppliers constructed the prefabricated units. The timescale in which the sites were completed is presented in Figure 2. The distribution of the unit-types in relation to the sites was done randomly, depending mainly on the times of delivery by each supplier.

At this stage no real interest was given to the utilities and services necessary for the effective functioning of each site. There were many problems caused by this with demands for improving utilities and services being a continual source of conflict between the inhabitants and the authorities. This forced the Municipality to undertake some programmes for the improvement of the sites. About two years after the earthquakes the services and facilities in most sites were at an acceptable standard.

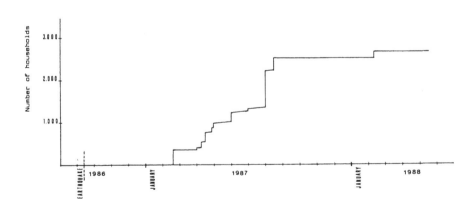

FIGURE 2 *Timescale in which the prefabricated units were delivered to homeless people after the earthquake*

The distribution of the units to the homeless

The distribution of the units proved to be a considerable task due to the intense pressure placed on the system by the homeless. A task undertaken by the Municipality of Kalamata, to avoid any accusations of favouritism they endeavoured to set certain criteria:

- neighbouring location of homeless permanent houses to match the location of sites
- the size of the household
- special problems experienced by members of the household (disabilities, sickness etc)
- units to be distributed on a ratio 7/3 for households whose houses were classified as collapsed/heavily damaged.

Special care was given, so that relatives or friends would be able to stay in nearby units. Following the completion of each site, the units were allocated to the homeless fulfilling these criteria by a lottery system. Once allocated a unit, a contract was signed between the head of the household and the Municipality. Among the contract's terms was that residence in the unit was permitted only until the repair or reconstruction of the permanent house was completed and for no more than two years, and that during their residence subletting or the use of the unit by another household or for a different use was not allowed.

Despite the enormous pressures exerted by the homeless on the authorities, distribution of the units was completed very rapidly after the completion of the sites and there were few complaints about the procedure itself. Allocation of the first completed sites came six months after the earthquakes.

When, one year after the earthquakes, the last sites were completed, many of the homeless had already found other solutions to their accommodation problems and therefore the real need and demand for prefabricated units declined. Nevertheless, there was a gap in the system as regards monitoring the units after they were inhabited, with subletting, use of units as storage facilities and illegal occupancy occurring.

The sites' function after they were occupied

A year after the earthquakes all the sites were occupied. Although they were deemed completed, many technical problems arose. The problems concerned:

- the technology, quality and construction of the units, for example leakages, problems in the electrical system, bad foundations
- mistakes or insufficiencies in the services constructed, such as drainage problems in the site
- lack of services and facilities, such as telephone and postal services, garbage collection, schools, nurseries, community centres

- the location of the site, for example, bad accessibility to the city or the shops.

Not every site had the same set of problems and in the same intensity, but in each there was a need for greater investment to make living conditions more tolerable. Informal committees representing the people were formed on some sites to put pressure on the authorities to improve the quality of services and facilities. Some months later, committees were officially elected in all sites. Following pressure from site-residents there was a noticeable improvement in the services and facilities provided, and within two years they were at an acceptable level.

The technical problems of the temporary housing were easy to identify. Less obvious were the sites' human and social problems. While residents and authorities accepted that there were problems, practically no help was offered and no research carried out on the dynamics of these problems.

The sites dismantle

As stated by the Mayor of Kalamata during the second anniversary of the earthquakes 'the existence of prefabricated units is the most severe political and social problem of the city'. A deadline, the end of 1989, was announced for occupants to abandon the units.

The problem proved rather difficult to resolve. Although the repair or reconstruction of the permanent houses was rapidly achieved and despite the fact that it was well known to the residents, even from the distribution of the units, that they would be allowed to stay in them for no more than two years, they were not willing to return them to the Municipality. According to the outcome of an official investigation carried out at the beginning of summer 1989, by that time only 1,500 out of the 2,870 units were inhabited. The units were being used as storage or as temporary houses for relatives and friends of the household. It was also a reality that the units were sublet or used as homes for family members such as grandparents.

As an incentive to abandon the units, a form of housing benefit was given to residents moving from a unit into a permanent house. The measure had some positive effect but did not solve the problem.

It seems that the dismantling of the sites is related to the housing problem in the city. The earthquakes particularly affected the old building stock which was rented by the low-income population who could not afford the new illegally high rents of the buildings after they were repaired or reconstructed. A percentage of this population found, as a solution to the housing problem, the use of prefabricated units for subletting or illegal occupation. Since authoritarian methods to make people leave units comes at a high political cost, the deadlines have no meaning. Although, according to the numbers of units returned, noticeable progress has been made, the sites are still in use in Kalamata.

In addition to the social and political problems arising from dismantling the sites, there are also serious technical problems. A major argument for the use of prefabricated units was that they could be reused to meet a future need. In practice this means that all the different types of units must be carefully dismantled, transported and stored in such a way that they can be reused. The problems arising are many, for example the storage space required for such a number of units is huge. The spare parts of units even of the same type are not compatible after dismantling. Damaged parts are not replaceable because most of the supplying firms no longer exist. Different types of units need different storage conditions and control. It should also be mentioned that in some types of units the level of damage after dismantling is so high that they are not reusable.

This last phase of the temporary housing process is essential for the justification of this form of sheltering strategy.

Conclusions

After the 1986 Kalamata earthquakes 22 sites with 2,870 prefabricated units of 18 different types were constructed to shelter temporarily the homeless. Some conclusions can be made after examining the temporary housing provision process:

- the land appropration procedures seem to have influenced drastically the timing of the temporary housing provision. So, although the speed of supply and construction of the prefabricated units was a main argument for the selection of this strategy, it seems that other parameters can be crucial for the speed of the whole project
- a realistic estimation of the number of units really needed is essential for the success of the temporary housing provision. But this is not easy to make soon after an earthquake, since the real need for prefabricated units is related to the timing of temporary housing provision and the expected progress of permanent housing reconstruction.

It seems that in Kalamata, by the time the last sites were completed a year after the earthquakes, there was no longer a real need for units to shelter the homeless. On the other hand, the high number of units·was a major cause for project delay because of the sizeable need for land and the large scale of work required.

It has also been a crucial factor on the total cost and the quality of temporary housing. Because of the number of units demanded, the Greek market could not respond. So, a variety of types of prefabricated units of different standards and suitability from seven countries, were used.

Dismantling sites is a serious political and social problem. The temporary housing tends to become permanent. And although the measures already taken, like the housing benefit, have had some positive effect, the problem is not yet solved.

The feasibility of the reuse of prefabricated units in a future sheltering need, as it was argued for the choice of this sheltering option, is yet to be proved. But so far it seems that there are many technical problems due to the dismantling, transportation and storage of such large quantities of units of different types.

The prefabricated units' temporary housing strategy has been tested in many events and in different countries. It is an important consideration why previous experience has not been transferred and why the same mistakes are repeated. The answer to that is maybe the key-issue in disaster planning.

References

ARGIZAKIS, K. and KOUNDOURIS, S. (1990) 'Evaluation of Damages in Buildings of Kalamata after the 1986 Earthquakes', 9th Greek Conference of Reinforced Concrete, Kalamata (in Greek).

DANDOULAKI, M. (1989) *Reconstruction of Kalamata after the 1986 Earthquakes: Some Issues on the Temporary Housing Provision*, Master thesis, Panteios University – Institute of Regional Development (in Greek).

Institute of Technical Seismology and Earthquake Engineering (ITSAK) (1986), *The Kalamata Earthquakes* (in Greek).

NSSG (1980) *The 1980 Population Census* (in Greek).

POMONIS, A. (1989) 'The October 1988 Elia Prefecture Earthquake (S.W. Greece): Seismic Environment, Building Types and Damage patterns,' *Disasters*, **13** (2).

Urban Plan of Kalamata 1986 (in Greek).

CHAPTER 18

Disaster Aid: Equity First

ERIC DUDLEY

The Martin Centre for Architectural and Urban Studies
University of Cambridge, UK

Introduction

This paper was prompted by a trip to Ecuador in July 1990. The area
affected by the March 1987 earthquake was revisited in order to assess the
impact of the aid programmes for the reconstruction of rural houses. It was
found that despite material benefits to some of the villagers and indirect
benefits of skills developments to the building professions there was also
evidence of damage to the broader developmental process. The principal
conclusion is that in order to avoid such damage there should be more
equitable distribution of benefits and consequently the promotion of
technologies in ways which facilitate such equity.

An Ecuadorian Earthquake

In March 1987 the north-east of Ecuador was struck in quick succession by
two earthquakes. The incident cannot be described as a major disaster when
set against some of the catastrophic earthquakes which have since occurred
around the world. Estimates of casualties vary but probably no more than a
hundred people died. The UNCHS estimated that 3,000 houses were
destroyed and 15,000 more were in need of repairs (UNCHS 1987:1). Most of
these houses were in rural areas and though the epicentre was in the tropical
jungle zone the bulk of the damage was to the heavyweight constructions of
the Andes (Figure 1).

In Ecuador, apart from a variety of state institutions which are involved in

FIGURE 1 *Map of the northern Ecuadorian Andes*

rural development, there are many NGOs. Consequently, there were a large number of different reconstruction projects launched in the area. The immediate response to the reconstruction needs created by the earthquake have been discussed elsewhere (Dudley 1988:111–121). In July 1990, several of the earthquake reconstruction projects were still under way.

Positive Impact

The benefits which have come from the post-disaster aid have taken a number of forms.

Technological improvement

Various authors have suggested that in developmental terms any re-construction programme is worthwhile only if it results in a lasting change of building practices which extends beyond the scope of the immediate needs of reconstruction. In the Ecuadorian case there now seems to be adequate evidence to believe that the use of 'L' shaped moulds to strengthen the corner of rammed earth buildings, a practice introduced after the earthquake, has now been adopted as part of the building vocabulary of the area (Figure 2). People building houses with their own resources for reasons other than reconstruction were observed to be using the moulds.

Perhaps more important than the introduction of new technologies has been the process which many villagers have gone through of re-evaluating their traditional technologies. There is no doubt that due to modern influences the use of earth and timber for walls has become unfashionable. Five years ago it was hard to find a builder who could make a rammed earth wall or who would admit to it. It was seen as something from the old days. Yet due to the presence of various institutions promoting the use of these traditional technologies, albeit with minor changes, people are realizing that outsiders value these techniques and so perhaps they are not so unacceptable. However, this change of attitudes is not solely attributable to the earthquake. Among the upper middle classes, earth houses are starting to become fashionable and the trend is percolating down.

Cadre of experienced architects and engineers

A similar process has been undergone by many Ecuadorian building professionals. Conventional architectural and engineering education in Ecuador has not dealt with the indigenous building techniques or with the special skills needed for working in participatory ways with rural communities. At the time of the earthquake it was hard to find experienced professional staff for the various reconstruction projects but now there is a substantial group of young professionals who have two or three years' hard field work behind them. The formation of this group is arguably the greatest single benefit to have come out of the disaster aid. The earthquake accelerated a process which was already under way and has probably brought it forward by several years. The immediate worry is whether or not there will be sufficient opportunities for these professionals to exploit and build upon these new found skills. Hopefully, the heightened awareness among development institutions of the possibilities for development initiatives related to housing will lead to a continuation of work in this field in other regions of the country.

An opening for other initiatives

The relationship between disasters and general development has been clearly spelt out (e.g. Cuny 1983). In the Ecuadorian case, reconstruction initiatives led to projects for roads, irrigation channels, community buildings and other benefits. More practically, the heightened awareness of housing issues

FIGURE 2 *The corner of rammed earth walls were made more seismically resistant by the use of an 'L' shaped mould*

encouraged funding agencies to encourage follow-up housing related projects. In the wake of a successful community based project to rebuild 2,000 low-cost houses the *Centro Andino de Accion Popular (CAAP)* are now undertaking a wide scale rural housing improvement programme tackling issues of environmental health which are unrelated to seismic considerations.

Transfer of resources

In terms of perception of benefit by the villagers themselves it is clear that they see material gain as the principal benefit. Whatever criticisms one may be able to make regarding how much money appears to have been eaten up in salaries, imported vehicles and the making of videos, there has been a significant transfer of resources to a large number of the villagers. It is possible that the perception of and preoccupation with material gain resulted in the subtler benefits of enhanced technical knowledge being overshadowed or lost.

Negative Impact

Despite the benefits of the aid there have also been some harmful effects.

Confusion of responses

In the first days following the earthquake, the principal NGOs working in the area were talking with each other and local Government agencies to determine who should be responsible for assistance and reconstruction work in which areas. Particularly around the town of Cayambe, this arrangement appeared to function reasonably well for the first few months. However, two problems started to become apparent. Firstly, there were remote areas which were not previously served in any comprehensive way by any NGOs and so tended to be largely ignored by the established NGOs who understandably wanted to reinforce their links with their existing constituencies. Secondly, after four or five months there was a new wave of aid funds. These were sums which were not immediately available as emergency aid at the time of the earthquake but which came as the result of applications for funds which needed to pass through various stages of formal approval. Once this money arrived, the pressure was then on both NGOs and state institutions to spend that money. Consequently, various institutions started to move into areas already being served by other reconstruction projects. Generally, the different projects would each have their own technical and organizational line and so the villagers would be faced with different and sometimes contradictory messages from the collective aid establishment. This competition created an even bigger incentive for the locally established NGOs to stick to their existing project areas in order to defend their patch.

The effects of these two problems was most marked where the two coincided; that is to say, remote communities not served by the first wave of aid but which largely because of this neglect attracted the attention of several members of the second wave. The most dramatic example of this problematic conjunction is in and around the village of Mariano Acosta. The village itself is small with no more than 300 households. Five different institutions were running reconstruction projects in the village two of which were still operating in July 1990. The five institutions each reflect a different thread of the rural development story in Ecuador:

- *Ministerio de Bienestar Social (MBS)*: the Ministry of Social Welfare, a state organization which has little previous experience in rural housing but which, with the support of UNCHS, is now emerging as the lead state agency in the field. Their houses have walls of rammed earth.
- *The Ecuadorian Red Cross*: the Red Cross project was the most top-down of the projects since it involved contractors erecting imported steel frames with concrete block infill and asbestos-cement roofs.
- *The Diocese*: the church remains an important influence in rural Ecuador and they had to be seen to be responding. Their solution was a design for a large concrete block and reinforced concrete frame house. Many of these are currently sitting unfinished due to lack of funds.
- *Federacion Indigena de Campesinos de Imbabura (FICI)*: FICI is a typical example of the new breed of NGOs which claim not only to serve the villagers but to represent and be of the villagers. With many of these organizations their credentials for being truly representative are questionable but, like the church and the state, they have to be seen to be responding. They attracted funding from an International NGO along with the services of an Ecuadorian architect, Manuel Perez, who is skilled in locally appropriate technologies. Their design was a timber frame with mud brick infill.
- *Fundacion Ecuatoriana del Habitat (FUNHABIT)*: this group of Ecuadorian architects and engineers attracted international funding for rammed earth houses which though similar to those of the *Ministerio de Bienestar Social* differed in a number of important details.

These five projects had or still have not only different technologies but also different work practices, such as free materials with paid labor, or subsidized materials with donated labor, or in the case of the Red Cross outside contractors. It was reported, though not verified, that one family had received five different houses. This may be apocryphal but there were numerous reports from various areas of families who had received three houses.

151

Conflicting or erroneous technologies

The phenomenon described above is not simply wasteful duplication of effort. The villagers are exposed to different officials each explaining that the offer they are making is an example of fair and just development and that the technology they are promoting is the correct one. It could be argued that there will always be more than one answer to any technical problem and that there is no harm in exposing the intended beneficiaries to a variety of solutions and allowing them to make their own choice. However, the choice is strongly influenced by the degree of material gain, the development institution's sweetener, and some of the technologies appear not to be technically sound and so are potentially damaging.

The steel frame design provides a seismically strong house yet it is a technology which is irreproducible in the economic context of rural Ecuador. If it cannot be reproduced not only is the technology not a positive gain for the local knowledge-base but also it could create the idea that imported high technology is the only adequate response available. Fortunately these houses are being rejected on the grounds that they are cold. If they had proved to be popular they may have done lasting damage.

At the other end of the spectrum are the 'appropriate technologies', but for a technology to be appropriate not only must it make use of indigenous materials and skills but it must also work. In some cases technologies which are being promoted are of questionable worth and may be actually harmful. One example is the practice of casting the ends of thin vertical wooden poles into the foundations which pass up through the rammed earth wall in order to provide a key between the foundations and the wall and to increase the overall tensile strength of the structure. In laboratory tests it has, apparently, been demonstrated that this can provide a significant improvement. However, in practice since the earth available in the area for construction had a higher than desirable clay content the poles tend to act as crack inducers and foci for drying cracks. This was noticed and commented on in some of the first houses to be built using this technique in 1987 yet in July 1990 the technique was still being widely promoted by various institutions. On interviewing builders, when asked if they thought these poles would help strengthen the walls, they generally replied, 'Oh yes, the engineer said so'.

In another instance, a state reconstruction project with international funding has built small houses with simple unreinforced concrete block walls. The design envisaged by the funders included integral concrete block buttresses as a contra-seismic measure. An evaluation by the funders revealed that the houses had been built without the buttresses. In response to the ensuing criticism the state institution has instigated a remedial programme of applying concrete block pilasters to the outside of the houses. These pilasters are not bonded into the wall and so cannot be expected to effectively strengthen the building. There is now evidence that some villagers are adopting this erroneous technique.

Dependency

Dependency has spread beyond technical dependence on the 'expert'. In the first few days after the earthquake many people started to rebuild their houses but as the novel idea spread that there were institutions proposing to give material help for house building people abandoned their reconstruction work and in some cases reverted to demolition. Now, three years on, the immediate memory of the earthquake has passed yet still there are institutions giving away houses. Increasingly in the area it is becoming part of the normal expectations which a villager has of an aid institution that it will provide substantial material help with housing. Local NGOs have been working patiently over many years to increase the sense of self-determination among rural communities struggling to recover from five hundred years of serfdom on the large *haciendas*. Many field workers now feel that the work of years has been brushed away by the often paternalistic aid of here today gone tomorrow agencies. Whereas before, self-help and independence were the watchwords of development, now handouts are the expectation.

New houses instead of repair

The initial damage estimates indicated that for every house which would have to be rebuilt there were five houses in need of repair. Although some of the intervening institutions did produce educational material on repairing houses and in some of the small towns there were urban repair programmes, generally the institutions failed to develop an adequate response to repair needs. The emphasis was on the construction of new houses built to the design of the intervener's architects. A programme of new identical houses is easier to manage than a programme of one-off repairs. In the village of Mariano Acosta with its five competing reconstruction programmes there are still many houses with cracked and partially collapsed gables. Their owners have received new houses yet the old buildings still stand and are still being occupied. It is reasonable to guess that when the next earthquake comes many of the casualties will result from these already weakened structures.

Factional penetration

It has long been recognized that aid is frequently a vehicle for political penetration and control. At a local level, various reconstruction projects have undoubtedly been used by individual politicians, but perhaps more significant have been the activities of evangelical groups. For instance, in the area of Canguagua the Protestant evangelical groups have not formerly had a significant presence. Shortly after the earthquake the evangelical based funding agency World Vision moved in to a small area with an offer of three-bedroomed concrete block houses with reinforced concrete frames. They now have an established foothold in the area. Throughout rural South America the conflict between Catholics and evangelical Protestants is a major cause of division which has now, in a small way, been further aggravated.

Divisions

A more widespread cause of division has been the manner in which aid has been disbursed within villages. At worst, there were examples of aid workers driving into villages and announcing that there were X number of houses available for that village and that the village president should draw up a list of who should receive the houses. Not surprisingly, in many instances those on the list were friends and relatives of the president. Even where sensitive and experienced field workers in collaboration with conscientious village leaders helped draw up a just list, a couple of years later that list has become a bone of contention. Some people who were excluded felt that because they had been careful in how they had built their house before and had, perhaps, invested more money in the building and had worked harder to get more money to pay for it, that they were now being penalized for their industry. In most other forms of rural aid concerned with agriculture, forestry, health or education there is a chance for all to benefit or those that do not benefit are at least not losing out too much in material terms. With housing, large sums of money are involved and potential divisions are consequently deep.

Experience from working with other rural communities in Ecuador, before and since the earthquake, has repeatedly revealed the principle that if material aid in any form is to be brought to the community then it should be received in equal measure by all households. This simple principle reflects the indigenous community work practices of the region in which each household would be expected to contribute equally in labour and resources to communal works and receive equal benefits irrespective of differing needs. On occasions this practice has been seen to be enforced with brutal rigidity resulting in, for instance, an elderly lady living on her own having to contribute as much as a household containing several fit young men. Such anomalies are the price of such a simple and readily understood system of equity. Similar practices have been observed in rural communities elsewhere in the world. Aid programmes which cut across this system by trying to target the individual affected families are trampling over an ancient system of rough but recognized justice and so seriously weakening the fabric of society.

Developmental imbalance

Many local aid workers have become frustrated by the disruption to their ongoing work caused both by the earthquake and the subsequent aid. One institution initially aimed to finish its reconstruction programme in six months then return to its normal work. In practice, the programme took a year to conclude but it attracted funding for a follow up housing improvement project; and whereas before the earthquake housing formed no part of the institution's work, now it has a major role. Many field workers feel that because funding for housing was suddenly available, the broad programme of the institution has got out of balance. Even more disruptive has been the influence of the housing projects of other institutions in their traditional project areas. Such projects are competing for the attention of the client population. Virtually all rural development projects now require input from the villagers, in the name of self-help and participation. The villager is expected to enter into a contract where he or she invests time and labour in return for technical and material aid. If one institution is offering a few seedlings for what is intended to be a developmentally sound self-sustaining agricultural programme then that is liable to appear to be a less attractive deal than a newcomer's offer of a free house.

In terms of priorities of development it is not clear that the risk presented by earthquakes in Ecuador justifies giving a high place to contra-seismic rural domestic construction at the expense of other interventions aimed at improved productivity, health, and education. Simply because an earthquake creates an opportunity for introducing programmes for contra-seismic construction does not necessarily mean that such programmes are the most developmentally appropriate. Even within the field of housing there may be cases where the criteria of rapid rehousing to facilitate economic and social recovery or continuity should be seen to be of greater importance than the introduction of contra-seismic technologies of marginal benefit.

Approximate distribution of earthquakes in Ecuador over a period of hundred years (derived from Egred 1968 and CRSAS 1985)

Magnitude	4.0<4.9	5.0<5.4	5.5<5.9	6.0<6.4	6.5<6.9	7.0<
No. of incidents	1,350	400	90	20	6	1.5
Percentage	72%	21%	5.3%	1.2%	0.4%	0.1%

A geographical imbalance has also developed. It used to be the case that the *indigena* areas of the north-eastern Ecuadorian Andes around Cayambe were suffering from similar problems to the other predominantly *indigena* areas in the central provinces of Cotopaxi and Chimborazo. However, over the last three years a disproportionate quantity of international funds have flowed into the disaster area whereas the other impoverished areas continue in their normal state of neglect. There are now indications that some of the unspent disaster money will be used on housing initiatives in the central provinces.

Equitable Aid?

Through reconstruction aid many new houses have been built, yet it is hard to prove that people have been rehoused any quicker than they would have been without aid. Indeed there is evidence from Ecuador and elsewhere that the knowledge that aid is coming slows down or stops the autonomous reconstruction process. In one isolated location, the community of Rumipamba found itself floating without help between the more or less arbitrary lines on the maps of various reconstruction projects. Two and a half years after the earthquake they had received no aid. Finally in frustration they bought some land and built themselves a totally new village of forty-five houses. Eight months later the village was largely complete without any technical help and only some laggardly financial aid to buy roof tiles. In this instance the catalyst for change was anger with the inefficacy of the aid machinery. As a consequence their communal cohesion and self-confidence is probably higher than any of the surrounding beneficiary communities.

It is, perhaps, already a cliché to refer to the disaster of aid. It is too easy to snipe at aid and point to its faults. However, in the case of a relatively minor disaster such as the 1987 Ecuadorian earthquake it is worth asking whether the aid did more harm than good or at least not sufficiently more good than harm to justify the expense? Also, accepting that the aid did both good and harm how can we manage things in the future to maximize the good and minimize the harm?

Balance

Worries about increased dependency may be misplaced or exaggerated. It could be that the shrewdness and robustness of the villagers is being underestimated by outside observers. It may be that many people are taking advantage of the jamboree while it lasts and when the supply of easy aid dries up things will return to normal more rapidly than may be expected. Concerns about divisions, however, are more serious. Some villagers have undoubtedly benefited but it is questionable whether in the broader perspective of development those benefits were equitable and just.

In normal circumstances, housing related issues often seem to be largely neglected by the aid community yet in the wake of a disaster the pendulum often seems to swing to the opposite and equally unhealthy extreme. Many of the problems which disaster aid attempts to tackle are not caused by the disaster but only highlighted by it. Paramount among such problems are those of poverty and inequality. Reconstruction projects are often faced with the dilemma of whether to truly *re*construct, albeit with contra-seismic improvements, or whether to establish and impose a new minimum standard of housing provision. In the wake of an earthquake the material losses sustained by the relatively wealthy inhabitants of the towns may be considerable simply because they have so much more to lose than their impoverished rural neighbours. In the Ecuadorian case many of the basic rural houses were rebuilt within a few days of the earthquake since they were so elementary in the first place. Indeed, some of the families concerned were excluded from the lists since by the time the damage was assessed and the lists drawn up they had already rehoused themselves. A reconstruction project which makes good the actual damage inevitably has to give substantially more aid to the wealthy. This cannot be correct. Yet, an equitable scheme pitched at a level sufficiently high to meet the perceived basic needs of the urban population and the wealthier rural families will result in a provision considerably higher than that which is the norm for the rural poor. For the poorer families included in the project this can result in a significant improvement in living standards yet for those on the other side of the arbitrary line on the map the only change is increased marginalization, bewilderment and resentment.

Clarity

There is little use in academics proposing ideal models of intervention unless they can be implemented. Experiences elsewhere have suggested that technical aid often works best where a single actor dominates the field so that even if the policy is not perfect then at least the beneficiaries are clear about what is on offer (see, for instance, Harrison 1987:314). Such a situation more often seems to exist in the less developed regions of Africa and Asia where institutions sometimes enjoy the luxury of intervening in territory which with respect to their area of aid is virgin. In Latin America and certainly Ecuador this is rarely the case. There are a wide range of different agencies of varying capacities and persuasions competing in an open but crowded market. Conflicts and confusions are inevitable. One approach to rationalizing the offers of the collective aid community would be more rigorous state control of the NGOs but in the current climate this would probably be both unrealistic and undesirable. The alternative of simply calling for greater co-ordination between NGOs seems rather lame and indeed it sidesteps the embarrassing fact that there does not exist an accord between development institutions about what development aid is actually for let alone how to do it. The situation is further confused by the career climbing aid bureaucrats who like the state, church, and political groups need to be seen to be producing tangible and, above all, photographable results.

Among a plethora of reconstruction projects it is likely that there will be some institutions which are sufficiently like-minded and committed to that nebulous concept of bottom-up development that there can be some degree of co-ordination. In the Ecuadorian case there were four or five NGOs which despite differences established a relationship which permitted practical mutual assistance and a steady interchange of ideas. However, this was not sufficient to eliminate the confusion of other overlapping and contradictory offers. In such circumstances, it would seem to be even more important for a locally based development institution with a long-term development perspective to identify one or maybe two simple low-input offers and then to pursue that line with single-minded determination over a wide front. Whatever the other institutions may do, the institution which acted in this way would both be understood by the beneficiaries and perceived to be acting in an equitable way even if in the short term they were seen by the lucky few as less generous than the newcomers.

Technological principles

If disaster aid should be more thinly and equably spread then there are implications for the technologies which should be selected and promoted by development institutions. In Ecuador's reconstruction, there have been too many examples of isolated groups of 'model' houses while the majority in the hinterland have gone on being neglected and another category of haves and have-nots has been created. Whether the houses are of steel and concrete or consist of the standard basket of 'appropriate' technologies is largely unimportant. The model house is inappropriate since it cannot be reproduced on a sufficiently large scale and, anyway, we have no business to be imposing model house designs on villagers.

Among building professionals there is a laudable concern for maintaining high technical standards. Yet, standards are not absolute. They have meaning only within a context. What is a basic requirement in San Francisco may be absurd in a situation where the price of a single reinforcement bar may represent the cost of a life-saving course of drugs or the fees for a term at school. The villager who rebuilds his house without a reinforced concrete ring beam may not be ignorant and in need of a dose of education. He may be making a rational choice based on a considered and informed opinion. The standards need to be defined in light of the actual circumstances. There is no point in advocating the eating of cake when even bread is beyond the intended beneficiaries' needs.

Where an institution's resources are limited, a technocratic concern often tempts a technically orientated institution to reduce the number of beneficiaries rather than 'lower' technical standards. Where it is a choice between lowering technical standards and excluding a proportion of those in need the choice should always be a reduction of technical standards. To support such a policy, there is a need for studies of traditional construction which suggest a range of progressively more sophisticated and expensive contra-seismic improvements so that aid implementers have clear cost/benefit criteria for determining at what level to pitch their interventions (see Spence and Coburn 1987 for an example of such a study).

The approach designed to minimize divisions and dependency while maximizing equity and long-term benefits is that of building education. The most successful building education projects seem to have concentrated not on model designs but on technological principles. Once a builder has assimilated a principle he can make his own designs. The approach is encapsulated in the slogan adopted by the Dhamar reconstruction project in Yemen: '*Think Before You Build*' (Leslie 1987:43–49).

Material aid

One of the elements behind the success of the Dhamar project was that, despite the impoverished nature of the country, the bulk of the individual families were relatively wealthy and could afford to make the necessary material inputs of steel, cement and imported timber. In many other circumstances an institution which wished to make an effective intervention could not follow the ideologically pure route of only providing building education. Where the villagers are poor, the natural resources limited, and the damage severe, there will be a clear case for some form of material aid albeit accompanied by building education.

Material aid does not have to mean houses or materials. In Ecuador, some of the most important aid was in the form of transport for materials, salaries for local builders, and communal tool kits. Such aid is a significant contribution to the costs of reconstruction while still leaving the key decisions of what materials to use, what design the house should have, and which families should receive how much assistance firmly in the hands of the community. It is material aid which strengthens rather than undermines principles of self-determination. Similarly, building education is about broadening people's range of choice by providing options which they may take or leave. The salaries for the local builders have the added advantage that by being for a fixed period, say six months, the villagers have an added incentive to reconstruct quickly.

There is potentially scope for the aid institution to intervene in the materials production process without fostering divisions and dependencies at the village level. However, in practice it remains an open question as to how viable such an approach is in a disaster context. Is it worth a small entrepreneur or an aid institution making investments in new plant to increase production if in a year's time demand will fall off again? There is probably no general answer to this question since it depends on the nature of the disaster, the location, and the society. In Ecuador, due to shortages of baked clay roofing tiles a number of institutions looked at possibilities for establishing new workshops or of increasing the productivity of existing workshops. In the end these initiatives came to nothing as it proved to be more viable and much more rapid to truck tiles in from other provinces for the duration of the peak period of the reconstruction.

If the aid is going to go beyond the types of material aid described above then the intervener is crossing a dangerous threshold beyond which the risks of division and dependency are greatly increased. Experiments have been carried out to increase the element of self-determination in such aid. The parish team of Ayora, near Cayambe, introduced what was effectively a voucher system where the individual families could choose between a range of available materials. But, however it was presented, there were still some people eligible for aid and others who were not and thus divisions were inevitable. Where material aid is given to the community as a whole leaving it to the villagers to sort out there is the potential for a strengthening of the community's internal mechanisms but equally where large sums of money are involved there is plenty of scope for rumours and accusations of pilfering and corruption which whether they are true or not can divide the community.

It may be that in a rural earthquake in a developing country there should not even be an attempt to produce lists of damaged houses but that, where material aid is going to be given, villages should simply be crudely classified under light damage, medium damage, heavy damage. Three packets of materials or three different values of vouchers would be prepared and every household in the village would receive the same package appropriate to the village's classification irrespective of individual need. The way would then be open to horse-trading between households and for aid between relatives. There would certainly be cases of hardship but overall the system would probably be perceived as conforming to the understood system of equity.

Conclusion

- There are three dichotomies which need to be kept in balance:

concerns for contra-seismic construction	⟷	other development issues both of rapid economic and social recovery and of on-going development
housing issues in a disaster context	⟷	housing in other places and times
project beneficiaries.	⟷	those excluded from the project

- One or maybe two simple low-input offers should be identified and then pursued with single-minded determination across a broad front.
- Building education programmes should be initiated with an emphasis on technical principles rather than model designs.
- Cost/benefit studies of a graded range of improvements to traditional construction should be carried out in seismic regions without waiting for the next event.
- Where material aid is to be given it should first be allocated for transport of

160

materials, salaries for local builders, and the provision of communal tool kits.
- If material aid beyond the above is felt to be necessary it should be kept to a minimum and disbursed across the broadest front and in accordance with indigenous principles of equity.

Acknowledgement

The author would like to thank Diego Jordan for his time and patience in showing the author around the reconstruction programmes in July 1990.

REFERENCES

CUNY, F. (1983) *Disasters and Development*, Oxford University Press, Oxford, UK.

CRSAS (CENTRO REGIONAL DE SISMOLOGIA PARA AMERICA DEL SUR) (1985) *Catalogo de Terremotos para America del Sur*, Lima, Peru.

DUDLEY, E. (1988) 'Disaster Mitigation: Strong Houses or Strong Institutions', *Disasters*, 12.2, Basil Blackwell, Oxford, UK.

EGRED, J. (1968) 'Breve Historia Sísmica de la República del Ecuador', *Boletín Bibliográphico de Geofísicay Oceanografía Americanas*, IV, Mexico.

HARRISON, P. (1987) *The Greening of Africa*, Paladin, London.

LESLIE, J. (1987) 'Think Before You Build, Experiences After the Yemen Earthquake', *Open House International*, University of Newcastle upon Tyne, UK.

SPENCE, R. and COBURN, A. (1987) *Reducing Earthquake Losses in Rural Areas*, The Martin Centre for Architectural and Urban Studies, University of Cambridge, UK.

UNCHS (1987) *Cómo Hacer Nuestra Casa de Tapial*, Junta Nacional de Vivienda, Quito, Ecuador.

CHAPTER 19

Introducing Disaster Mitigation in a Political Vacuum: The Experiences of the Reconstruction Plan Following the Alto Mayo Earthquake, Peru, 1990

ANDREW MASKREY

Tecnologia Intermedia (IT Peru)
Lima, Peru

Introduction

In a country where the word disaster has become synonymous with the state of the economy and of society in general it might seem perverse and irrelevant to focus our attention on a small earthquake in a remote part of the jungle. The Alto Mayo region, like most of the Peruvian Amazon, has been systematically ignored in the official version of Peru's history and has little or no prominence in the country's political and economic life. If it wasn't for the spread of coca plantations, the actions of armed groups and the impact of the earthquake of 29 May 1990, it is improbable that the Alto Mayo would figure prominently in the national imagination at all.

However, while the concept of disaster in Peru expands to engulf even family and personal relationships, it is essential not to lose sight of the lessons that we can learn from so-called natural disasters. Because, at the same time as the dividing line between disaster and society in Peru becomes fuzzier, an analysis of the causes and impact of the disasters and of experiences of disaster mitigation can be very useful. Perhaps, from the specific experience of a natural disaster we can project outwards lessons valid for the ever elusive reconstruction of society as a whole.

This paper, on the Alto Mayo disaster, tries to emphasise what has been learned there, in the belief that the experience is useful and suggestive for anyone involved in mitigation and reconstruction, in any sense of the word.

FIGURE 1   *San Martin region, Peru*

Setting the Stage

The Alto Mayo, in Peru's San Martin region (Figure 1, Figure 2), was the first area of the Amazon lowlands to be urbanised by the Spanish after their arrival in Peru. Moyobamba the principal city was founded by Juan Perez de Guevara in 1540 and from then until the late nineteenth century was the political and economic capital of the Peruvian Amazon. In the colonial period, the region was only weakly articulated to the rest of Peru, being administrated for 85 years from the Virreynato de Nueva Granada (actually Colombia and Ecuador).

After 1851, when steam navigation began on the Amazon, the region intensified its commerce with Brazil and the Atlantic. A handicraft industry of

163

FIGURE 2   *Populated areas affected by the earthquake*

'panama' hats sprung up, using a palm fibre called bombonaje. The dynamism of this industry is demonstrated by the fact that in 1870, 191,521 hats were exported via the river port of Iquitos and that Brazil, Argentina, Italy and France opened consulates in Moyobamba. Unfortunately, the development of this incipient industry was cut short by the rubber boom, which moved the economic and political centre of gravity of the Amazon to Iquitos.

Because of its isolation, the Alto Mayo's economy started to recuperate only in the 1940s when airports were built in Moyobamba and Rioja, allowing trade with the Pacific coast. However, it was when the road from the coast (Carreterra Marginal) reached the Alto Mayo in 1974 that a particularly rapid and violent process of change began.

Until the 1970s, the economy was characterised by a dualism between the production of coffee, cocoa and cotton for the export market on the one hand and a wide range of native food crops for regional consumption on the other. However, once the Marginal arrived, both were swept aside by rice fields and the development of a cash crop economy linked to the urban markets of the coast. The region and its people became heavily dependent on external factors beyond their control: the availability of credits, fertilisers and pesticides; price policies and controls imposed by successive Governments and the maintenance of the Marginal.

The Marginal also stimulated the immigration of peasants from the Andes and the coast. In the late 1970s, the urban population of the province of Rioja, for instance, was rising by 9% a year and the district of Yuracyacu by 16%. Once the best land for rice growing had been used up, continued immigration pushed the agricultural frontier into fragile rain forest environments, with increasingly low yields.

Ecologically, the Marginal spelled disaster for the Alto Mayo. The loss of the natural resources on which the region's population previously depended (timber for building; medicinal plants; fish and animals and regional fruits etc.) made people more dependent still on imports and pushed people's living patterns into forms which were not appropriate to the ecology of the area. As the traditional protein sources (wild animals) became scarce, malnutrition became a serious problem for the rural population, especially the migrants from the Sierra. New building forms, in brick and concrete for those with money and mud bricks for those without, were ovens in the heat in the first case and seismic death traps in the second.

In the 1980s the illusion of development which the Marginal had brought to the Alto Mayo was shattered and the region entered into an unprecedented crisis. The Government enterprises, responsible for buying and selling all the area's rice production, went bankrupt. At the same time, no maintenance of the Marginal was carried out meaning that the road became unpassable. As a result the rice production could not be transported to the coast and the region's producers were not paid. The whole development model rested on enormous subsidies and with the fiscal crisis of the Peruvian state in the 1980s these could not be sustained.

With the destruction of the rainforest, the area's hydrological regime was altered, causing droughts on the one hand and violent floods and aluvions on the other (Río Gera 1989, Ríó Indoche 1989, San Miguel del Ríó Mayo 1990).[1] In order to survive economically, the small farmer introduced coca growing and processing, which further intensified the destruction of the forest. These specific processes in the Alto Mayo evolved in the context of the worst economic, social and political crisis in Peru's history, with over 3,000% inflation in 1990, a dramatic fall in living standards and the institutional disintegration of the state. To make matters worse, the creation of new regional Governments was paralysed in the Alto Mayo due to a conflict between San Martin with the coastal region of La Libertad.

Nonetheless, despite or perhaps because of the crisis, positive tendencies were also emerging in the region.

Because of the conflict between the agricultural producers and successive Governments over prices and commerce, an upsurge of community based organisation took place, consolidating itself as Frentes de Defensa de los Intereses del Pueblo (FEDIP).[2] These organisations started to represent the interests not only of the agricultural producers as such but also of entire districts and provinces. They became increasingly legitimised in the region as central and local Government weakened and collapsed. In the Alto Mayo the Frente de Defensa de los Intereses del Pueblo de Soritor (FEDIP-Soritor), in particular, achieved a very strong organic structure and effectively exercised authority in the town and district of Soritor.

Paradoxically helped by the appalling state of the Marginal which made the importing of manufactured goods very expensive, a growing micro and small industry sector began to supply the regional market with products as diverse as building components, lorry batteries, furniture and other goods. At the same time, agricultural producers started to develop fish and dairy farming to attend the growing urban market in the region.

Technologically, an incestuous mix of modern and traditional elements created a particularly favourable and dynamic context for the adoption and adaptation of new innovations.

Cocaine and micro enterprise; political violence and social organisation; environmental destruction and a diversification of agricultural production are all characteristics coexisting in the Alto Mayo. The urbanisation process provoked by the Marginal led to the accelerating vulnerability of the region in the 1970s and 1980s. But at the same time it set into motion other processes, which create new perspectives for the region's future. It was in this paradox of decadence and new growth that the earthquake of 29 May 1990 occurred.

The Disaster of 29 May 1990

The earthquake struck at 9.35 pm with a magnitude of 5.8 on the Richter scale. In the Alto Mayo, there were a total of 65 deaths and 607 injuries and over 3,000 houses destroyed. The town worst affected was Soritor with 26 deaths, 310 injuries and 1,100 houses damaged or destroyed, representing nearly 90% of the total housing stock.

The Alto Mayo has a long seismic history, the last serious earthquake occurring in 1968. Evidently, the intensities produced by the earthquake varied from area to area according to local geology and soil conditions. However, the disaster itself was due above all to the vulnerability of the building forms and structures which predominated.

Most of the houses which fell down and killed their occupants were built from rammed earth (tapial) and had serious structural deficiencies. The lack of maintenance, deficient building methods, the effects of rain and humidity and damages from the 1968 earthquake which had never been properly repaired were all factors which contributed to weaken foundations and walls. At the same time brick and concrete buildings were also damaged due to structural

166

weaknesses and deficiencies such as an absence of reinforced concrete columns and beams.

While the vulnerability of the housing can be partly explained by the precarious structures thrown up by migrants along the whole length of the Marginal, the collapse of old houses in the centre of Soritor, Moyobamba and Rioja showed that the system of rammed earth construction introduced in colonial times was in itself highly insecure.

The vulnerability of the housing is fairly obvious: it was the collapse of houses that killed people in the Alto Mayo earthquake. However, people's response to this specific disaster can be interpreted properly only in the much wider vulnerability and on-going disaster engulfing the area. It is only in this wider context that we can understand the roles played by the different social actors in the area after the earthquake.

The Social Acts and the Disaster

The analysis of previous disasters, in Peru and elsewhere,[3] shows that the different agencies (Governmental, non-Governmental and international) that intervene during and after emergencies often do so following a pre-elaborated and fictitious script of how the drama is supposed to unfold. This now familiar kitsch[4] version of disaster relief seems to respond more to the expectations of the mass media and its readers than to the reality in which the disaster has occurred and in turn reinforces those expectations by providing and feeding the same comforting images. Because the Alto Mayo jungle was remote and exotic to most of the agencies intervening, some of the emergency programme managers were able to let their imagination run riot.

One of the basic suppositions of the kitsch version of disaster relief is that food supplies are basic necessities after any catastrophe, no matter what the hazard type, the region where this hazard occurs and the impact it produces. It is no surprise that the agencies, coordinated by INDECI,[5] concentrated much of their efforts into getting food into the area in the first weeks after the disaster. These supplies arrived, however, in a real and not kitsch situation.

In the months before the earthquake, the population of the Alto Mayo had participated in a 25 day long regional strike organised by the Frente de Defensa de los Intereses del Pueblo de San Martin FEDIP-SM (the regional community based organisation). One of the central demands of FEDIP-SM was that the Government buy and transport to the coast the tens of thousands of tons of rice and maize which were starting to rot in overflowing warehouses throughout the region. It is evidently debatable, therefore, the wisdom of investing scarce resources in sending food supplies to a region, made highly vulnerable by its inability to consume or sell all the food it produces. At the same time, the earthquake, as a hazard type, had not affected crops or agricultural production. It is particularly ironic that, according to local people's own version of events, the emergency supplies included sacks of imported rice.

The emergency supplies in greatest demand and which were most useful in the area were corrugated iron sheets and medicines. Both items corresponded to a real felt need, in the first case to reinforce and extend the tambos or garden kitchens, which most families were using as provisional refuges and in the second to treat injuries. However, this apparent success must be interpreted in the context of the wider vulnerability of the area already existing before the disaster. Before the earthquake, most hospitals and health centres had exhausted their supplies of medicines, due to the virtual bankruptcy and collapse of public finances. Rather than dealing exclusively with the effects of the earthquake, therefore, the medical supplies allowed the health sector to recuperate from a much deeper and more long-term problem. Similarly, corrugated iron sheets were useful not only for provisional refuge but also as roofing in permanent housing and thus responded to a much wider housing problem in the towns, which again existed well before the earthquake struck.

However, while much of the emergency operation must have seemed to local people like a black comedy it is important to stress that, to our knowledge, the transport and distribution of supplies was conducted efficiently, albeit authoritarianly by INDECI. It is to INDECI's credit that there was neither evidence nor complaints of the massive corruption and embezzlement of resources, so frequently seen in disasters, both in Peru and abroad.

The response to the disaster by people and their organisations in the Alto Mayo also failed to fit the kitsch version of events projected by the action of the relief agencies and reinforced by the media. Rather than being helpless, stunned and shocked, what the disaster brought to light was people's capacity to respond effectively and quickly through their organisations. In Soritor, where 50% of the victims and 30% of the total damages were concentrated, FEDIP-Soritor had already carried out its own detailed evaluation of damages and of relief needs by the day after the disaster. This evaluation was handed over to a surprised ex-President of the Republic, in front of the national television and press in Soritor, on 30 May 1990.

Visitors to the Alto Mayo in the weeks following the disaster were surprised by the apparent normality with which the population was continuing with its daily activities (and problems). Again it must be understood that the seismic disaster was only another additional factor in an existing and on-going economic and political disaster which the population as facing and which worsened considerably in the months following the earthquake. People did not let the earthquake distract their attention from other equally dramatic problems being faced on an on-going basis. It is fascinating to see that in the Asamblea Regional del Alto Mayo[6] held only two weeks after the earthquake, most of the debate and discussions continued to revolve around the problem of the rice and maize growers rather than around the reconstruction of damaged houses.

It is unfortunate that the different FEDIP and other community based organisations were left on the sidelines by INDECI in the organisation of the disaster relief operation. Again the kitsch version of the disaster, which presupposes a structure of Government and local authorities capable of organising and channelling relief and which ignores the existence and legitimacy of autonomous community based organisations prevailed over reality. The social vacuum created by the absence of deficiency of the state at the regional and local level could not be filled by the ad-hoc creation of Comités de Defensa Civil[7] set up by INDECI and which bypassed already existing organisations. Only in specific cases such as Soritor, where FEDIP-Soritor absorbed the Comité de Defensa Civil was this contradiction overcome. But even there, no mechanism existed to ensure that the relief aid provided really corresponded to people's needs.

The Alto Mayo Reconstruction and Development Plan

The Alto Mayo Reconstruction Plan emerged as an initiative of Tecnología Intermedia (IT Peru), which had a critical position with respect to the kitsch version of the disaster.

The Plan attempted to present both to local organisations as well as to other NGOs, Government and international agencies a strategy for the reconstruction and sustainable productive development of the region, in particular on the best technological alternative for rebuilding houses.

Throughout July 1990 micro-level field work was carried out, in coordination with community organisations, in order to identify available resources for reconstruction in each district and on the basis of these define the best technological alternatives for rebuilding houses. For Moyobamba and Soritor, this alternative was an improved version of quincha using unsawn local hardwoods, which could allow the rebuilding of economic, attractive and seismic resistant houses, and at the same time maximising the use of resources, such as timber and bamboo, to which most of the population still had access.

In August 1990, two months after the disaster, the Plan was presented to all the community organisations, authorities and institutions. Nationally, the Plan was presented to Government agencies such as INDECI, ENACE, SENCICO, funding agencies such as CARITAS, International Red Cross, and those technical assistance agencies such as ININVI and PREDES that were committed to supporting the reconstruction. It was also important that the Plan was officially approved by INDECI, INP and the Ministerio de Relaciones Exteriores.[8]

At the end of August, the Plan was presented in public to an audience of several hundred people and community leaders in a Seminar Tecnología Apropiada para la Mitigación de Desastres held in Moyobamba.

Another range of activities were carried out to achieve the dissemination of the Plan: radio programmes on local stations; an itinerant photographic exhibition on quincha, which was exhibited in town squares in Soritor, Moyobamba and Havana; a series of articles on the Plan in national newspapers; training courses for local builders, attended by 80 participants; a panel on building technologies, for local institutions; the construction of a demonstration module in quincha in Soritor; and a series of technical meetings and coordinations in Lima with Government agencies, NGOs and funders.

To promote environmental management and protection a forestry nursery was established in Soritor, with native hardwoods suitable for building, together with radio programmes, training of local promoters and a panel on reforestation.

Six Months After the Disaster: the Results of the Reconstruction Plan

In the region, the motor behind the Reconstruction Plan was and until now is FEDIP-Soritor: the community worst affected by the earthquake. In other areas of the Alto Mayo, while there was interest and support of the Plan by individual authorities, community leaders and individuals, there was not that organic relationship with the community which in Soritor allowed a massive response.

In Soritor the quincha was massively accepted by people as the alternative for rebuilding their houses. While the photographic exhibition and the building of the demonstration module were important factors in the adoption of the technology, the decisive point was that the proposal was based in months of detailed discussions with people and their leaders and on a detailed evaluation of available resources. Many families are now rebuilding their houses in Soritor in quincha on the basis of what they have seen and learned. At the same time people begin to revalue the forest as a source of building materials. It is particularly interesting this adoption of the technological proposal if we compare it with the negative results experienced in most disaster reconstruction projects in Peru.[9]

The dissemination of the Plan and the coordinations with technical assistance agencies led to agreements with ININVI jointly to carry out training activities. At the same time it was an agreement with a local NGO, CEIMAA, which led to the promotion of reforestation in Soritor. These horizontal coordinations between different Governmental and non-Governmental agencies enabled the activities of the Plan to cover an area far wider than that which would have been possible from a single institutional perspective.

The dissemination of the Plan through the mass media had a decisive impact on the support obtained from Government, private and international funding agencies. Through media dissemination, the Plan gained legitimacy as the planning instrument for the reconstruction of the region. As a result of the Plan CARITAS committed financial resources for the reconstruction of 180 houses, beginning in Soritor and applying the Plan's quincha technology. Similarly, UNDRO committed itself to supporting the training activities to be carried out by ININVI and IT Peru.

Altogether then, the' Plan as an instrument stimulated and catalysed a dynamic development and reconstruction process in the Alto Mayo, which gradually incorporated and involved the local population and its organisations, different Government agencies and NGOs and funding agencies. The Reconstruction Plan became the axis around which all the processes became articulated.

Lessons from the Alto Mayo Experience

It is still far too soon after the disaster to reach any definitive conclusions on the success or limitations of the Plan and on its medium- and long-term impact in the area. Previous disasters have shown the importance of evaluations five or ten years after the programmes have been implemented to see whether there has been more than a transitory impact in an area. However, the experience provides important insights into both the role of NGOs in disaster mitigation and reconstruction and into the institutional variables surrounding the introduction of technological innovations into local housing.

In countries like Peru, conventional assumptions on disaster mitigation do not make sense. In Peru, the Government's disaster mitigation programme cannot be critically analysed because disaster mitigation as an institutionalised activity does not exist. Instead of mitigation, a kitsch version of disaster relief is applied with the kinds of results described in this paper. A passive population is converted into a recipient of relief aid which mass media expects them to need and a spectator of a procession of evaluation missions, whose purpose is unclear. People's own organisations and their capacity to define needs and priorities are unfortunately invisible in the kitsch version. Quite simply, people are objects and not subjects in a frequently rehearsed drama in which they are expected to play their part but over whose script they have no influence. Happily in the Alto Mayo, the drama was put on stage efficiently and with the best of intentions, but even so it is still an ineffective and inefficient waste of very scarce resources.

The total absence of a mitigation or reconstruction plan or programme, organised by the state in the Alto Mayo, has a fairly obvious explanation. The state has never had a significant presence in the Peruvian Amazon. With its internal decomposition over recent years (aggravated in the Alto Mayo disaster by the simultaneous change in national Government and the paralysis in the creation of the regional Government), the state completely lacked the coherence and the consistency necessary to lead a coordinated response to the disaster, once the emergency was over and INDECI had retired from the region. Individual Government agencies attempted to intervene in reconstruction activities but without having the gravity and terms of reference necessary to involve the state as a coherent whole and without having channels of communication with the local population. For their part, local people and their organisations were so heavily hit by the overall economic and agrarian crisis (as well as being confused by the expectations raised by so many agencies), that they also lacked the level of centralisation needed to catalyse the reconstruction process. In other words, there was a political vacuum between people and the state in which it is very difficult for mitigation or reconstruction processes to take place.

In other words, the problems surrounding the reconstruction of the Alto Mayo are political or institutional in origin rather than technical. Under these circumstances, the role of an NGO cannot be reduced to simple technical adviser or project implementor on behalf of either people or the state but must strive for something much greater. That something is the reconstruction of a social, political and institutional framework within which all the different actors – the state, people and their organisations – NGOs and funding agencies, can converge and discover and establish new relationships. It is necessary to write a new script for a new play.

The Alto Mayo Reconstruction and Development Plan turned out to be the axis around which it was possible to reconstruct the loose fragments of state and society into this new script. The role of the NGO was to put forward clear objectives and goals and gradually build bridges between all the actors, tying together loose threads and weaving a web of new relations. Only in the context of this framework of new relationships between all the different actors, however fragile and provisional they may be, is it possible to promote reconstruction.

The problems involved in working in this way are immense. In order to function as a centralising axis, the Plan had to be seen as legitimate by all the parties. An inherent problem of all NGOs is their lack of legitimacy, both with respect to the state, and to be honest, more often than not with respect to people and their organisations as well. In this context, communication was a crucial variable: especially the speed with which the initiative of the Plan was launched and the attempt to cover the whole spectrum of actors involved. In the case of the Alto Mayo Reconstruction Plan, the familiarity with the region and its people and the coverage achieved in the mass media were factors which contributed substantially to the Plan's success.

Only due to this emphasis on communication was it possible to implement a technological alternative for the reconstruction, which was both accepted by the local population and supported by funding agencies and the state.

In conclusion, the experience of the Alto Mayo, to date, reinforces the conviction that real disaster mitigation becomes possible only through a complementary participation of people and their organisations, the state and non-Governmental organisations. At the same time, it shows the importance of local organisation as a vehicle through which people can take control over not only disaster mitigation but also the process of development as a whole. With the crisis of the state in Peru, local people and their organisations are the only stable point of reference around which any mitigation or development programme can be implemented. It is in this context of social vacuum that NGOs have to act as mediators, communicators and technical advisers searching out new consensus and relationships between all the actors and patching and reweaving the broken threads of Peruvian society. Only in this way is it possible to launch development initiatives which go beyond mere survival in the face of the on-going disaster which envelopes us all.

Postscript

On 4 April 1991 at 11.20 at night, the Alto Mayo was rocked by a new earthquake with a magnitude of 6.2 on the Richter scale causing 35 deaths and 183 injuries in Moyobamba, Yantalo, Calzada, Rioja and Nueva Cajamarca: 9,663 houses were damaged. Many of the tapial houses which had been badly damaged in the 1990 earthquake but which had not been demolished or repaired fell down. Fortunately an earlier tremor at 10.24 on the morning of 4 April had alerted people to the risk and casualties were very few compared to material damages.

By the time this second earthquake occurred, over seventy houses had been rebuilt in quincha mejorada in Soritor with partial loans from CARITAS and technical assistance from ITDG. A further forty houses had been rebuilt by families using the new technology, but without loans. None of the quincha houses suffered even light damages demonstrating both to local people as well as to the professionals that the technology worked well under quite high seismic intensities. It is not often that promoters of improved technologies find their proposals put so thoroughly and so soon to the test.

The experience of the second earthquake evidently increased the credibility of the technology in the eyes of the population and by the beginning of June 1991 there were 180 quincha houses rebuilt in Soritor (120 with loans and 60 without loans). In July 1991, ITDG and CARITAS began new housing programmes in Yantalo and Moyobamba, both areas seriously affected in the April 1991 quake.

Between the first and second earthquakes, the social and political context in the Alto Mayo also changed. In February 1991, after more than three years of campaigning by the FEDIP and local organisations, a referendum was held to determine the creation of an autonomous regional Government, a decision which was upheld by the majority of the population. When the second earthquake occurred, the regional development corporation (CORDESAM) had been reactivated leading to a more consistent response to the reconstruction by Government agencies. However, at the same time the area was put under military occupation and control in May 1991, following the kidnapping of seven policemen by guerrillas. It is necessary to underline that the continuation and expansion of housing reconstruction programmes in the Alto Mayo, coordinated by local organisations like FEDIP-Soritor, was carried out in an atmosphere of tension and fear due to the worsening of political violence in the region.

Apparently, the second earthquake increases the chances of the technological innovation of quincha mejorada housing taking root in the region, substantially reducing vulnerability to future disasters. However, as the experience of other programmes shows, an exhaustive re-evaluation of the Reconstruction Plan will be needed in five years or so, to assess up to what point the objectives were fully attained or not.

NOTES AND REFERENCES

1. Juvenal Medina (1990) *El Desastre de San Miguel del Río Mayo*, IT Peru (manuscript).
2. FEDIP means Community Based Defence Fronts. In San Martín these organizations exist on a district, provincial and departmental level. It is peculiar to Peru that these organizations have been formed by communities to defend themselves against the state!
3. Andrew Maskrey (1989) *Disaster Mitigation: A Community Based Approach*, OXFAM Publications, Oxford. Also published in Spanish as *El Manejo Popular de los Desastres Naturales*, IT Peru, Lima.
4. The word kitsch in this paper is used in the sense defined by Milan Kundera in his unforgettable book *The Unbearable Lightness of Being*.
5. INDECI – National Institute of Civil Defence.
6. Asamblea Regional del Alto Mayo was a meeting for community leaders organized by FEDIP-SM held in Rioja on 13 June in order to coordinate a community based response to the disaster.
7. Comites de Defensa Civil – INDECI theoretically services a structure of Civil Defence Committees, at district, provincial and departmental levels. However, in practice the district and provincial level Committees are formed as ad-hoc organisations only after disasters occur and have no permanent personnel or budget.
8. ENACE (Empresa Nacional de Edificaciones – National Building Company); SENCICO (Servicio Nacional de Capacitación para la Industría de la Construcción – National Building Industry Training Service); ININVI (Instituto Nacional de Investigación y Normalizacion de la Vivienda – National Institute for Housing Research and Standards); INP (Instituto Nacional de Planificación – National Planning Institute); Ministerio de Relaciones Exteriores – Ministry of Foreign Relations; are all Government organizations. CARITAS; International Red Cross and PREDES (Centro de Estudios y Prevención de Desastres – Disater Prevention and Research Centre) are church based, international and non-Governmental organizations respectively.
9. Flor de María Monzon and Julio Oliden (1990) *Tecnología y Vivienda Popular*, IT Peru, Lima.

CHAPTER 20

Wind Effects on the Tongan 'Hurricane House'

GREG REARDON

James Cook University
Townsville, Australia

Introduction

Traditionally, man has built his shelter from the elements by placing materials one on top of the other to form walls and then bridging across the walls with beams to support the roof. The original materials for the walls were stone, earth, clay blocks or wood. The material was heavy so the main purpose of this form of construction was to 'stay up'. That is, the structure was built to resist gravity loads. This philosophy still obtains in the colder countries of the world. Dwellings are built with walls of significant mass to provide insulation and with roof structure of sufficient strength to withstand severe snow loading.

As most of today's more affluent and technically advanced countries either are in the temperate zone or have European origins from that region, that tradition of building has tended to survive.

Building to resist wind forces needs a different philosophy. The dominant force is not gravity, but the uplift pressures associated with wind flowing over the roof. It is the same concept that is used in the design of aircraft. Thus the action of the wind is to try to lift the whole building up by the roofing. These uplift forces must be resisted not only by the structural members forming the roof and walls but especially by the joints between those members. It is in this aspect that designing a building to resist wind forces is quite different from designing one for gravity loading.

Most joints between structural members resisting gravity loading need only sufficient bearing area to transfer the compressive forces between them. In such instances fasteners are needed only to locate the structural members and keep them in the correct position during construction. As such the fasteners are of a nominal nature and have little function after the building has been constructed. However, the uplift pressures from wind loading want to pull the structural members apart at the joints. The joints must be sufficiently strong to resist the forces generated by these pressures.

Wind on Buildings

Building geometry

Wind pressures on a building are influenced by its shape. A building of circular plan would experience different pressures from one of rectangular plan in the same wind field. Likewise the pressures on a tall thin building would be different from those on a short fat one. In general, the windward face or wall experiences positive pressure pushing against the structure whereas the side walls and leeward wall experience negative pressure (suction), wanting to pull the cladding away from the wall structure.

The main geometric feature affecting wind pressure on building elements is the roof slope. For winds blowing normal to the ridge line, the windward section of roof will experience negative pressures if the roof slope is low whereas if the roof slope is high the pressure will be positive. The pressure on the leeward section of the roof is always negative. The intensity of the suction pressures on the roof is usually greater than that on any other part of the building.

Although it may seem a logical conclusion to build houses with steep roof pitch to reduce the overall suction forces on the roof, it would not totally solve the problem. For wind blowing parallel to the ridge of the building, both slopes of the ridge experience uplift pressures, irrespective of the roof pitch.

Wind pressures

It is well known that the pressures acting on a building are a function of the wind speed. The faster the wind speed the higher the pressure. However, it is often not appreciated that pressure on a building is proportional to the square of wind speed. That is, if the wind speed is doubled the pressure is increased fourfold.

The actual wind speed that impacts a building is not necessarily the speed that is measured as representing the wind storm. Anemometers, devices which measure wind speed, are normally located at airports or similar locations in a flat open environment. The maximum gust during a wind storm is measured relative to this open terrain. Most buildings are not located in such open terrain but are surrounded by other buildings of similar proportions. Thus the speed of the wind impacting a building is usually less than the gust speed measured by the anemometer. Closely spaced buildings, such as occur in a typical suburban environment, shield each other and effectively reduce the wind speed to about 75% of its open terrain magnitude. Thus the pressures are effectively reduced to about 50% of the pressures on a similar building in open terrain. Therefore it is the speed of the wind impacting the building that is important, rather than the intrinsic speed of the wind storm.

The total effect of wind uplift is often underestimated. For example, a wind gust of only 25 metres per second (90 km per hour) hitting a building 14 m long, 7 m wide, with 600 mm eaves overhang could cause a total of 6.2 tonnes of uplift force on the roof. A wind speed of 50 m/s would cause a total uplift force of 25 tonnes on the roof of the same building.

Resistance to wind forces

The above example illustrates that it would be virtually impossible to resist uplift wind forces by virtue of the mass of roofing alone. By the same token the placement of weights (usually bricks) on a roof to increase its wind resistance is somewhat optimistic, as the first example shows that at least 6 tonnes of weights would be needed to secure the roof against a wind gust of only 25 m/s.

Uplift wind forces should be resisted by structural members forming a chain of strength from the roof to the foundations. This means that not only must the structural members be adequate but also the joints between them must be capable of transferring the wind force between members.

In countries of Western civilisation where steel is readily available, joints are normally made using bolts, metal rods or steel straps. In developing countries that do not have a supply of steel components, adequate joints can be made using traditional techniques such as natural rope or the like.

Building materials

In developing countries there appears to be a social status associated with masonry construction. It has been referred to as the 'Noble Material' of construction. While masonry may be more aesthetically pleasing to some, it does not have any intrinsic properties that make it better able to resist engineering stresses associated with wind storms or earthquakes. From the engineering viewpoint, masonry is a brittle material that has virtually no tensile strength. If used without reinforcing it has very low resistance against wind or earthquake forces. Steel reinforcing bars can be built into masonry construction to provide the necessary tensile strength, and give the system some flexibility. However this technology is usually not used for low-rise domestic buildings in developing countries, probably because of the cost of the steel and the lack of understanding of its role in providing strength and flexibility to the masonry.

In contrast with masonry, wood is naturally flexible and it can readily be used to construct wind resistant buildings. The main concern with wooden construction is to provide adequate joints between members. This has been addressed above.

FIGURE 1 *House testing rig*

The Cyclone Structural Testing Station

The Cyclone Structural Testing Station was established in 1977 within the Department of Civil and Systems Engineering at James Cook University of North Queensland, Australia. The role of the Station is to conduct research and investigations into the effects of wind on buildings. The research programme has been directed at low rise buildings, usually houses.

The research programme has included investigations into the structural performance of various building elements such as walls, roofs, ceilings and the like as well as investigating water transmission through masonry walls. The Station also makes investigations into the damage caused by wind storms and tropical cyclones. Damage investigations have been made in Pacific island countries as well as in Australia.

Results of the Station's research have been incorporated into building codes and regulations in Australia and Pacific Island countries.

House testing programme

The Station has also developed the expertise for conducting tests on full size, low-rise buildings. To date seven such buildings have been tested, for either cyclone wind conditions or thunderstorm wind gusts. The Station has fabricated a large test rig capable of applying simulated wind loading to full size buildings. A combination of uplift and lateral forces can be applied to the building by large loading frames that are erected along each side. The buffeting effect of tropical cyclones can be reproduced by cycling the applied loads.

Figure 1 illustrates the loading system. To apply uplift loading the hydraulic rams 'a' pull down on one end of the large 'see-saw' beams 'b' causing uplift forces on load spreaders 'c' attached to the roof. Each load spreader distributes the applied force over an area of roof to simulate the pressure acting on that area. Horizontally mounted rams 'd' were attached to a large RHS steel beam 'e' fixed to the uplift loading frames at wall height. A cable was extended from the ram to a load spreading system 'f' at top plate level on the windward wall. Each ram load was distributed to four loading points approximately one metre apart.

Test programme

When conducting tests to simulate the effects of tropical cyclone winds, it is essential to reproduce the effect of the buffeting forces that are produced by the wind gusts. As it is virtually impossible to reproduce the real gustiness within the tropical cyclone an approximation is made. Because of loading constraints the load cycling regime must be kept as simple as possible. The accepted standard for cyclone wind simulation in Australia requires 10,200 cycles of uplift loading to be applied to the roofing and 1020 cycles of lateral load to be applied to the walls.

For roofs the following sequence is adopted:

8000 cycles	0–5/8 design pressure – 0	
2000 cycles	0–3/4 design pressure – 0	
200 cycles	0– design pressure – 0	
One application	2 × design pressure – 0	

For walls one-tenth of the number of cycles is applied for each load level, based on wall pressures rather than roof pressures. The uplift and lateral loads are applied simultaneously, using the sequence of nine cycles of uplift only followed by one cycle of combined uplift and lateral loads.

Testing the Tongan Hurricane House

The 'Hurricane House'

In 1982 the tiny Pacific Island Kingdom of Tonga was devastated by hurricane Isaac (Oliver and Reardon 1982). Two thousand families were left homeless. The world community reacted very generously to the Tongan plight, with donations of building materials for the homeless. The Tongan Ministry of Works embarked on a reconstruction programme and, in consultation with the Building Research Establishment UK, designed a cyclone resistant house. New houses were made available to families whose houses had been destroyed by Isaac. Special subsidies from overseas and aid agencies meant that the families had to pay approximately one quarter of the cost of the houses.

179

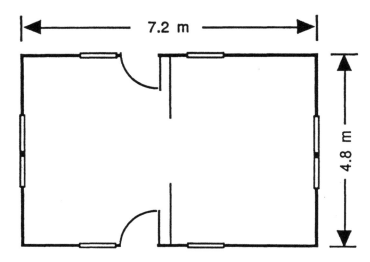

FIGURE 2   *Floor plan of 'Hurricane House'*

The house was of panelised timber and plywood construction, with all of the panels being made by Tongan labour at Nuku'alofa, the capital. The 2.4 m square panels were then transported either by land or sea to the villages where local labour assembled the components into houses. A standard house was two panels wide and three panels long (4.8 m × 7.2 m). An elevation of the house is included in Figure 1 while the plan is shown in Figure 2. The corrugated steel roofing was supported by trusses at 1.2 m spacing. The standard house was supplied without any ceiling or internal wall lining. While the panelised construction allowed the house to be extended at a later date, the concept relied on the owner ensuring that the addition had the same structural strength as the original design. The owner may not always recognise the importance of this.

To verify its structural integrity one of the 'Hurricane Houses', as they became known, was shipped to the Cyclone Testing Station in Australia for testing. A Tongan construction supervisor was also sent over to ensure that the construction was exactly the same as it would be in Tonga, rather than how the Australian researchers may think that the house should be assembled.

Performance

Full details of the performance of the Tongan 'Hurricane House' have been given elsewhere (Boughton and Reardon 1984). In summary, the house in its original configuration resisted about 4000 cycles of 5/8 design pressure before failure occurred. Some of the metal straps securing the roof trusses to the walls failed in fatigue. That is, the continuous loading and unloading programme

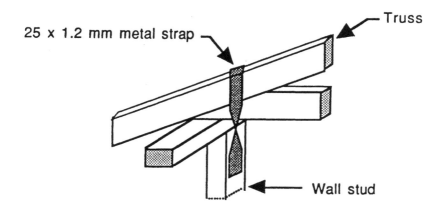

FIGURE 3   *Truss hold down detail*

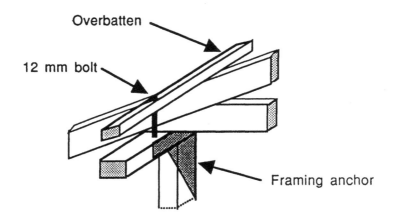

FIGURE 4   *Remedial tie down*

caused the metal to crack and eventually break. Figure 3 shows the truss hold down detail and the strap that failed.

As some 1200 'Hurricane Houses' had already been built in Tonga, the Station felt obliged to recommend a solution to the Tongan Government that would overcome the problem of fatigue of the tie down strap. While not all of the houses would need to be upgraded, those that were in exposed locations would need to be. A repair system using overbattens on top of the trusses was chosen, mainly because it could be implemented in existing buildings. By removing the barge boards at the end of the roof, the overbattens could be fitted without having to remove the roof sheeting. The overbattens were bolted to the wall adjacent to each truss. Figure 4 demonstrates the principle.

The modified house performed much better than the original one. It resisted the full complement of load cycles, although there were some failures of truss joints. In fact, although the apex joint of some trusses had virtually broken, the house was still able to resist the applied load. This was because the ridge capping started to act as a structural member and provided an alternative apex joint for the trusses.

On completion of the load cycling, the building was loaded statically until failure occurred. It happened at about 1.7 times design pressure when one of the rafters broke in bending. While this performance does not quite meet the requirements of the Australian standard test it should be viewed in the light of the economy of Tonga, and in the acceptance of risk to buildings that may be appropriate in that country.

The results of the test programme were sent to the Tongan Government together with recommendations for increasing the strength of houses in very exposed locations. The Station also recommended that those houses already in very exposed locations be strengthened in the same manner that was used for the test house.

REFERENCES

BOUGHTON, G.N. and REARDON, G.F. (1984) 'Simulated Wind Load Tests on the Tongan Hurricane House', Technical Report No. 24, James Cook Cyclone Structural Testing Station.

OLIVER, J. and REARDON, G.F. (1982) 'Tropical Cyclone Isaac: Cyclonic Impact in the Context of the Society and Economy of the Kingdom of Tonga', Disaster Investigation Report No. 5, Centre for Disaster Studies, James Cook University of North Queensland.

CHAPTER 21

Disaster Resistant Construction for Small Dwellings in Solomon Islands

CHARLES BOYLE

Pacific Architects
Honiara, Solomon Islands

Introduction

The purpose of this paper is to present some of the ideas for building construction improvements that emerged as a result of research undertaken after cyclone Namu in Solomon Islands, May 1986.

Solomon Islands with a population of some 350,000 is one of the least densely populated countries of the South Pacific. Located in the genesis area of tropical cyclones for the South West Pacific and spread over some 150,000 square kilometres the risk and intensity of cyclone activity increases as one travels east. There are some 2,500 seismic movements a year, perhaps two or three being strong enough to be felt.

The capital Honiara (pop. 40,000) is the only well-developed urban area, while there are a series of seven provincial centres (pop. 1,000–3,000) in the islands. About 80% of the population live in rural or peri-urban mainly coastal fringe areas being dependent on subsistence economy utilising materials to hand and other available resources for building purposes. The term 'small dwelling' is an accurate description of the majority of buildings in these areas.

Cyclone Namu

In mid-May 1986, Solomon Islands was severely affected by tropical cyclone Namu. Its effects were exacerbated by the un-preparedness of the rural communities in the construction of their homes; some 10,000 homes were destroyed and another 30,000 were damaged (these statistics are imprecise and are derived from the National Disaster Council survey). Over 100 people were killed, mainly by landslide and flooding on the low-lying plains of Guadalcanal and its elevated hinterlands. The larger urban areas were for the most part unaffected as the cyclone did not pass directly over, for example, Honiara (distant by some 60 miles).

Response to cyclone Namu

As a result of the cyclone, large amounts of assistance in the immediate form of medicine and food, and in the longer term of roof sheeting and other technical advice was made available. It was the first major disaster event since independence (1978) and this was the first opportunity for the national community to look at the question of building construction and related issues on its own terms.

Notable amongst the initiatives taken were the formalisation of Solomon Islands National Disaster Council, a low-cost building materials council organised through the Foundation of the Peoples of the South Pacific, a national 'Rural Reconstruction Programme' which was to advise and implement the Government programmes, and independent though associated initiatives taken by various non-Government organisations such as Hybrid Technology, established as a response to a ground-swell of opinion that traditional techniques seemed an inadequate means of rebuilding. No organisation was then involved in longer-term study and direction or were more concerned with the immediate response of rehousing.

Study and Findings

Solomon Islands population is traditionally nomadic and depends on a subsistence economy: that is, its food, housing and medicines are derived from resources immediately to hand rather than through any financial medium. Bartering is a common feature of inter-communal trade. Communities were established and relocated depending on the availability of productive food gardens. Buildings were only expected and required to stand for a period of some 10 years: a product of community resettlement and natural depredation. With abundant resources and manpower it was easier to rebuild than repair or make more permanent dwellings.

During the past century this pattern has changed: populations have increased greatly (annual growth is presently about 3.5%) and the desire for education, health facilities and a cash income (replacing the old trader-bartering system: few people will now exchange copra for axes or other implements because of logistics). There is less interest in traditional medicine coupled with a rise in modern pharmacopoeia. As a result there is an increasing need for more permanent settlements and buildings. Traditional construction is not suitable for this: you cannot run a trade store from a leaf house for obvious security reasons, nor expect the same level of hygiene or insect protection from leaf construction as from materials such as concrete block or fibrous cement sheet.

Newer construction techniques such as timber framed housing were developed particularly over the past 20 years mainly in the urban areas. Many of these techniques were brought back to the village community, often with only a partial understanding of how they were to be built to resist natural forces such as earthquakes and cyclones. The use of new materials such as roof sheeting and fibrous cement was seen as the way to make them more permanent; but it is more the manner in which something is built than the materials used that makes it permanent.

As a result much of the destruction of cyclone Namu derived not from an inherent weakness, but through the neglect of traditional building techniques and the improper application of modern construction methods to both modern and traditional materials. This was borne out from our travels to the various communities and discussions at the village level: where traditional techniques were more fully employed, notably the use of timber poles from roof to ground and effective bracing and the use of vines for tying, the buildings fared better. Buildings which fared less well were built without adequate bracing, and with insufficient continuity between roof, wall, floor and foundations, usually through the minimal provision of strapping, or a reliance on nails for fixings particularly when placed in the direction of separation rather than across, this coupled with an inadequate appreciation of uplift forces rather than gravity loads. It is not possible to give statistics since the micro-conditions (topography, adjacence of other structures, etc.) varied greatly; however this was the general pattern that emerged.

The desire for improvement and permanence and the need to provide for such non-subsistence activities as education, medicine and transport effectively provide the motivations for change.

The journey from subsistence to permanence in building construction cannot be made in one leap, but gradually, so as to match economic growth and the gradual increase in technical ability and without disrupting cultural continuity. The rate of change is a direct product of the population's desire for change and its shifting priorities. In order to make this change, the following options have to be considered. These form the substance of the second part of this presentation.

Review of Construction Techniques

The choice of construction technique depends on three factors which are all under pressure in the move towards a more permanent and cash-based economy:

(1) *Availability of materials*

Traditional sources of materials are threatened by increased population demands on the resources available, and the conversion of land to cash crops (cocoa, copra etc).

(2) *Availability of manpower*

The delights of paid employment by comparison to the continuous effort of village life result in urban drift as well as a loss of interest in things rural. Communities are fragmented with the willing and able working for a cash wage for the Government or in the fishing, mining and logging sectors often remote from the village, all at the expense of maintaining the community.

(3) *Ability to finance the work*

The long-term obligations of loan finance do not come easily if one is used only to day-to-day resource management: the sudden availability of cash (from a good crop or a loan for agricultural development for example) may be used for non-productive activities such as a building rather than re-investment. Importing building materials from overseas at the expense of locally generated finance is only now becoming a feature of macro-economic planning. An individual may quickly find himself in deep financial trouble and the marginal profitability of his cash crop, again dependent on world market prices (copra and cocoa have dropped by some 50% in real terms over the past ten years), is often insufficient to meet his debt. As a result, finance is harder to come by, rates of interest increase, the period of repayment decreases and methods to cut costs are sought, often at the expense of construction standards.

The options for construction development may be classified thus:

(1) *Traditional construction*

Utilising materials immediately to hand such as timber poles, sago and pandanus leaf for wall and roof coverings. When combined with loya cane strips or liana creepers this type of construction characterises most of the rural buildings in the country. Ablutions are usually carried out remotely in the bush, and cooking is done in a separate cooking house.

A working knowledge of techniques, regular maintenance and sufficient manpower to complete the work (often through joint community effort: the majority of rural communities are family or tribal based) is essential. Construction costs are effectively zero.

Sustainability requires the transfer of skills between generations. This may best be achieved by sustaining the skills by one of the following means:

- making a record (written and/or visual of the tradition)
- discussing the realistic needs of the community
- building a database from which further study can be conducted

- keeping the value of these traditions alive and so allowing for a gradual evolution of construction techniques.

Some simple improvements have already been identified such as three-way jointing and vertical ties on the exterior of interlocking wall panels.

(2) *Hybrid construction: mixing old and new*

This type of construction is a little like Pijin (a local grammar with foreign words): using traditional construction systems but employing them in conjunction with more permanent materials.

The mixing of techniques and materials can sometimes lead to a deficiency in construction: for example properly fixing a steel roof on a pole frame will place added strain to the wall-roof connections. Likewise nails will rot and the pole will shrink away from the fixing. These and similar technical problems must become the subject of further research and experiment.

Given adequate support, this area has the greatest potential for realistic development and resource utilisation as a response to communities' needs, and their technical and financial abilities.

The development (and continuing evolution) of basket-weave construction through joint collaboration between Pacific Architects and Hybrid Technology has been one product of this study which provides for a structural frame that can be overlaid with leaf, timber, steel or boarding and needs only basic construction skills to accomplish.

(3) *Modern construction*

Timber framed housing construction through use of gauged, sawn, nailed and strapped timber framing with timber, steel or boarded cladding is the perceived ultimate goal of permanent housing.

The technique relies on considerable sophistication and training and is expensive. The limited availability of machining equipment and transport to remote locations restricts its use to coastal and peri-urban areas. Non-penetrable cladding means increased wind pressures therefore necessitating higher standards of assembly and fixing.

Intensive training and carpentry skills are required as well as a thorough grounding in the principles involved in basic engineering.

Recommendations

Based on the above, it is possible to make specific recommendations for construction development both within Solomon Islands and as broader initiatives for this decade of natural disaster reduction:

- encourage programmes to record traditional building construction before such skills are lost, preferably conducted through non-Government organisations who have a closer and more intimate association at community and village level;

- carry out a survey of significant buildings in the provincial areas – to which the community will turn in the event of disaster – to ensure that they will be adequate and relatively safe;
- develop a simple, non-technical rural building construction code illustrating principles as much as details to assist in basic construction improvement;
- establish a centre for specific research into the use of rural building materials with particular reference to insect and decay resistance, reaction with metallic fixings, alternatives to strapping and, additionally, establish a publicly available database;
- develop a programme to construct models to illustrate construction principles as an adjunct to visual and written materials and as a supplement to hands-on training;
- develop incentives for the production of local building resources through commercial support and local industrial development;
- find new ways, mainly through financial support, to integrate the work of local expertise into the larger programmes of development agencies at all levels whether international, regional or local.

CHAPTER 22

Occupant Behaviour in Earthquakes

MANSOUR RAHIMI

Institute of Safety and Systems Management,
University of Southern California,
Los Angeles, USA

Introduction

The objective of establishing guidelines on planning and preparation for occupant safety in earthquakes is based on the premise that the shaking forces drastically affect and alter living and work environments. For example, it is estimated that the First Interstate World Center (in downtown Los Angeles) is designed to sway five feet in an earthquake of magnitude 8.3. The accelerations from such shaking may be high enough to produce projectiles from most objects in the building. This higher risk should be managed by the provisions of specific planning, preparation and information dissemination to assure that occupants who survive the collapse of buildings are not seriously injured by the building contents.

Earthquake preparedness and recovery frequently stress the idea that individuals and households should expect to be on their own for at least 72 hours after an earthquake. The need for self-help and autonomy of activities is also stressed because emergency response agencies are expected to be greatly taxed immediately following an earthquake by demands such as care for the injured and suppression of the secondary hazards. In order effectively to integrate the efforts of the emergency personnel with the needs of the occupants, one needs to know the underlying behavior of occupants in relation to their built environments. Little is known about the behavior initiation and sequencing of building occupants in time of earthquakes. Even less is known about the behavioral factors that contribute to occupant injuries.

Current Knowledge

The issue of risk of injury to occupants of small dwellings in earthquakes is multifaceted and complex. There are numerous factors that play important roles in the injury outcome of an earthquake. The three main elements are related to human factors, structure and earthquake. The generally accepted hypothesis is that occupants have difficulty negotiating the interior environment of buildings during and immediately after earthquakes. There is evidence that non-structural elements and building contents pose significant life and safety hazards during earthquake shaking. For example, the percentage of injuries related to non-structural and building contents (e.g. glass, furniture, fixtures, appliances, chemical substances) appear to be significantly higher than previously expected (Ohta and Ohashi 1980; Ohashi and Ohta 1984). Previously innocuous elements of the interior environment, such as light fittings and filing cabinets, become hazardous in an earthquake. Additionally, building contents that are dislocated by earthquake forces may block exits, restrict access to emergency supplies and cause secondary hazards (Archea and Kobayashi 1984). Therefore, life safety in an earthquake may depend on a number of interacting variables including the ability of occupants to take the desired self-protective actions. Furthermore, Aroni and Durkin (1985) reported that 50 out of the 133 persons (about 37.6%) injured in the 1983 Coalinga earthquake had some type of disability. This study did not consider the factors of age, type or condition of structure, type and position of non-structural elements, and sequences of occupant behavior. Also, Hutton (1976) and Parr (1987) emphasize that in disaster situations, the needs of children and the elderly may be similar to disabled individuals. This notion will significantly increase the number of people who may be at higher risk in the course of negotiating their built environments for safety.

Archea (1990; Archea and Kobayashi 1984) investigated human behavior after the 7.1 M off-Urakawa (Hokkaido, Japan) and Loma-Prieta (California, USA) earthquakes and concluded that contrary to common belief, people are able to engage in much more activity during the period of strong ground motion than has been thought possible. The average distance travelled during the 10–12 second Loma Prieta earthquake was 13 feet and 10 inches. In the off-Urakawa earthquake occupants travelled an average of 27 feet during the 30 seconds of shaking. The Japanese subjects were more conscious of a secondary fire hazard than the American subjects. In the Urakawa sample, 80.8% stated that taking care of a fire was among the first two actions taken. They were also more protective of personal property; 39% attempted to save personal possessions walking directly past available zones of refuge. Based on the Loma Prieta sample, almost 42% remained totally vulnerable during the shaking. It was also concluded that there are cultural differences that may affect the actions of occupants in earthquake emergency situations.

While there were no deaths in three significant earthquakes in California

(Santa Barbara 1978, Imperial County 1979, Coalinga, 1983), the number of injuries reported ranged from 78 to 211 per quake (Aroni and Durkin 1985). The majority of earthquake induced injuries occurred in residential buildings. Rahimi and Azevedo (1990) hypothesized that a large proportion of deaths occur due to the collapse of the structural elements, while the majority of injuries are related to non-structural, building contents and human behavior. Arnold et al. (1982) indicated that all 47 injuries in the Imperial County Services building occurred due to occupant behavior and building contents; there was minimal damage due to non-structural elements and mechanical and electrical components. Ohashi and Ohta (1984) also concluded that building contents were important in injury causation. Archea (1990), Aroni and Durkin (1985) and Arnold et al. (1982) showed that moving about during the earthquake may increase risk to injury rather than the intended action of self-protection. Ohta and Ohashi (1985) state that occupants' reaction to the onset of shaking is highly significant in possible avoidance of injury. About 50% of the 47 injuries reported by Arnold et al. (1982) occurred when occupants engaged unnecessarily in evasive behavior. For example, occupants suffered injuries by 'bumping into objects' in an attempt to protect themselves. If a doorway has a door swinging on its hinges, it may not be the safest place for self-protection during the shaking period. Several occupants experienced buckling or swinging doors while standing in a doorway (Aroni and Durkin 1985). It was also mentioned that a majority of occupant injuries for the elderly are related to falls due to cluttering of floors (Watzke 1989). These results indicate that there is a need for models and strategies of human behavior so that significant interactions may be noted and specific strategies designed to successfully train occupants and to avoid risk of injury or death.

Research Objectives and Importance

Our research attempts to provide some explanation on how human behavior interacts with the building contents and interiors. More importantly, a detailed description of this interaction can help us to better understand the needs of occupants and means by which these needs can be addressed. An attempt was made to highlight this interaction with a survey from 33 disabled individuals experiencing the Loma Prieta earthquake of October, 1989, in four northern Californian cities. Some results will be examined in this presentation.

Behavior of individuals during and after earthquakes is an important issue in the design of educational materials for building occupants with regard to earthquake preparedness, survival and recovery. These requirements must begin with a general description of behavior and become specific on how these behaviors can be modified or adapted for safety. Specific training and preparation material must also take into account the impression of denial of potential hazards prior to the event. To deal with denial, it is suggested that perception of controllability of the hazardous event must be modified so as to undermine emotional management of the event before the event occurs. In order to change the perception of controllability of event, training and educational programs should be explicit on self-protective actions and procedures. The behavioral training strategies should address not only the behavior modifications and the needs of the occupants but also the efficient search and rescue operations by the emergency personnel.

Acknowledgement

This research is being supported by a grant from the National Science Foundation (BCS–8910457).

REFERENCES

ARCHEA, J.C. and KOBAYASHI, M. (1984) 'The Behavior of People During the Off-Urakawa Earthquake of March 21, 1982', *Proceedings of the 8th World Conference on Earthquake Engineering (San Francisco, California)*, Prentice Hall, Englewood Cliffs, NJ, USA.

ARCHEA, J. (1990) 'The Behavior of People in Dwellings During the Lomo Prieta California Earthquake of October 17, 1989', *NCEER Bulletin* 4(2): 8–9.

ARNOLD C., EISNER, R., DURKING, M. and WHITAKER, D. (1982) 'Occupant Behavior in a Six-Storey Office Building Following Severe Earthquake Damage', *Disasters* 6(3): 207–14.

ARONI, S. and DURKIN, M.E. (1985) 'Injuries and Occupant Behavior in Earthquakes', *US and Romania Joint Seminar on Building Research, Engineering, and Earthquakes*, September.

HUTTON, J.R. (1976) 'The Differential Distribution of Death in Disasters, a Test of Theoretical Propositions', *Mass Emergencies* 1: 261–66.

OHASHI, H. and OHTA, Y. (1984) 'Importance of Indoor and Environmental Performance Against an Earthquake for Mitigating Casualties', *Proceedings of the 8th World Conference on Earthquake Engineering*, Prentice Hall, Englewood Cliffs, NJ, USA.

OHTA, Y. and OHASHI, H. (1980) 'A Field Survey on Human Response During and After an Earthquake', *Proceedings of the 7th World Conference on Earthquake Engineering*, 9: 345–52.

PARR, A.R. (1987) 'Disasters and Disabled Persons: An Examination of the Safety Needs of a Neglected Minority', *Disasters* 11(2): 148–59.

RAHIMI, M. and AZEVEDO, G. (1990) *Physically Disabled Occupants: A Survey From the Loma Prieta Earthquake of October, 1989*, University of Southern California, USA.

WATZKE, J., SMITH, D., SOMERVILLE, N. and VERRAN, A. (1989) 'The Study of Home Safety Problems for Older Disabled Persons: a Multi-Dimensional Approach', *Proceedings of the Human Factors Society 33rd Annual Meeting*, Denver, Colorado, USA.

CHAPTER 23

The Rebuilding of Fao City, Iraq: A Case of Central Government Post-war Reconstruction

SULTAN BARAKAT

Institute of Advanced Architectural Studies
University of York, UK

Introduction

This paper explores the exceptional effort made by the Iraqis in their nationwide reconstruction campaigns for the southern cities of Basrah (the second largest city after the capital, Baghdad) and Al-Fao, as a case study of rebuilding settlements after a man-made disaster. The two cities were devastated during the eight-year war with Iran.

These reconstruction campaigns were completed in record time, based on a predetermined timetable, despite having to work in adverse weather conditions and the remoteness from the points of supply. The author visited the war-destroyed areas of Basrah soon after the cease-fire in August 1988. Later on, in November 1989, he was invited by the Iraqi Government to participate in the 'First International Symposium on Post-war Reconstruction in Basrah and Fao'. Basrah's reconstruction was started in December and lasted until June 1989, when the Fao work started. This city was rebuilt in a surprisingly short time: 114 days.

This paper attempts to examine the efficacy of Iraq's reconstruction policies, principally through exploring the rebuilding of Al-Fao city. While recognising the positive aspects this paper will however discuss the less worthy aspects of Iraq's reconstruction policies, both as admitted by the Iraqi authorities themselves and by the author's constructive criticism.

It is necessary to make clear that in doing this the author is concerned to learn the valuable lessons of Iraq's experience in reconstruction, so that others who suffer from war may benefit in the future. The author in no way means to understate the achievement of the Iraqi Government in the reconstruction of Al-Fao; he simply suggests that, generally, what has been built should not be seen as an end in itself. On the contrary, it should be seen as a first step in a long process of rebuilding. At the same time, reconstruction should be considered as an 'open experiment' for local discussion and involvement, not least for the Government planners themselves.

War and Destruction

Creation and demolition, construction and destruction have always been an integral part of human life and activity. Almost every nation, culture and civilisation throughout history has acted both as a 'founder' and 'destroyer' of human settlements. Many societies all over the world have experienced devastation and dispersal. Some have disappeared altogether, others have rebuilt, in one form or another, their new lives from the rubble of the past.

To mankind, security has always meant the construction of his habitat and shelter. However, 'national security' for some societies has at times meant destruction for others. This tragic and ironic consequence of so much 'security' in recent times has too often resulted in the destruction of defenceless settlements. It seems the bombardment of human settlements has become one of mankind's principal activities, often lavishly supported by 'public funds'. Moreover it also seems that the 'horrific' events associated with destruction are given more prominence than the founding and rebuilding of communities.

War, with its misery and ruin, is the most demandingly painful test of a people's commitment to the nation state. The larger and more bitter the conflict becomes, the greater the test of the true mettle of a nation's spirit and the solidarity of its people. However the author believes that the concept of 'Post-war Reconstruction' could likewise furnish a unifying theme that provides society with an opportunity for solidarity and participation, even greater than the prosecution of the war itself. If the people's interests could be truly represented by their Government then peaceful development is what they would surely choose.

The City of Al-Fao

The whole city of Al-Fao in the south of Iraq was razed to the ground in the war with Iran (Figure 1). Its people and buildings suffered terribly during its two year occupation, both from Iran and later on during its liberation by the Iraqi forces. The city is said to have been struck by an unbelievable seven million shells during the period of hostilities.[1]

'Blessed Ramadan'[2] or the so-called 'Battle of all Battles' was the huge Iraqi operation that was suddenly launched on 17 April 1988, by the 'Seventh Army

195

FIGURE 1 *The Iran–Iraq border*
[Source: Grummon, 1982]

Corps' supported by the 'Presidential Guards'. They reached deep into the Iranian defences at Al-Fao. It was a successful 35-hour operation, that drove the Iranians out of their positions and terminated two years of occupation. This operation had a very decisive impact on the course of the whole war. Iraq claims that it was the battle that eventually forced Iran to accept the cease-fire that was declared by the UN Security Council resolution 598 in August 1988.

Before that, under cover of darkness on the night of 9/10 February 1986, Iran attacked Fao peninsula with a great number of forces. They managed to occupy the whole triangular area taking the shape of a bridgehead and protected on the

196

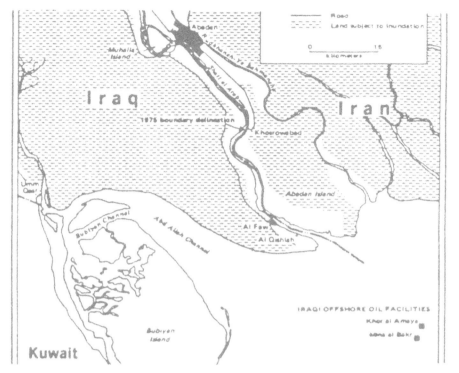

FIGURE 2   *Shatt al-Arab and the location of Al-Fao city*
[Source: Grummon, 1982]

sides by salty marshes and soft soil, thus cutting Iraq's access to the sea. This occupation was seen by Iran as the first step towards occupying the city of Basrah, the second largest Iraqi city after the capital Baghdad.

Iraqi sources claim that the number of Iraqi troops killed in the battles for Fao, from 1 September 1980 until 18 April 1988, were 52,984. The same sources also claimed that Iran lost 120,000 soldiers during the occupation of Fao and more than 30,000 during the Iraqi liberation.[3] Thus almost 200,000 people excluding civilians were killed on the earth of Fao in less than 26 months.

The city of Al-Fao lies 90 km to the south of Basrah's city centre, on the western bank of the Shatt al-Arab waterway, very close to the Arabian Gulf (Figure 2). Its people maintain themselves mainly from agriculture as the area is famous for its fertile fields. Before the war the palm tree plantations dominated the region. Fao owes a great deal of its wealth to its leading port and oil exporting terminal, through which Fao became the only Iraqi access to the sea and its main gate towards the rest of the world. Unfortunately, this strategic commercial importance was to become the cause of its suffering and destruction during the war.

197

'Utopian' Reconstruction

Still, for the Iraqis, Fao represented the 'Gateway to their Grand Victory'. For them the miracle of the liberation of the 'City of Sacrifice' was to be followed by another reconstruction miracle to suit their symbol of pride and achievement. A city was to be reconstructed to represent the perfect and ideal victorious Iraqi society. In other words a 21st-century Iraqi 'Utopia'.

Although we are living in exciting days of rebuilding after eight years of destruction, we should not be blind to what is taking place in the globe around us. I believe that the world is at a historical juncture, where a number of eras· have drawn together at the same time: the end of the 1945 'Cold War' represented by the destruction of the Berlin wall; the disintegration of Russian domination and thus the end of the 1917 era. Even more significantly, the era of Western dominated capitalism is said to be under considerable strain. All of these eras have influenced architecture and town planning all over the world for the last century and Iraqi cities were no exception. All these cultures coming to an end at the same time does suggest that the world has an opportunity to remake itself in the image of its different societies over the next years and into the 21st century.

It becomes increasingly evident that no matter how 'good' the intention of a Utopian dream, as long as the stated policy is exclusively the *authorised* version, there will be clashes between those who believe in it and the masses who know little or nothing about it. In other words, 'the Plan' and its execution will come into conflict with the people's democracy. Many will say, 'What is so very wrong with that? Where in the world does formal development and natural democracy really go hand in hand?' In Gorbachev's USSR, with its pursuit of glasnost and perestroika, freedom and restructuring, they have admitted that not to build with the active participation of the people is bad economics and socially unworkable. Today, Mr Yuri Murzin, Chief of the Architectural Department at the Central Scientific Research and Design Institute in Moscow could stand and say, '. . . for decades we have been ignoring the people's opinion and forcing our ideal dreams on them, and for decades we have been faced with continuous failures'.[4] Wimmer (1989), an East German planner, claimed that 'We in the GDR are now living through dramatic changes (November 1989). It is now a matter of humanitarian socialism linked with the progressive elements of democracy.[5] The majority of the people of the GDR want to have a State born with a high degree of responsibility and opposed to the "elbow society" implied by any adaptation to or variation of the capitalist structure of society. This is of vital importance to future reconstruction; to the objectives of urban development and to the definition of architecture' (Wimmer 1989:5).

Even in the so-called 'democratic countries' and at the planning and architectural levels such a '. . . notion of utopia has really led more to disasters than great cities' (Leon Krier, 1989).[6] For instance in post-war Britain, the various Governments wanted to usher in their version of a brave new world and turned the future over to the planners and developers with all their ideal solutions, only to discover a few decades later that these were not ideal for the users and clients. The biggest let down of all is that faith in the capitalist approach to economic and industrial development is beginning to be seen to fail the peoples of the world and indeed the very planet itself.

Central Government Reconstruction

So, have we learnt from experience and are the answers reflected in the quality of our rebuilt environment? For instance, we have not learnt from experience in the case of reconstructed Fao. The author believes that Fao is a true case of reconstruction by central Government alone. Right from the beginning four military divisions were used to clear the city of its rubble. The first step was to compose an Executive Central Committee for the Reconstruction Campaign under the chairmanship of the Minister of Local Government, with members from different Ministries and staff from the Ministry of Local Government.

'Al-Fao was the first city to be planned and reconstructed. The decision was made by the Government in August 1988 as a symbol of liberation and victory. Millions of dinars were set aside for that purpose. The structural Plan of the city was ready within 45 days. Then in October 1988 the Government asked private architectural offices to contribute to the effort of rebuilding by not charging for their design services . . . the Ministry of Local Government arranged for them to visit Al-Fao' (Barakat 1989b:63–64). Mr Namir Zenal, Chairman of the Regional and Urban Planning Department at the Ministry of Local Government, had talked to *Al-Qadessia* newspaper on 20 October 1988 about the new design and planning of Al-Fao city. He said that they took into consideration the political importance of the city as a symbol of liberation, as well as its economic role as a secondary port for the Basrah Region. He also said that another four plans were completed for new residential settlements around Al-Fao, as substitutes for the villages destroyed in the war.

Obviously, in the rebuilding of Al-Fao Iraq followed in the steps of some other socialist countries; planning by decree, assuming the needs and desires of the inhabitants and ignoring the participation of the users. How can the authorities gain the confidence of the people if they do not involve them? Human settlements make up societies and are expected by Governments to provide a stable base for social and economic development.

The Iraqi Government by taking over the individual properties in Fao ensured that future urban reconstruction would be free from any land speculation. This approach might be a contributory factor towards successful post-war reconstruction if seen as a means of rationalising land use, in order to create an environment favourable for daily life and production. On the other hand, this approach will reinforce the official central planning model and will threaten, as well as underestimate, the people's role. Such an approach can only be carried out against the individual's wishes and will, eventually, make people feel insecure.

In terms of urban design and the overall image of the city, the Government attempted to reflect Islamic and Arab identity. This desire was expressed by the President when he addressed the Iraqi Association of Engineers on 10 October 1984: '. . . where is our own identity and the architectural character of this era that is to be inherited and talked about by the coming generations? . . .'[7]

But this concern can be and has been interpreted in different ways in Al-Fao where reconstruction was based on large-scale clearance. The author drew attention to this aspect in 1989 when he wrote '. . . the intended reconstruction plan of Al-Fao has at its centre a great open space, surrounded by the city's main administrative and commercial buildings. Within this space the two surviving mosques are to be preserved as a memorial to the war and another modern civic monument, representing the Iraqi victory, is to be added. This paved open space will function, "apart from a vast heat store", as a festival square with only a small green area, plus a military museum, cinema, theatre and restaurants. It is also the place in the city where the roads from Basrah and Shatt al-Arab cross.[8] All very symbolic but whose symbols and from where do they come? They are certainly nothing to do with Islamic or Arabic architecture and do not in any way provide any reassurance to the President's question concerning the "coming generations"'. (Barakat 1989b:81).

Such a 'symbolic' and 'festive' approach towards reconstruction was implemented in some Eastern European countries. But, as recently as 1981, the reconstruction of areas destroyed in the Second World War, for instance in East Germany, has been resumed on the foundations of the old urban structures. Before that 'Modern International' modules '. . . that corresponded to the thesis of the "Athens Charter", dominated the reconstructed urban areas, resulting in "bold" structures, but no actual buildings' (Wimmer 1989:6). This was particularly so during the first phase of reconstruction, that was identified by Wimmer (1989:5) to be from 1945 to 1957. He also claimed that even during the second phase which lasted until 1971 '. . . the city's streets and squares remained to be overdimensioned'. Such cases could be found in Dresden's Altmarkt (Old Market) and in Berlin's streets: Rathau and Liebknecht.[9] The 1980s reconstruction phase is said to demonstrate the 'socialist' view of urban development and architecture, in which new construction, post-Second World War reconstruction and conservation of 'monuments' are proceeding as an integral whole. Successful examples of this approach can be seen in the 'Nicolai' quarter and the 'Rostock University Square' in Berlin (both projects completed early in 1987).

This approach influenced even the prefabrication industry; although the GDR like elsewhere in Eastern Europe did not give up the industrialised housing systems, still '. . . panel construction introduced in 1956, has as from 1981 been differentiated, for purposes of downtown area reconstruction, in such a way as to permit both adaptations to existing architectural styles and completely new and modern replacement construction' (Wimmer 1989:9). Thus reconstruction ought to proceed side by side with careful urban renewal.

Another aspect of reconstruction concerns building materials and techniques. Although it is a relief to find that prefabrication systems were not widely used in Al-Fao, still some housing apartment blocks in Basrah were constructed in pre-cast panel systems. Are we repeating the mistakes of the 1950s, 1960s and 1970s? A careful look at previous similar projects built in Basrah makes it quite clear that such building materials and techniques are not appropriate either to the local environment or to the local social and cultural values.

Vietnam's experience in this field gives us a very good example to learn from. It is said that since the end of the war many multi-storey, prefabricated housing projects were built in Hanoi, using the 'montage' building method of large wall-sized concrete panels. Although this method demonstrated, as elsewhere, the possibility of supplying a high number of dwelling units in a short time, it failed to answer the local social and technical conditions of Vietnam.

The long-term problems associated with industrialised building systems are well established; these tend to be highly dependent on imports, and a high quality transport infrastructure is needed to move the finished panels. Also inexperienced management of large high-tech industrial plants is hampered by Government restrictions. On the other hand, conventional methods use local and appropriate building materials and can be easily upgraded to meet modern needs.

In terms of reconstruction policy, I believe that the Iraqis had the right priorities in their campaign for Basrah. Here the rubble-clearing was followed by replacing the infrastructure; streets, bridges, water and electricity supplies and opening and clearing rivers. This programme lasted for four months and encouraged the city's inhabitants to come back, rebuild or repair their houses and start their normal life again. Whereas in the case of Fao the authorities tackled the problem in a different way; possibly because of the different scale of devastation and because of the previously mentioned moral, economic and political reasons (Figure 3).

Al-Fao Reconstruction

A careful look at the reconstructed city of Fao raises more questions. First of all, what does a reconstructed city that has no inhabitants but contains more than enough administrative, cultural and Governmental facilities represent and whom does it really serve? Where are the 25,000 pre-war population?[10] Why haven't the previous inhabitants returned to their city and been involved in

FIGURE 3 *A view from the reconstructed city of Fao*

rebuilding and resettling it themselves? Moreover, who is really going to benefit from this reconstruction? And does it actually represent all of the ideal concepts of an Arab city that was intended in the decision to rebuild the city in the first place?

The city was divided into several self-dependent sectors each containing 2,000 residential units. The main features are the 'Festival Square' and the 'Triumphal Gate'. The Square takes the shape of an octagonal star with a diameter of 170 m surrounded by a crude pre-cast colonnade with 92 columns (Figure 4). The Gate contains two main arches for vehicles, each 8.1 m high and another two pedestrian arches each 6 m high. The 30,000 pieces of stone that cover its concrete structure were installed by a special team of engineers and technicians brought from Yemen!

The responsibility for reconstructing the city was shared between several bodies. The Ministry of Local Government was responsible for the projection of the city's master plan, the implementation of water and sewage work as well as traffic engineering and road paving (Figure 5). While the Ministry of Transport and Communications was charged with the task of installing a telephone network, an electronic exchange and connecting Basrah and Fao with a microwave communications system. It was the duty of the Ministry of

FIGURE 4   *The 'Festival Square' in Al-Fao*

Housing and Construction to implement all the required buildings in Al-Fao city. In its turn this Ministry divided the work on a competitive basis between four contracting companies owned by the Ministry itself.

As far as the residential buildings were concerned, the Government adopted, as we said before, the policy of independent sectors, each of which was to be called after an Arab country and the houses of that sector were to represent the 'traditional' houses of that country. For this purpose house designs were imported from Jordan, Palestine, Tunisia, Egypt, Libya, Syria, Saudi Arabia, Morocco and Yemen. Nevertheless these designs are said to have been undergoing some modification in order to ensure their suitability for the local environment. These designs will be imposed on the people to implement them, in order to ensure the intended unified image of each sector.

Another important factor that should be considered, especially with such rapid reconstruction that must have affected building quality, is the repair and maintenance factor. I believe that by the time Al-Fao becomes an inhabited city, all the buildings will need maintenance. Some signs of deterioration are visible now. We should be aware of the fact that reconstruction and repair work in many developing war-devastated countries takes up considerable funds in the budgets of Development Plans and at the same time their reconstruction is challenged by different aspects such as continuous population growth,

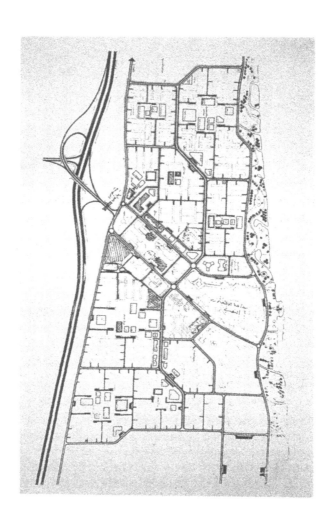

FIGURE 5   *The master plan of Al-Fao city*

political instability, natural disasters, along with the growing need to improve living and working conditions.

It is believed that 'in socialist countries, from a socialist's point of view, housing may be understood as social income. Housing is both for living and consumption, which means it is an instrument for everybody to join in private ownership. It is also production, to produce and reproduce social labour strength and a social property' (Nguyen 1989:4). For instance, what principally distinguished East Germany from West was that '. . . housing construction [was] seen as a basic need of all people without having to pay exorbitant rents' (Wimmer 1989:5).

Recently, in an attempt to choose the right approach towards a solution for the housing problem that could be suitable for the country's economic and social conditions, the Communist Government in Vietnam directed its policies towards 'self-help housing' and joint activities with the people and the local Governments. Nguyen (1989) claimed that 'self-help has a very important role to play in the strategy of the contemporary transitional stage towards socialism'. In this approach the provision of the physical infrastructure, such as water supply, electricity, roads, etc., is the responsibility of the local or central Government, for which the user pays an annual land tax.

Conclusion

World-wide experience suggests that for the success of any reconstruction plan an order of priorities must be stated to minimise waste. Reconstruction policies must be pursued at national, provincial and local levels. Each aspect should be planned sufficiently to answer both short- and long-term needs, depending on the priorities and available funds. Thus successful planning is that which can cope with the immediate and urgent needs of reconstruction and at the same time look ahead to the continuum of development. We must move away from a project-by-project based view of reconstruction, which sees things only for the short-term on a one-off basis and imposed from 'above and outside'. It is the author's view that reconstruction is an 'incremental learning process' for the people and in that respect not that different in theory from any improvement work. If it is to be by and of the public, reconstruction must of necessity take much longer: 'learning through doing' takes time. And it has to be remembered that it is the lives of the people themselves that are also being reconstructed.

REFERENCES

BARAKAT, S. (1989a) 'Considerations of cultural heritage in post-war reconstruction', *Second York Workshop on Settlement Reconstruction After War*, IoAAS, University of York, UK.

BARAKAT, S. (1989b) *Conservation of Architectural Heritage in War-damaged Urban Areas of Iraq, the Case of Basrah*, MA dissertation, Institute of Advanced Architectural Studies, University of York, UK.

BARAKAT, S. (1989c) 'Opportunities to achieve national identity through post-war reconstruction in Iraq', *National Identity in Contemporary Arab Architecture*, 16–18 October 1989, Baghdad, Iraq.

BARAKAT, S. (1989d) 'Some recommendations for the reconstruction of Basrah and Fao', *First International Symposium on Post-war Reconstruction in Basrah and Fao*, 17–20 November 1989, Baghdad, Iraq.

DITTMANN, E. (1989) 'Munich, 40 years of reconstruction', *First International Symposium on Post-war Reconstruction in Iraq*, 17–20 November 1989, Baghdad, Iraq.

IRAQI MCI (1989) 'Fao, the City of Sacrifice and the Gateway for Great Victory', Ministry of Culture and Information, Department of Information, Baghdad, Iraq.

NGUYEN, M.K. (1989) 'Vietnam's experience in post-war reconstruction', *First International Symposium on Post-war Reconstruction in Iraq*, 17–20 November 1989, Baghdad, Iraq.

PESCHICH, P. (1989) 'The reconstruction of Belgrade', *First International Symposium on Post-war Reconstruction in Iraq*, 17–20 November 1989, Baghdad, Iraq.

WIMMER, M. (1989) 'Experience gained in the reconstruction of war-destroyed towns, cities and areas in the German Democratic Republic', *First International Symposium on Post-war Reconstruction in Iraq*, 17–20 November 1989, Baghdad, Iraq.

NOTES

1. As it is stated on the memorial Gate of Al-Fao.
2. After Ramadan, the Islamic holy month of fasting.
3. 'Fao, the City of Sacrifice and the Gateway for Great Victory', a publication of the Ministry of Culture and Information, Department of Information.
4. From a personal discussion with the author during a meeting in Sofia, November 1989.
5. Even now, one wonders whether the first cries of humanitarian socialism will survive the headlong rush into so-called Western democratic capitalism.
6. A BBC2 programme, 'The Late Show', 1 February 1990.
7. This quotation was considered in October 1989 the theme of the 'Symposium on National Identity in Contemporary Arab Architecture', held at Baghdad, where the design and planning of Fao was released publicly for the first time.
8. According to a personal interview with Mr Mozafur Al-Yamori, a senior planner at the Ministry of Local Government, Baghdad. In January 1989, he proposed the structural plan of the new city of Al-Fao.
9. According to the author's own observation in a visit conducted in September 1987.
10. According to a survey done in 1977, by the Central Statistic Body, page 24.

CHAPTER 24

La Zurza: A Unique Experience in the Integral Urban Development of ` Santo Domingo, Dominican Republic

DAVID SCOTT LUTHER

Instituto Dominicano de Desarrollo Integral (IDDI)
Santo Domingo, Dominican Republic

Introduction

The Dominican Republic is presently undergoing a phenomenon found to be very common in the Third World: a massive population shift from the rural areas to the urban centres. Though the country's total population is growing at a rate of 2.6% annually, the cities are increasing at 6.5% and, in particular, the slums of the capital city of Santo Domingo are exploding at a 10% yearly rate. The situation is made even more critical because though these same slums contain 64% of the inhabitants of 'La Capital', they occupy only 19% of its total land area.

Description of La Zurza

Of all the slum settlements in the city, the worst are, no doubt, those that are situated in a strip alongside the two rivers (Ozama and Isabela) that run through Santo Domingo. In all, this area possesses close to 400,000 people. One of the 'barrios' that is located within this strip is La Zurza which is fairly typical in its characteristics in relation to the rest.

Among the most outstanding characteristics of La Zurza are the following:

- extremely high density (658 persons per hectare);
- young population (only 36% of the heads of households are over 40 years of age);

- very transitory population (30% have been there a year or less);
- precarious topography (only 6% of the houses are out of danger of landslides);
- small homes (58% of the houses have only one room and 87% have two or less);
- poor quality of construction (fully 40% of the houses are in bad or extremely bad condition);
- chaotic physical and spacial organization of the slum;
- no organized infrastructure or community services (for example, only 26% of the houses have individual water outlets);
- high degree of unemployment and under employment (only 20% have steady jobs and close to 60% make less than the minimum salary as defined by Dominican law);
- poor education (only 47% have reached sixth grade and 23% are illiterate);
- inadequate health care (La Zurza, with 400,000 inhabitants, has no established health care services of any kind).

The only a-typical characteristic of La Zurza that sets it apart from other slums is the fact that 54 industries dump their chemical wastes into a ravine that runs through the slum creating almost indescribable health problems for the inhabitants that live there.

IIDI's Development Project in La Zurza

In response to this situation of almost total abandonment and anarchy in which the population of La Zurza lives, the Instituto Dominicano de Desarrollo Integral, Inc. (IDDI), in coordination with the community and its representative organizations, is co-implementing the first and only large-scale integral development project carried out by a private non-profit organization in the slums of Santo Domingo.

Project objectives

The primary objective of the project is to help improve the quality of life (in all senses of the concept) of the community of La Zurza by way of transferring to it the required financial, educational, material and organizational resources and skills so that the population can make the necessary decisions and take the corresponding actions regarding their own development.

The secondary objectives of the project are to assist with the following:

- strengthen the capability for self-development of the community of La Zurza;
- improve the health and environmental sanitation conditions in the settlement;

- improve infrastructure and community services in the 'barrio';
- generate sources of income and improve the productive capability of the community;
- promote the personal, academic and vocational education of the population;
- improve the housing conditions in the slum;
- provide a model for the integral development of a marginal urban settlement of Santo Domingo that can be replicated in other slums in the city;
- promote the collaboration of formal organizations with informal (grass roots) groups thus creating the necessary trust to permit the two to work together fruitfully.

Description of the project activities

The project is divided into four programmes which are:

(1) Social Programme.

Without a doubt the principal problem of La Zurza is that it is not a community in the traditional sense of the word but rather an agglomeration of migrants from all parts of the Dominican Republic. There is no sense of collective consciousness and the inhabitants are, therefore, very individualistic in their attitudes and actions. In fact, La Zurza could be considered a no-man's land, a dog-eat-dog world.

Because of this, no true form of development is possible if the population does not find some way of organizing itself and working toward some definable, coherent and sustainable collective goal. This axiom is true for all development projects, no matter where they might be implemented.

This situation required that the social/organizational component of the project be of the highest priority. The activities that compose this programme are:

- community organization,
- personal formation,
- informal education,
- vocational training,
- awareness building in the community (including identification of the problems that affect them and possible courses of action to resolve these).

The major task was to encourage the creation of a representative community organization, the Sociedad para el Desarrollo Integral de La Zurza, SODIZUR (Society for the Integral Development of La Zurza), through which all the activities of the project would be channelled. The principal objective of the creation of SODIZUR was to promote the capability for self-development within the 'barrio' after IDDI eventually leaves La Zurza thus enabling the community to stand on its own two feet as an organized and coherent entity. Over the long term this will tend to reduce the rampant paternalism to which the country has always been subjected. At the same time, local organizations are almost always more efficient in implementing development projects than are the external ones, simply because of the knowledge they have of the 'barrio', the people, the local conditions, and in this case, also because of the credibility SODIZUR has in La Zurza.

One of the basic components of the social programme is the training and institutional building of SODIZUR so as to enable it to carry out the required project activities. This organization is a democratically elected body and is incorporated under Dominican law as a non-profit and private entity.

(2) Income Generation Programme.

Aside from the principal problem of not being a coherent, cohesive and organized community, the major problem in La Zurza, as with almost all other slums of Santo Domingo, is the lack of sufficient income to cover the cost of buying even the most basic daily needs such as food, clothing and housing. Many of the residents of the 'barrio' cannot take part in the activities of the project simply because they have to preoccupy themselves with finding enough money to survive.

In response to this, a two-pronged income generation programme is being implemented, these being:

• to foster the creation of new cooperative micro-enterprises,
• to strengthen the existing micro-enterprises.

For this purpose several revolving funds have been set up and channelled through SODIZUR to the micro-enterprises of La Zurza. SODIZUR identifies potential candidates, evelutes and, if appropriate, then recommends them to IDDI as potential beneficiaries of low-cost loans.

One of the requirements for obtaining a loan is that the candidate participates in self-help activities such as construction of infrastructure and community services projects. In this way, experience in collective work is achieved and, of course, community needs are met.

(3) Construction Programme.

One might say that the principal physical characteristic of the environment in La Zurza is spatial anarchy and chaos subjected to a continuous deterioration. To confront this situation IDDI/SODIZUR had to design a three-staged strategy to be implemented progressively. These stages are:

(a) Consolidation of the existing physical environment to prevent it from deteriorating further. This stage is composed of the following activities:

• stabilization of slopes
• consolidation of the internal pedestrian system

210

- consolidation of the storm drainage system
- cleaning the ravines.

(b) Improvement of the existing environment once it has been consolidated. This includes the following:

- water supply
- storm drainage
- pedestrian access and communication
- waste disposal
- housing improvement
- improvement of existing latrines
- improvement of the electrical energy supply.

(c) The construction of new installations and services that takes into account the following:

- construction of houses, latrines, etc.
- construction of centres of sanitary services of latrines, showers, clothes washing and public water taps
- construction of infrastructure services
- construction of communal buildings
- construction of a cover for the ravines thus isolating the human and chemical wastes
- construction of a chemical treatment plant.

At present the project is implementing the second stage and initiating some of the activities of the third stage.

(4) Health Programme.

The health programme is based on three fundamental objectives which are:

(a) Improving the environmental sanitation conditions within La Zurza that includes:

- assuring clean water supply
- disposal of human wastes
- disposal of household garbage.

(b) Preventive health care that includes:

- education in personal hygiene and nutrition
- community cleaning campaigns
- vector control.

(c) Maternal infant health care involving the following areas:

- nutrition

- supplementary feeding
- breastfeeding
- prevention and treatment of diarrhoea
- personal and family hygiene
- prevention and treatment of respiratory diseases
- oral rehydration
- birth spacing and other related topics.

Vulnerability to Disasters Within La Zurza

As was described previously, La Zurza is part of a strip of land that is almost a kilometre wide and eight kilometres long that borders the Isabela and Ozama rivers in the northern part of the city of Santo Domingo. This area of land of approximately 400,000 inhabitants is of a very irregular topography and extremely hilly making it very difficult to build on or inhabit. Also into these slums is discharged the rain and storm drain-off plus the industrial and biological wastes of the entire northern part of the city. This situation along with the fact that the ownership of this whole area of land has been in litigation (legal limbo) for more than thirty years, has made the territory most undesirable for all but the rural migrants who have illegally settled on it.

As a result of this, these 'barrios' live in a state of almost total abandonment on the part of the Government having no formal water supply system, garbage collection service, human waste disposal system, vehicular access, electrical energy, little or no medical, academic or vocational attention, etc.

Vulnerability to natural disasters

La Zurza is vulnerable to a series of natural hazards, some frequent, almost regular or seasonal (such as floods and hurricanes) and others that occur as a result of the living conditions in the slum (such as landslides that are a result of poor construction and fires that happen due to the extreme density of the structures that they call their homes).

(1) Vulnerability to Fires

Because the vast majority of the houses located in this area are built of wood and are so closely packed with no possible access by fire department units, these communities are very vulnerable to all kinds of fire hazards such as electrical fires (due to the pirating of the lines outside of the area which, inevitably, produces frequent short circuits), those caused by open fire cooking, etc. This situation is aggravated by the fact that there are no adequate exit routes for the population making them very susceptible to becoming trapped by any potential disaster.

212

(2) Vulnerability to Landslides

As was previously described, the topography in these settlements is very irregular, the soil tends to be unstable and there is no organized rain or storm drainage system. When the migrants settle into the areas, they build anywhere, anyway they can and very fast (usually at night so as to avoid being caught and imprisoned by local police, who are normally paid off anyway). The houses are set into the hillside, one almost right on top of the other, usually without any really adequate foundations or efficient structures. As is common during a heavy rain, a house on the top of the hill or slope will collapse and fall on another house below it which in turn falls on still another in a 'domino' like way. The real disaster comes from the fact that even though a family has gone to all the effort of building a sound foundation (investing a lot of money and time into it), if those that live above them have not bothered to do so, they potentially can slide down onto them destroying their house, no matter how well built it might be. So, in a sense, one pays for the irresponsibility of others. (That is a familiar characteristic of these areas.)

However, the reason that people do not build adequately is not because they do not know how to or are irresponsible, but rather are unwilling to invest their money into building permanent structures if they feel (rightly so) that the Government can forcibly remove them. So, as a consequence, they invest in those items that they can take with them such as colour televisions, stoves and refrigerators.

(3) Vulnerability to Flooding

Immediately alongside the two rivers and bordering the slums is a strip of flat land (basically composed of silt deposited there by the rivers) that varies in width from a 50 to 100 metres that is completely and densely inhabited. Almost yearly there are flash floods caused by rains in the interior of country which, by the way, are accentuated by the rampant deforestation to which the country is subjected. On a regular basis the structures in this area are washed away. As a consequence, the quality of construction is extremely poor simply because the families know that the houses are temporary at best. This is very common in this narrow strip. At the same time, those areas that are on either side of the numerous ravines that run through the slums are also vulnerable to flooding on account of the storm drainage flow of the northern part of the city.

(4) Vulnerability to High Winds

Though the Dominican Republic (and specially the south coast) is extremely vulnerable to high winds, these 'barrios' in general have not suffered the damage one would have expected. This is basically due to the fact that the terrain is irregular with much of the area to some degree protected from these winds. Nonetheless, because of poor construction practices and use of waste or scrap material that they build with, many roofs are blown off and occasionally whole houses will collapse.

213

In general it could be correctly argued that the vulnerabilities to the so-called 'natural' disasters described above are nothing more than 'man-made' (or man-imposed) conditions that when confronted with natural hazards (such as high winds and flooding) become disasters. So, in effect, these are not 'natural' but 'man-made' disasters. Such is the case with almost all the marginal areas in Third World countries, whether they be urban or rural.

Vulnerability to 'man-made' disasters

Aside from those 'man-made' conditions of vulnerability that become disasters when provoked by the occurrence of natural hazards, when speaking of the slums of the Dominican Republic one must also refer to those situations that are strictly imposed by a society that is unjust in its treatment of the poor and undemocratic in not allowing the population adequate opportunities to participate in the decision-making process of how the country is to be governed and how to distribute its resources.

These are basically social and economic conditions that manifest themselves in numerous ways within the slum settlements. Among them are:

- no guarantee of steady or fixed incomes;
- no guarantee that they will not be forced off the land they are living on (as is presently happening on a large scale in Santo Domingo);
- no guarantee of protection from youth gangs, thieves or other similar menaces common in these areas;
- no real mechanisms through which to express their opinions, aspirations, desires or needs within the present socio-political context;
- no guarantee of a clear, secure or comfortable future for them or their children;
- no guarantee of being protected from the multiple health hazards caused by poor quality of water, no garbage collection, no effective human, biological or chemical waste disposal system, etc.

What cannot be under-estimated is the effect these conditions play on the psychological state of the people who live in these slums. One can perceive a sense of frustration and desperation almost universal in the 'barrios'; and though it is not the purpose of this paper to exaggerate living conditions in these areas, anyone who has spent some time there will well understand that the above description is pretty much reality.

These and other factors have created among the population a sense of being exploited and rejected by the Government and the mainstream of Dominican society and this is reflected in their attitudes about life and how they maintain their communities. As stated before, to a large degree there is no collective consciousness (as occurs in more 'traditional' communities), but instead there exists a very individualistic world where almost everyone is out for themselves. People also feel to be very transitory and temporary with regard to their permanence in the 'barrio'. The natural outcome of this is the creation of a very vulnerable (in almost all senses of the word) situation that can be translated into a disaster with the slightest spark, be it a price hike by the Government, food scarcity, political trouble or even a rumor. The problem is aggravated even further by the fact that it is also the urban poor who are usually the most affected by the adverse consequences of any resulting disaster (a riot, a strike or whatever) thus impacting that much more negatively on the quality of life in the slums. In a sense, what we have here is a continuous downward spiral with the inevitable increase in the vulnerability of these areas to natural and 'man-made' hazards.

Coping with this Situation

The inhabitants of the 'barrios' cope with the situation simply because they have to; there are really few other alternatives for them. Some of these are:

- return to the rural areas of their origin. This, however, is almost inconceivable simply because no matter how bad the situation in the cities can become, it is preferable to being in the countryside for a number of reasons, primarily economic, but there are also social pressures to move to the city.
- leave the country via 'yolas' (small boats) for Puerto Rico. This is an option that is being used more and more by the Dominicans due to the fact that the economic situation in the country is deteriorating constantly.
- remain as they are presently with no real means of self-defence or promise of a more secure future.
- organizing themselves into grass-roots groups so as to be able to help one another more effectively and also to have more influence in terms of their relationship with the Government and other external bodies. This is the option that is at present being promoted by IDDI and its collaborating organizations. (The primary criticism of this approach is that it is merely a palliative and does not resolve the overriding situation of structural inequality that exists in the Dominican Republic.) Over the short term, this alternative is the only viable way for the slum dwellers even though the process is slow and full of obstacles. Consciousness raising is always slow, especially in a society where there is no real and historic community action tradition (as occurred in other countries) and where the population has been subjected to a rampant paternalism and state of dependency for centuries.

In coping with life in the slums, the main objective of the inhabitants is simply to survive. However, there is always the drive to improve their lot and they are able to do it very creatively, not only in their use of building materials and construction techniques, but also with regard to how they make their

215

living and set up socio-economic structures. Necessity imposes that on them. Nonetheless, few of them really have the luxury of thinking about how to improve their living conditions much less reduce their vulnerability to disasters. Those of us in this particular field of disaster related risk reduction must face up to that fact.

Conclusion

In conclusion, several points can be made, none of them new or innovative, just difficult to implement. They need to be constantly reiterated:

- the need to dedicate more time, energy and resources towards resolving the problems of that 64% of the city's population that only occupies 19% of this land area. This is not to say that less attention must be given to rural areas but the balance in focus should be more even.
- experience has taught many of us who have worked in slum areas that often the only way to attract resources towards resolving the problems found there is by putting public pressure on the Government and other formal organizations to respond to the situation. It is unfortunate that the system must be forced to react instead of acting in a planned and carefully thought out manner, but that is the way it sometimes works. The hope is that the reaction can be transformed into a long-term programme that really focuses on the needs of the beneficiaries. Public pressure is created by means of attracting attention to the problems in the slums through using the press, pressure groups, protests, etc.
- because vulnerability to disasters and underdevelopment are so closely linked, it is not possible to deal with one without treating the other; the two go hand in hand. At the same time one must remember that it is useless to talk about risk reduction and disaster preparedness to those whose main objective is just to survive (of course, this has its exceptions, for example those who are constantly subjected to flooding). But the point must be made because we, the 'experts', so frequently mislead these often gullible people, who are anxious for a helping hand, with our constant insistence regarding disaster related programmes.
- it is imperative in any development or disaster-related programme to include the people involved in every aspect of the decision-making process thus helping them to become conscious and willing participants. Nothing imposed really works; they must be involved if any true development and structural transformation is desired.
- the intermediate support organizations (whether they be called PVOs, VOLAGS or NGOs) must understand that their role in assisting the lower income population is not to become the primary actors in any project or activity that they promote, but rather to be a catalyst or facilitator of change.

216

One cannot substitute a population's capability for self-development but instead foster it.

- whatever technology transfer, materials used or level of education is employed, they must be in accordance with the social and economic reality of the people for whom they are intended. If not, they are bound to fail.
- it is necessary to reinforce the concept of integral development which is an indispensable component in any effort to aid our fellow men. It is not enough just to increase a person's income, or educate him, or protect him against disasters, or improve his home. These efforts always tend to be disconnected and only partially resolve his problems. Man's needs are many, indivisible and should be treated as such.

CHAPTER 25

Housing in El Salvador: A Case Study

DÉBORA C. VÁSQUEZ-VELÁSQUEZ

Architecture Department, School of the Environment
Leeds Polytechnic, UK

Introduction

El Salvador is the smallest country in Latin America (21,000 sq km), has approximately 5 million inhabitants and is the Central American country with the highest density of population (257 inhabitants per sq km) (Figure 1).

Like most Latin American countries, El Salvador is characterized by housing shortages and poor living conditions which affect 60% of its population (Fundacion Habitat de El Salvador). About 3 million Salvadorians have inadequate income due to a lack of permanent employment and live in shanty towns which do not provide adequate living standards, services or infrastructure.

Approximately 60% of the population in El Salvador is below the age of 20 years (Ministerio de Planificacion, Gobierno del El Salvador) and the annual rate of growth of the total population is 2.3 per thousand. Taking into consideration this statistic, it is possible to estimate the increase of the population over the next ten years as 1,300,000 (319 inhabitants per sq km).

According to Government figures, the urban population in El Salvador by 1985 was 46% and the rural 54%. These figures are being affected by the migration to urban areas in the central and occidental zones due to the economic crisis and the continuing civil war in the country. The urban population is mainly concentrated in the capital city of El Salvador, San Salvador, and constitutes 35% of the total population of the country, over 1.7 million inhabitants (Stein 1989).

Official figures provided by the Ministry of Housing of El Salvador suggest that less than half of the housing in the city can be classified as of 'acceptable' standard, based on the criteria of location, materials and use of basic services.

FIGURE 1   *Central America*

The poor housing conditions for the majority of the population in El Salvador have deteriorated since 1980 with the upsurge of the civil war and the earthquake of 1986. The official report published by the UN Economic Commission for Latin America – ECLA – and the World Bank state that the houses destroyed by the earthquake number 60,000 units, of which 50,600 belong to the informal sector or shanty towns; 7,260 families were left homeless.

According to information from the Institute of Social Investigation of the University of Costa Rica, the population of El Salvador that lived in accommodation from the informal sector was in 1947 40.5% and by 1975 this figure reached 58%.

An official report presented by the Salvadorian Government indicated that:

219

- 63% of the urban population in San Salvador live in accommodation of the informal sector (shanty towns);
- by 1986, housing shortages accounted for 572,000 dwellings, of which 30% were in the urban areas and 70% in the rural areas;
- the rural accommodation is of much lower quality than that in the urban areas;
- only 44% of the total houses in the country have water supply systems;
- only 66% of the dwellings have electricity;
- only 59% of the houses have some kind of floor, the rest have just the ground soil as a floor;
- 44% of the dwellings do not have sewage systems;
- in 39% of the dwellings, people suffer overcrowding of more than three persons per room;
- 42% of the dwellings are of unsecured tenure;
- the materials used in the construction of the majority of the dwellings are of poor quality;
- 25% of the dwellings in the rural areas are made of adobe, bamboo, straw and mud.

These official figures reveal the serious problems of housing shortages in El Salvador as a result of the economic, political and social crisis throughout the country. The housing shortage is so severe that the actions taken by the Government to provide housing for the homeless have not solved the problem. An official report presented by the Salvadorian Government established that 'the improvement in the social conditions has been small, not only in San Salvador, but in all the cities and the rest of the country' (Informe de el Gobierno del El Salvador 1989).

El Salvador does not have an adequate policy of urban planning that organizes, regulates and controls the disorderly expansion of its cities and their future development. The plans for improved communications and public services have not taken into consideration the accelerated growth of human settlements and therefore there exists poor sanitary conditions, bad quality and acute shortages of water supply, drainage systems, transport, roads, energy, fuel, portage, and telecommunications, as well as deficiencies in health care, education and lack of leisure provision all over the country (Informe de el Gobierno del El Salvador 1989).

The Government then faces the problem of:

- where to locate the homeless as a result of the earthquake and the homeless migrants who are product of the civil war and economic crisis;
- how to provide accommodation and dwellings to meet the present demand.

In search of a solution to the problem, the Salvadorian Government has implemented, with the participation and aid of national and international institutions and organizations, emergency programmes for the provision of basic accommodation for the homeless, but these programmes lack financial and physical resources, particularly land which is necessary to housing schemes.

The apparent scarcity of land is caused by the speculation and the concentration of land in the hands of a few private owners (Stein 1989). Therefore land tenure is one of the main obstacles to solving the housing problem of thousands of poor families. Then, the housing programmes provide accommodation only to a small percentage of the affected population, leaving the majority, the poorer families, with only the possibility of the shanty towns as a solution to their accommodation problems.

Therefore, the only two possibilities for the homeless to find accommodation are:

(1) Shanty towns: they start as land invasion and the construction of a temporary shelter. Their population is severely affected by unemployment and the residents of these areas do not have any security on land tenure.
(2) 'Programas de Ayuda Mutua' (Self-help, self-build programmes): they are implemented by non-Governmental or Governmental institutions with loans or donations from national and international institutions and organizations. The main purpose of these types of programmes is to guarantee security of tenure of land and to provide a basic shelter with the construction of a low income unit for families in need, allowing areas in each housing site for the future development of communal facilities, creating the conditions for community organization and possibilities to improve people's living conditions.

It is fundamental to guarantee a good level of organization among the community for the success of these types of projects. The projects are not subsidized and therefore need to be self-financing and thus have the disadvantage that the poorest sectors, those most in need, cannot benefit, because it is a requirement that at least three members of the family must have a regular job to guarantee the payment of the long-term loan (up to 20 years).

Example of Self-Help, Self-Build Programme: Habitat Comfien Project

The main purpose of this project, developed by the 'Fundacion Habitat' (Habitat Foundation) of El Salvador, was to provide dwellings for the families affected by the earthquake (Figure 2).

- site location: Canton Milingo, Ciudad Delgado
  4 miles north of San Salvador.
- number of dwellings: 1,100
- total area of site: 0.82 Ha.
- total area/dwelling: 121 m^2
- size of each unit: 20 m^2

Objectives of the project development:

- acquisition of an accessible site;
- service provision: water supply, drainage, electricity;

221

FIGURE 2   *The Habitat Comfien Project*
[Source: Ernesto Barraza Ibarro]

- construction of a basic unit consisting of: one room, bathroom, wash-house;
- technical assistance to guarantee improvements in living conditions.

The site location is a fundamental factor in the development of any project because it has a strong influence on the users' budget. The long distances from work prolong the users' working hours because public transport is infrequent and expensive. For economic reasons, the site gradient should not be more than 30%, the pedestrian circulation should be perpendicular to contours, and the vehicular circulation parallel to contours. Environmental amenities must be preserved. The aim of the project is to provide low-cost constructions that guarantee an adequate quality of materials and adequate living conditions.

Conclusion

Taking into account the financial problems and the present situation in El Salvador, it is possible to conclude that the self-help programmes are a valid principle for the solution of the immediate shelter needs of the homeless. Projects such as Habitat Comfien for the construction of 1,100 units represent 0.19% of the total housing deficit in El Salvador. In order to supply housing for the present demand, 520 projects of the same magnitude would be required. Therefore, considering the present population and its annual growth, it can be estimated that in ten years time, the population of El Salvador will be 6,600,000 inhabitants and the housing demand (assuming the number of members per family to be 5) would be 1,320,000 units. If the present percentage of the deficit remains constant at 60%, the shortage in houses would be 792,000 units and therefore 79,000 units would have to be built every year to meet this deficit.

Taking into account the difficult situation in El Salvador, the implementation of 'self-help' programmes could be the solution to the provision of basic shelter for the homeless if the Government develops integral programmes throughout the country.

REFERENCES

Informe de el Gobierno de El Salvador (Report presented by the Salvadorian Government) (1989), 'Conferencia Internacionale Refugiados centro-americanos' (International Conference of Central American Refugees) Guatemala, May 1989.

BARRAZA, E. et al. (1985) 'Manual para Proyectos de Ayuda Mutua', Instituto Nacional de Vivienda, Santo Domingo.

LUNGO UCLES, M. (1988) 'San Salvador: Habitat Popular despues del Terremoto', Medio Ambiente y Urbanizacion, No. 24, September.

STEIN, A. (1989) 'The "Tugurios" of San Salvador: A Place to Live, Work and Struggle', Environment and Urbanization, 1(2) October.

CHAPTER 26

Mitigation Program Selection and Evaluation: Assessing Effectiveness

PATRICIA A. BOLTON

Battelle Human Affairs Research Centers
Seattle, WA, USA

Introduction

Over at least the last two decades it has become possible to discern an increased concern on the part of policy makers about the need to take action to prevent losses from natural hazards rather than to simply engage in palliative efforts after disasters to ease the discomforts of those who have lost their homes and neighborhoods. An examination of various types of research and program documents describing disaster reconstruction projects and development programs reveals a variety of approaches for reducing losses (examples include Bates 1982; Davis 1981; Haas et al 1977; Kreimer and Zador 1989; United Nations Centre for Human Settlements 1989). Most typically, however, loss reduction measures are considered in post-disaster situations, where there is some pressure to use the opportunity to replace damaged and destroyed housing with housing that will be safer in the face of similar future events. Interest in these measures is lower in areas that have not recently experienced a disaster.

In more affluent areas, there may also be some concern after a disaster for improving the resistance of still existing housing now viewed as particularly vulnerable to future events (for example, in Mexico City following the 1985 earthquake). Likewise, there is some interest in considering dwelling safety, i.e. dwelling resistance to some natural hazard, in the course of providing new housing as part of development programs.

The central guiding objective of the International Decade for Natural Disaster Reduction (IDNDR) is the reduction of losses to the built environment that occur as the consequence of natural events such as floods, hurricanes and typhoons, earthquakes and other similar meteorological and geophysical extremes. The Advisory Committee on the IDNDR (1987) in its delineation of the concept for the Decade acknowledges the importance of hazard and disaster reduction, both in anticipation of destructive natural events, and as a program strategy in the aftermath of disasters.

The initial Decade statement suggests physical and social adjustments that include:

• planning and building to withstand a hazard;
• identifying and avoiding the sites where a hazard is likely to occur;
• restricting the uses of land and establishing minimum standards for avoiding hazardous sites and conditions;
• instituting public awareness campaigns in areas prone to hazards;
• reconstructing a community so that it is less vulnerable to the next hazard.

It should be noted that many hazard reduction measures are most easily applied where new development is involved, and in instances of post-disaster reconstruction. Altering the conditions of existing development in order to achieve a greater degree of resistance of the built environment to a natural hazard can be a most difficult political and social endeavor, but critical to consider if high death tolls are to be averted in the future.

This paper addresses factors related to the decision-making about adopting disaster loss reduction measures. Whatever the circumstances for the initiation of a housing program – reconstruction or development – any program design short of providing total autonomy to the prospective residents involves a series of formal decisions about the project location, cost, design, materials, and oversight. The same factors that go into the deliberations about the loss reduction approach to use for a particular program will also underlie the design of an approach for evaluating its effectiveness when selected.

Designing Housing Programs

Examination of studies of post-disaster housing reconstruction projects indicates that three important criteria for housing programs are that the housing:

• be provided quickly and with a minimum of ambiguity about location, cost, and tenancy rights;
• be socially as well as physically habitable, that is, that the design be consistent with familiar and culturally acceptable traditions so that the residents' social status and interaction patterns are not greatly altered by virtue of their new residence; and
• provides some degree of hazard resistance appropriate to the locale.

In general, these same criteria can apply to development housing projects as well as to cases of post-disaster reconstruction. In either case, these criteria cannot all easily be met to the same degree. There are inevitably trade-offs among them. In particular, the provision of hazard resistance is often the most likely to entail a longer planning period and the need to control in some way the participation of the prospective residents, especially if they are involved in the construction of the housing. While prospective residents might agree that hazard resistance is an important criteria, they will quickly forgo it in preference to traditional housing (housing which, in their view, is the most socially habitable), or immediately available and cheaper housing (especially if it also provides social habitability). Thus housing program developers, whether they be local officials or social agency staff, or implementors of housing being donated or financed from external sources program, will have to take the major responsibility for promoting and for building hazard resistance into the housing. At the same time the residents are more likely to be satisfied if they have a high degree of participation in the planning and execution of the project.

The Decade report observes that:

- many known disaster reduction procedures cannot be applied worldwide because experience in their application or critical data for their effective use in a particular region is not available;
- many promising approaches lack the ongoing research effort required to develop them for future application.

I would propose a variation on the issue suggested by the first of these two cautions, less related to effective application of known technologies, but more directly related to human organization and behavior. The following is true in both developed societies and in less developed settings:

- many promising approaches ultimately will not be as effective as theoretically possible, because their implementation requires changes in behavior that can be difficult to bring about on a wide scale.

This premise is not meant to discourage the consideration of previously unfamiliar strategies for achieving reduction in losses and disruption from future disasters. Rather it is meant to call attention to the need to separate out the policy maker's or program donor's *objectives* for the selected approach from the *likely outcome* of implementing the selected approach. Typically, several options can be considered for incorporating hazard reduction into a housing program, so the planning process entails choosing among options. Effectiveness in reducing the hazard should be one of the criteria when options are being compared. However, in the process of comparing hazard mitigation options, the use of the theoretical effectiveness of a particular measure can lead the decision makers to select an option that ultimately may have less actual effectiveness than was assumed in the selection process. Previous work by a

226

colleague, Peter May, and myself addresses this dilemma faced by decision makers (Bolton et al 1986; May and Bolton 1986).

Planning for Hazard Reduction

The variety of approaches for promoting the provision of safer dwellings can be wide ranging. Our earlier work focused on the setting in the United States, where regulatory approaches are the most common. I would propose that when hazard reduction is being considered for less developed countries the general approaches for its introduction are better depicted as follows:

- *exhortation* – urging a community or those responsible for building houses to engage in safer practices with respect to the location or construction of housing (for example, public education campaigns about hazards; distribution of literature illustrating improved building techniques);
- *requirement* – passing local ordinances, or conditioning financing, making it necessary for those constructing dwellings to adhere to certain standards and conditions (for example, new building codes in Managua following the 1972 earthquake; World Bank requirements for the Phase I housing program following the 1985 Mexico City earthquake);
- *enablement* – enhancing awareness of the hazard and providing technical assistance and training to homeowners or local building trades in the use of appropriate materials, designs, and construction practices (for example, the SENA-managed housing recovery program in Popoyan, Colombia, following the 1983 earthquake);
- *delivery* – building or delivering pre-designed and/or prefabricated permanent dwellings for the community in order to assure the new dwellings are hazard resistant (for example, League of Red Cross Cities housing program in Ecuador following the 1987 earthquake).

While varying with respect to the extent to which the local population is covered by the loss reduction measure(s) being applied, all of these approaches for promoting the use of loss reduction techniques have the same central goal: to reduce losses in future hazard events. Each of the approaches can be focused on achieving the application of one or more specific measures reducing deaths and losses related to the destruction or damage of dwellings.

Assessing Mitigation Options

There are many approaches to achieving a reduction in deaths and dwelling losses. Examples of loss reduction measures related to the earthquake hazard, but also relevant to other hazards, include such measures as reinforcing certain elements of existing dwellings to make them more resistant to seismic forces, applying designs, construction materials and standards for new dwellings to enhance their resistance to groundshaking, restricting development or re-development in areas susceptible to significant consequences in an earthquake (e.g. liquefaction, landsliding), requiring more stringent building standards for dwellings to be built in areas with some specifiable susceptibility to the consequences from the hazard, or providing some financial incentive or conditioning the financing to homeowners, local Governments or project developers to promote the construction of dwellings with a specified degree of seismic resistance. More than one of these may be applicable to a particular situation. Two major considerations must be weighed against each other in selecting the most appropriate measure or measures for the specific situation:

- *costs* – which will need to be considered for various stages of a program, front-end costs and long-term costs, and in terms of who will bear them, for example the donor or financier, the local Government, or the occupant;
- *effectiveness* – where three factors contribute to the relative effectiveness of a measure: coverage of the measure, its theoretical effectiveness, and the degree to which it is implemented (Bolton et al 1986).

The notion of 'coverage' refers to the extent to which a mitigation measure applies to the area at risk. For example, available data may indicate that an entire community is vulnerable to severe groundshaking; measures can be considered that will affect all dwellings, existing and proposed, or that will apply only to new development, or will apply only to a specific housing program, but not to all new housing being developed.

The notion of potential or 'theoretical' effectiveness reflects the objective of the technology being applied. Some measures, such as strict construction standards or design criteria, may have the objective of preventing virtually 100% of structural damage, while another technology may be recommended with the more limited objective of reducing loss of life, but not address overall building damage, such as the use of lightweight roofing materials in place of heavy tile.

The potential effectiveness of a specific technology will be reduced if it is not thoroughly and correctly applied. That is, its theoretical effectiveness must be discounted by the extent to which it is not operable in all of the dwelling units for which it was intended. For example, a housing program can be initiated for which specific guidance is provided for reducing virtually 100% of the structural damage by assuring seismic resistance through the requirement that each builder attach the roof and walls together in a specific way. The costs of the program will lie in providing the design, disseminating the techniques, and providing inspectors for the construction period. However, in practice the technique is only actually correctly applied in 60% of the houses. The potential effectiveness together with the extent of the implementation of the measure equals 60%, while the relatively high costs of the program remain the same.

On the other hand, some other type of technology may have the potential to reduce deaths by 80% through the use of lighter roofing materials even though some extent of wall collapse can still be expected. The relatively low costs are distributed between the program which subsidizes the cost of the roofing material, and the home owners who purchase and use the materials. The program's potential effectiveness is not equal to that of the first example, but 85% of the households involved purchase and use the roofing when rebuilding their homes.

Assessments such as this can be used as the basis for evaluating different programs designed to reduce death and loss from natural hazards. Rough calculations can also be used in a prospective manner, as part of the process of selecting an appropriate program design. Local value judgements about loss reduction should be taken into account as well as strict cost-effectiveness estimations. To do such an assessment, even in a qualitative rather than quantitative way, there are three main elements of implementation to examine (Bolton et al 1986):

- *the target group* – who is targeted for making a change in behavior; that is, whose behavior (practices) will have to be different if a certain hazard reduction measure is adopted? In many instances it will be the behavior of the 'builder', whether individual homeowners or a single developer. An estimation can be made of how likely the target group is to change its past practices.
- *the chain of implementing actions* – what steps will have to be taken to convince, require or enable this target group to engage in the new practice or practices? To what extent are each of these steps likely to have a high degree of success in being fully carried out?
- *intermediary implementors* – whose decisions are central to the implementation of the chosen reduction measure? For example, who will be responsible for establishing the design or standards or requirements, for enforcing the standards, or for providing the necessary expertise and information. What is the likelihood that they will agree to adopt or implement the program and will have the skills and motivation to do so in a comprehensive manner?

Conclusion

Planners and decision makers need to weigh carefully the trade-offs between the costs of some programs in conjunction with what they might actually achieve in the way of averting deaths and losses in future hazard events, if implementation of the measure is less than perfect. It may be that simpler but more easily implemented programs have equal or greater pay-off than seemingly elegant and highly effective solutions. This question can also be approached through the systematic evaluation of a variety of projects, in order to obtain insights about the relative effectiveness of various loss reduction measures that might be the basis for major reconstruction or housing development programs and about the factors that need particular attention in project implementation.

The implications of this discussion are:

- a calculation of prospective effectiveness can be important in the selection among potentially appropriate reduction measures;
- program planners and managers need to balance the trade-offs among cost, potential effectiveness, and implementation feasibility;
- the evaluation of effectiveness of a completed project can be made by an assessment of the extent of coverage and implementation, in lieu of having an actual disaster to indicate averted damage and losses.

REFERENCES

Advisory Committee on the International Decade for Natural Hazard Reduction (1987) *Confronting Natural Disasters: An International Decade for Natural Hazard Reduction*, National Academy Press, Washington DC, USA.

BATES, F.L. (ed) (1982) *Recovery, Change and Development: A Longitudinal Study of the 1975 Guatemalan Earthquake*, University of Georgia, Athens, USA.

BOLTON, P. et al (1986) *Land Use Planning for Earthquake Hazard Mitigation: A Handbook for Planners*, Natural Hazards Research and Applications Center Special Publication No. 14, University of Colorado, Boulder, USA.

DAVIS, I. (ed) (1981) *Disasters and the Small Dwelling*, Pergamon Press, Oxford, UK.

HAAS J.E. et al (1977) *Reconstruction Following Disaster*, The MIT Press, Cambridge, USA.

KREIMER A. and ZADOR M. (eds) (1989) *Colloquium on Disasters, Sustainability and Development: A Look to the 1990s*, Environment Working Paper No. 23, The World Bank, Washington DC, USA.

MAY, P. and BOLTON, P.A. (1986) 'Reassessing Earthquake Hazard Reduction Measures', *Journal of the American Planning Association*, 52 (4) 443–451.

United Nations Centre for Human Settlements (Habitat) (1989) *Human Settlements and Natural Disasters*, Geneva, Switzerland.

CHAPTER 27

Assessment of the Iranian Earthquake 20 June 1990: A Field Report

PATRICK STANTON
with
RODERICK JARVIS, MICHAEL MARCHANT and
ROBERT POVEY
Association of Pioneer Rescue Officers (APRO)
Northampton, UK

Introduction

This operational report of the Iranian Earthquake, 20 June 1990, was written by the UK Pioneer Rescue Team while on reconnaissance of the Zanjan and Gilan Provinces in North-West Iran, in order to make an assessment of the disaster response, following the 7.5 (Richter Scale) earthquake, on behalf of the Iranian Red Crescent Society. Patrick Stanton was senior APRO officer commanding, Roderick Jarvis was second in command and the two Under-Officers were Michael Marchant and Robert Povey.

Arrival

Monday 25 June 1990

The Association of Pioneer Rescue Officers (APRO) Team arrived at Tehran airport, Iran, at 01.30 hrs (Iranian time) four days after initial stand-by in UK. Formalities at the airport took approximately two hours. Iranians at the airport were very open and expressed their pleasure at our arrival. Many people thanked us for our help.

04.45 hrs. Iranian Red Crescent Society moved us by taxi to the Enghelab Hotel where we saw a number of personnel from Canada and Czechoslovakia. Two rooms were made available for our use. We checked our equipment and slept for two hours. Red Crescent officials were to deploy us as soon as they could.

12.30 hrs. The personnel from the lobby had disappeared. No one seemed to know what to do with us, despite the fact that we were invited by the Iranian Government. After lunch we bought some useful things at the hotel shop such as matches, disposable lighters, cigarettes and small knives, all of which could be used by survivors. We contacted Dr Medi Abbasi, who was the resident doctor for the injured war veterans cared for in the hotel. With his help Rescue Officer Stanton telephoned Dr Akbar Zargar, an architect friend of his, and an expert on reconstruction following wars and disasters.

Briefing

16.00 hrs. We were collected by Red Crescent officials and taken to their local headquarters. Dr Zargar, we were informed, had been in contact with them, and as a result they decided that the team could be useful in the disaster zone. We were introduced at this time to linguist Magid Alikhani. Through Mr Alikhani the Red Crescent officials asked us to undertake a reconnaissance and assessment mission of the impact area in the Zanjan and Gilan Provinces in North-West Iran. We agreed to leave at 05.00 hrs the following morning. In the meantime we obtained maps and other items for recording the information that we would be gathering.

One thing which stands out above all others at this time is that everyone we met had been extremely kind and had done their best to make our waiting as comfortable as possible. We were frustrated that time was slipping away for those who required help in the impact area, but we realised our needs were only a very small part of a massive mitigation effort.

Reconnaissance and Assessment

We understood that our task was to move through the disaster zone assessing whether the survivors had adequate access to the following:

- food
- water
- medical aid and SAR (Search and Rescue).
- small tools
- large plant
- shelter materials
- sufficient clothing

- domestic utensils
- financial support
- adequate transport and fuel
- disaster relief managers
- distress and stress counsellors
- facilities for disposal of dead
- adequate facilities for documentation
- emergency veterinary services

We needed to see what the survivors could supply to assist themselves:

- had the survivors made arrangements to meet their needs?
- what local assistance was available?
- were the above enough for their survival and well being?
- was the present level of assistance likely to decrease? Without outside help would things become worse?

If so we would investigate how outside assistance could be managed:

- could emergency supplies be obtained locally?
- if not, what alternatives were there?
- had the survivors already agreed a leader, who would assist in the coordination of delivery and distribution of relief resources and if so would this be effective?
- what were the logistics and how could they be met quickly?
- where would the necessary personnel and supplies come from?
- how would they be distributed?
- where could equipment and other supplies be stored?
- were there essential items, for example food, water, shelter, tools, medical supplies, which could be obtained only outside the impact area and if so, how long would they take to mobilize and deliver?
- had any attempt been made to organize an Emergency Headquarters and communications system?

To answer these questions it was agreed that this operation would take a minimum of five days. As each area was eliminated from the enquiry, our findings would be relayed back to Red Crescent headquarters, so that the information could be disseminated and acted upon as quickly as possible.

Activities in Iran

Tuesday 26 June 1990

05.00 hrs. The Red Crescent officials introduced us to our Iranian team; including Behroz Takfalh (driver) and Mehran Kalady (rescue team guide). We were also to have a journalist to accompany us. Initially he was suspicious and unfriendly although this attitude quickly disappeared as we discussed our previous experiences and our present task. Mohammad Reza Nematy (our other guide) informed us that the first area to be visited was the Red Crescent Centre at Qazvin. From there we would be travelling on the road to Manjil, a town which we were informed had been 100% destroyed.

The Red Crescent supplied us with a Mercedes mini-bus; unfortunately it was not equipped with radio communications. This was disappointing for it would slow down the speed with which we would be able to pass on the information that we would be gaining on our journey.

09.30 hrs. We arrived at Red Crescent headquarters at Qazvin. We were shown the problems that the Red Crescent managers were facing. It was observed that managerial personnel were exhausted and were making mistakes, especially in the handling of survivors. One manager was seen to become extremely angry, which in turn caused survivors to become emotional and agitated. The ensuing argument finally had to be controlled by armed soldiers. It must be understood that managers should be relieved at regular intervals in order to prevent such occurrences. No blame can be placed on managerial personnel. Their motivation and dedication is of the highest order; post disaster distress will, without doubt, cause them physical and psychological disorders unless they are treated sympathetically. It was also observed that fit survivors were not being used to unload incoming relief vehicles. A waste of a vital resource.

Our Senior Rescue Officer was able to obtain supplies in case we found survivors who needed food, water or medical supplies. He also expressed his admiration for the heroic efforts of the Red Crescent personnel at the Qazvin Centre.

After we had left there we travelled some distance before any damage to buildings was observed, the first seen was light and repairs were already being undertaken. Helicopters were flying in the direction of Rudbar over flat plains of scrubland and cornfields. The weather was sunny and fine.

10.05 hrs. We arrived in Agababa. Dwellings here were light single storey structures made of fired brick, with some residents carrying out repairs. Relief transport and ambulances were everywhere, in fact, so far there seemed to be no shortages in transport services or in fuel supplies. Large plant such as bulldozers, backhoes and rubble lorries were seen in large numbers.

In Kuhin damage was more extensive and a number of tents were seen in a field below the village. Survivors reported that they had no shortages of food, water, tents or medical services. They insisted on telling us their experiences which we listened to with great care. A village off the road, called Bakendy, was severely damaged. It could be seen in ruins at the foot of a mountain. The villagers there told us how they had dealt with the initial problems themselves, although they had been visited by emergency and relief services shortly afterwards.

From this point on, obstructions on the road were more numerous, and

FIGURE 1   *Total destruction of the town of Manjil, north-west Iran*

work was still going on to clear them. The results of mountain slippages were impressive (as large sections had broken away), as was the Iranian roadworkers' attempts to clear them. It was in this area that we began to hear from survivors, telling of their family losses. One of our tasks was to offer some comfort and aid towards the psychological recovery of the victims. We sat with the children sharing tins of fruit juice and listening to their stories.

After we had passed through Lushan no significant damage could be seen from the road.

11.30 hrs. We arrived at Manjil (Figure 1). As we approached the town a large lake could be seen off to our left and as we had been steadily climbing we could now overlook the valley in which the town of Manjil lay. Large cracks in the soil ran downhill. What remained of the town lay before us smashed and broken (Figure 2). The stench of death was carried to us on the wind. Close by, an olive-oil factory constructed of reinforced concrete had pancaked sideways (Figure 3). We made a close examination of the wrecked factory. There were no Search and Rescue team markings to indicate that it had been searched although a number of fire appliances stood nearby.

We drove down the hill towards the international compound on the periphery of the town, where we spoke to members of the international teams. Our guides told us that Médicins Sans Frontières (a French medical aid unit) had been the first to arrive. At the time there were ten Search and Rescue teams operating in the area, many of them French. There were two Field

FIGURE 2　*The remains of the town of Manjil following the 7.5 earthquake*

FIGURE 3　*The only standing section of the olive-oil factory: the rest had 'pancaked' sideways*

Hospitals and Casualty Stations established by the French as well as an Emergency Headquarters with the Tricolor flying over it. Further along the road the Spanish had an Intensive Care Unit (ICU) in operation: all were busy either dispatching search teams or treating casualties.

We saw twelve members of the British International Rescue Corps in their camp nearby, most of whom were standing around doing nothing. Their tents were inadequate for extreme climates. They did have however not one but two satellite communication systems which enabled them to talk to the UK. On the other hand they seemed individually under-equipped to carry out prolonged Heavy Search and Rescue work.

Colonel Manoury, the French controller of Sapeurs-Pompiers, gave us a detailed assessment of the teams deployed in Manjil. He also said that there was a triangular area that encompassed Bahrainabad, Daylaman and linked across the mountains to Rudbar, about which little was known as the international teams were finding it difficult to penetrate the zone. He also said that only Red Crescent personnel had visited this area and it was not known whether they had left.

We concluded that the French response was possibly the most efficient international mitigation effort that we had so far encountered, in spite of the French press personnel buzzing around the headquarters like bees around a hive, causing some disruption.

The Japanese team consisted of eight doctors and twelve rescue personnel. There appeared to be a fire brigade connection, as all were wearing belts with the same emblem on the buckle. The camp itself was a little untidy and there was an air of lassitude. The Japanese commander appeared to be awaiting orders. Past experience suggested this may not come. So in an effort to get them going we told the commander of the need for a team to penetrate the triangular area (mentioned above) and arranged for him to be briefed by the French commander. Rescue Officer Stanton suggested that the Japanese team should be air-lifted by helicopter into the area and said he would check with Red Crescent officials to see if this could be arranged. Before we left we gave the Japanese commander a map with the triangular area marked on it.

Our overall impression of the international camp was not favourable: there was an air of indolence, with too many people seeming to be sitting about not doing very much (with the exception of the French). Most teams had the attitude that they should wait for orders from the Iranians. In principle this might be the right approach but in practice it could be a waste of vital resources. *The problem here is that the international contingent did not operate as a coordinated group, but rather as entirely separate teams unable or unwilling to take the initiative or cooperate with other teams under the direction of an overall leader.*

We also discovered that international support was welcomed by survivors. Problems of coordination appeared to have arisen because some Iranians holding minor bureaucratic positions resented what they had seen as outside interference. Individuals of this kind had been small in number; however,

237

their attitude of polite non-cooperation caused bad manpower management the results of which denied the affected population resources that could have been used to their advantage. Perhaps this was all due to a shortage of interpreters in the area!

13.45 hrs. Whilst on route to the local Red Crescent headquarters, we passed through the remains of the town, examining buildings and talking to survivors as we went. Both old burned brick and new framed buildings had suffered a similar fate (Figure 4). We saw that the new buildings were made to a high standard using modern materials. However, the method of construction had remained traditional, leading to a large loss of life as the structures fell apart (Figure 5). It seemed that no one had educated the builders in up-to-date safe forms of construction. It was also observed that no marking of searched buildings had taken place by either Iranian or international teams, which we knew from past experience inevitably leads to inefficiency and unnecessary loss of life.

We stopped and spoke and listened to survivors' experiences. All of us were affected by what we saw and heard. We found the survivors kind and open in their expressions of grief and hospitality. At no time did we encounter hostility. Where Search and Rescue had been carried out the methods of shoring and trenching were used but because the town had not been mapped and gridded we feared that no systematic Search and Rescue operation had been done.

15.30 hrs. We arrived at the Red Crescent headquarters where Reza Moazeny was introduced as the director of the camp. (Yet another extremely exhausted man showing signs of stress.) There was some form of verbal confrontation. We were not sure what was happening. The conversation flowed with no apparent purpose. Individual participants came and went like attracted and repelled particles of matter. There were arguments over the use of the helicopters. Somebody was not available to give their permission. We had lunch with the Red Crescent Committee. Our guide Reza Nematy suggested that we should go to Rudbar about three-quarters of an hour's drive away as they had more helicopters there. We began to feel that for some reason the Iranians did not want foreign eyes in the mountain areas.

Before leaving Manjil, we returned to inform the Japanese of our lack of progress. On the way out of town we continued to examine destroyed buildings and speak with survivors. There were no shortages of relief supplies. Some survivors expressed their concern about living in tents because of snakes and scorpions.

16.10 hrs. We travelled towards Rudbar and were held up because earth tremors had caused rock slides that blocked the road. The methods of keeping the roads open were effective. As we headed for the helicopter base we could see the town of Rudbar on the far side of the river and there was a considerable amount of air traffic. Part of the landing area had been tarmacked. At the far end of the site there were a number of huts that were being used by civilian

FIGURE 4 *A family died in this framed dwelling*

FIGURE 5 *In this collapse five people died*

and military authorities to coordinate their efforts. We observed that survivors who needed supplies were being ignored and left on the road side. The area resembled a military fire-base rather than a relief centre.

17.30 hrs. Four from our joint group went into the base to meet Provincial Governor, Masudy. The meeting lasted an hour, the Governor was quite happy for us to fly over the area with the Japanese, but we would not be permitted to land. We stated that we were not tourists, but if that was the Governor's decision we would comply. It seemed that yet another official did not want us to talk to the people or see the damage at ground level. We received a letter of authority to give to the Air Force officer in charge of helicopters. Another long conversation ensued when we met him, before being terminated with the statement 'It is not possible! It is too windy for the helicopters to fly.'

We returned to the vehicle to discuss what our next move should be. We were approached by survivors who said that they needed food. We gave them some of our supplies. We noticed the friction between ordinary soldiers and the Revolutionary Guards: it was this friction that seemed to affect the response to the survivors' needs. The Revolutionary Guards here were totally different in their behaviour from those that we had previously met. These men were surly and threatening in their manner. We saw helicopters continuing to come and go despite the 'wind'. The level of expertise of the local authorities seemed less than adequate, a feeling that was reinforced by still hungry survivors. We felt that we had just encountered a committee of bandits rather than officers in charge of a relief effort.

18.30 hrs. We arrived back in Manjil and informed the Japanese that no helicopters were available and suggested they attempt to get into the mountains by road. A Government Minister who identified himself as being from the Foreign Ministry said he would try to get helicopters for the morning.

19.50 hrs. We were about to leave the Japanese camp when we heard a loud bang. An ambulance on the road had collided with an Iranian soldier causing him serious injuries. Our team dealt with his initial problems and called the French doctors to his assistance. He was taken by ambulance to the French field hospital with serious leg, knee and hip injuries. Like us he was a parachutist. We also dealt with the driver of the ambulance, another soldier, who was suffering with shock and heart attack symptoms. We took him to the Spanish Intensive Care Unit and left him with the doctors.

This incident reinforced our impression that despite the obvious expertise of many of the international teams most seemed mentally unprepared to respond quickly to such a simple event, for they and their Iranian counterparts seemed totally bemused by the incident. However, quick medical action did come from the French, Spanish, Japanese and Iranian Red Crescent personnel.

20.45 hrs. Reza arranged for us to sleep in a metal cabin in a field controlled by the Red Crescent adjacent to the international camp. The manager was kind, hospitable and extremely efficient. The cabin was good protection from the wind and the dust. The Red Crescent personnel joined us for a meal and the following debriefing session.

Rescue Officer Stanton held an open debriefing after the day's work; this is a summary of observations:

(1) The Red Crescent Society had dealt effectively with the supply of water, food, clothing and tents in all the areas visited along the main and side roads to Manjil.

(2) Survivors from the villages had no complaints, except concerning snakes and scorpions.

(3) Transport was adequate even to the point where some areas appeared to be saturated with vehicles. None were seen standing idle.

(4) Veterans of the war had organized roadside rest areas, where drivers could stop, wash, eat and rest before continuing with their work.

(5) Red Crescent response and management were effective.

(6) We were concerned that managers were working in extremely stressful conditions and many were totally exhausted.

(7) The value of their work should not be underestimated or forgotten once the emergency is over: many no doubt will suffer psychological problems.

(8) Domestic utensils were in short supply.

(9) Facilities for documentation of missing, injured, dead and survivors appeared non-existent.

(10) Children were seen spraying insecticide around the tented areas in a dangerous manner.

(11) Initial Search and Rescue was hampered by road blockages and terrain. Survivors' response was positive, saving many lives.

(12) Professional Search and Rescue activity lacked coordination and the searched areas had not been mapped, gridded or marked, nor were there aerial photographs available.

(13) However, evidence showed that in many cases, Search and Rescue techniques were carried out correctly, if only fragmentarily.

(14) The authorities have, largely through the efforts of the Red Crescent Society and ordinary citizens, achieved a remarkable degree of success.

(15) We felt that the impetus gained suggested that the reconstruction phase begin as soon as possible.

(16) In Rudbar at the Government helicopter base too many military and civilian personnel were standing around doing nothing.

(17) Survivors were reporting shortages of food and obstructive authorities.

(18) The response that reached out from Manjil and that which reached out from Rudbar were different in attitude and effectiveness.

(19) Although progress and relief on Day Six after the earthquake was remarkable, the survivors were showing signs of exhaustion and stress that urgently needed to be dealt with.

(20) There is some evidence of a bureaucratic stranglehold with a danger of the whole response becoming stalled.

(21) Survivors had not been shown where to erect their tents to avoid damaged buildings falling on them in the event of aftershocks.

(22) In the international camp many of the same past mistakes were evident (with the exception of the medical units); too much equipment, too many personnel, too much flag-flying, too many media, too many people standing around doing nothing. The French and the Spanish were the only ones to show any kind of organisational initiative.

Wednesday 27 June 1990

During the night our cabin was rocked by at least eight aftershocks.

06.00 hrs. Our Iranian team were doing a remarkable job. Only Reza Nematy (our guide) was causing us problems mainly due to the fact that he kept wanting to return to Tehran and his insistence that everything we did should be done at high speed, which of course was not possible if the mission was to be carried out efficiently. However, he worked hard at smoothing obstructions. The aftershocks during the night seemed to have disorientated him.

Under-Officers Marchant and Povey were sent to examine damaged and collapsed buildings adjacent to the Red Crescent site on the periphery of the town, to inspect the after-effects of the Search and Rescue operation. They reported that although there had been signs of Search and Rescue teams having worked there, none of the buildings had been marked. Survivors living in the area seemed confused when questioned about how many people had died or had been injured. They were also unsure of how many people were still missing or how many survivors there were.

06.30 hrs. We drove back into Manjil town centre to take a more detailed look at collapsed houses. Many of them still contained the smell of death. Traditional adobe buildings showed a number of voids that did not appear to have been searched. As we returned to our vehicle a sick survivor was discovered (stomach pains and diarrhoea plus severe post-disaster distress). We took the casualty to the international compound for treatment. Whilst there, we visited the British International Rescue Corps camp; they were still standing around doing very little except trying to get a message to the UK on their satellite communications equipment. We then went to the Japanese camp and saw the commander who informed us that the helicopters were still unavailable and they were being transported into the mountains by military vehicles. They expected to leave within half an hour

08.00 hrs. We decided to go to Rudbar to look at the response in the town. As we drove over the river bridge we noticed that people were working everywhere. Large numbers of armed soldiers were seen patrolling the streets. The contrast to Manjil was apparent to us all. As we drove along the main road we could see signs of the earthquake's work. Row upon row of houses that had been built on the side of the mountain had collapsed one on top of the other as they slid downwards towards the road. The dust in the air was very evident, with the stench of death and sewerage everywhere. Many men were digging in the remains. Revolutionary Guards were seen carrying out decontamination procedures. Half way along the main street we stopped to visit a field hospital run by the Red Crescent Society. Casualties with minor injuries were being treated in the open air. A Contaminated Dressings Unit (CDU) was disposing of used material in *a safe and hygienic manner*. Drivers' rest areas and Revolutionary Guards' Sanitation Units were also scrutinised. Considering the conditions, the response seemed efficient. The morale of the workers appeared high even though they were very tired. Once again we had been unable to confirm the level of casualties or the number of survivors from the people we questioned in the area.

Further along the same road we inspected a Pharmacy Unit being run by university students. This too looked efficiently organised. In this area, debris gloves and masks appeared to be in short supply. However, Red Crescent officials told us that although they had been issued, the survivors did not wear them. How true this was we had no way of knowing. However, many survivors and Military Rescue personnel were seen to be using cloth strips tied across their lower faces. There were no shortages of shovels or pick-axes, though hammers and chisels were not much in evidence.

Many of the survivors were still wandering around in a daze and seemed to be suffering from post-disaster distress. Others were extremely dirty and exhausted after digging in debris for six days. Tired rescue personnel paid little attention to the survivors' needs, although none seemed to have complained of being hungry or thirsty.

At an improvised Clothing Store on the roadside, clothing was being sorted and distributed by Iranian women, some of whom were survivors. We learned a number of things here:

- that the clothing had been donated by people from Rasht and Tehran;
- domestic utensils were in short supply causing difficulties in washing and cooking;
- that emergency veterinary services were available;
- no facilities existed for documentation of those missing, injured or dead;
- tents seemed to be in short supply;
- emergency supplies of food were being supplemented from locally obtained resources;
- many relief personnel were used on an 'ad hoc' basis, with each group apparently choosing its own working area rather than being directed by a coordinating unit.

Further along the same road we encountered a military road block that was apparently in place to prevent looting. We were allowed to pass after identifying ourselves. Several hundred metres further on we spoke to a Colonel from the Police Academy, who was there with his police cadets. They were carrying out police duties in place of the officers who had died in the earthquake. We received a warm welcome from both the commanding officer and his men, who were very tired.

As we continued along the road we examined houses on the mountain side that had been destroyed or damaged. The mountain in this area was badly fractured, so much so that the surviving residents stated that they were leaving as the area had little future.

After examining the houses, we returned by the river road back towards the town centre, where we found a field kitchen that had been organised by Tehran businessmen. Their leader, Mohammad Ali Farshchy, told us that the businessmen had closed their places of work and had brought food and equipment to the area and they themselves were preparing and serving 10,000 meals a day. The kitchen was impressive: hygienic and efficient under very difficult circumstances. They spoke of their experiences and said how glad they were to see so many people from so many countries that had come to help in the disaster.

Almost opposite the field kitchen we found the Armenian Medical and Rescue team camp. We also met the leader of the Red Crescent Society in Rudbar. We all went to the Armenian camp together. Their team consisted of eight doctors and twelve rescue personnel. The equipment was assembled in trailers towed behind three Lada vehicles. The equipment, they told us, was a gift from the West German Red Cross. They expressed their solidarity with the Iranian people in their sadness and were pleased to be allowed to give back something to others facing a similar situation to themselves.

The rescue team came from Yeravan, the Armenian capital, and was called 'Spitak' after the city that had been 100 per cent destroyed during their earthquake in 1988. Rescue Officer Stanton received a warm welcome from them as he had been a Casualty Extraction Officer in Leninakan.

10.15 hrs. We left Rudbar taking with us a casualty suffering from appendicitis. We delivered him to the helicopter base to be air lifted to Rasht. The helicopters were sensibly used for a dual purpose, not only to transport relief supplies and casualties but also to spot blocked roads. This information was passed by radio to the road gangs via the helicopter base, which enabled personnel to clear the obstructions quickly.

On our journey towards Rasht we observed that vehicles were being stopped at check points. It appeared that vehicles for obvious efficiency reasons were used in both directions, resulting in empty vehicles being sent back to pick up supplies.

Just before the village of Ganjeh the road was badly blocked by fresh falls of rock from the recent aftershocks and its surface had huge splits in it. Within half an hour the road gangs had it open again. On this mountainous road our vehicle was hit several times by falling debris. Fortunately we sustained no serious damage, though the roadside was littered with smashed and broken vehicles. At Rhostamabad we saw collapsed buildings including a reinforced-concrete framed factory that had suffered 100% damage.

As we got closer to the city of Rasht so the damage lessened and men were seen working on various sites along the road, especially at the dam and in and around factories.

On the road from Rudbar to Rasht, we found no shortage of fuel for transport. A number of Red Crescent radio-communication vehicles were seen; however, when we tried to pass on our information we found making contact with base extremely difficult because of the mountainous terrain.

11.35 hrs. Rasht. Our team was joined by a photo-journalist, Mahmoud-m-Haji Agai (the last journalist left us at Rudbar). His first reaction was to be deeply suspicious and antagonistic, but as we got to know each other and he saw we were no threat to the Government and that our only purpose was to be as helpful as possible to the people, he became quite friendly.

The city of Rasht sustained what we considered to be minor damage and, although distressing for the people involved, had not affected to any great extent the life of the city. One memorable sight was the town hall, where the roof had collapsed inwards leaving the walls standing.

The Red Crescent headquarters was very busy. We found no shortages of food, water or other resources. But, although the staff were extremely tired their morale was high and we were received with open and friendly hospitality.

13.45 hrs. At the village of Astaneh we stopped for tea on the road side and gave the journalist a brief introduction to ourselves and our Association. He was pleased when he learned that we were NGO volunteers from England. He seemed to become genuinely interested in our mission and asked us to help him obtain pictures of the damage in the mountain villages.

As we continued our journey most of the villages that we passed through had sustained little damage. We observed that most of the roofs were made of metal or tiles and were extremely light and durable.

15.34 hrs. We had been driving up a mountain road for some time, either side of which was temperate rain forest. Villages along the mountain road had sustained little damage. Our driver Behroz Takfalh was doing an excellent job as was our translator Magid Alikhani. Mehran Kalady had been extremely supportive. Our other guide Reza Nematy was by this time very tired and was in a hurry to return to Tehran. We felt that though Reza evidently cared a great deal about the state of the people he was suffering from disaster shock and tiredness. For instance, he kept telling us that '. . . *it was very dangerous and that the road was very bad*', in spite of the heavy traffic that continually passed us going down the mountains.

Ten kilometres before the village of Espeyii (Spili) we found the road badly cracked and that heavy lorries had been driving over the crescent shaped split, putting themselves in great danger. For safety reasons we narrowed the road with boulders and bright orange safety signs in an effort to protect other drivers. There was a very real danger that an aftershock or heavy rain would cause a major slippage, as the depth of the cracks in some places was at least three metres and could be traced down the steep side of the mountain.

17.20 hrs. Espeyii (Spili). As we entered the village, on our right there was a large vernacular timber and mud style house. The wooden roof had collapsed inwards causing major damage (Figure 6). The people here seemed withdrawn and suspicious as they did not come and greet us as they had done in other villages. There seemed to be a heavy atmosphere and the people seemed afraid to speak to us. A soldier approached us and our interpreter told him who we were and what our job was. The soldier came back several minutes later with some of the villagers; once again we explained our purpose.

Suddenly the villagers began to speak, telling us of their shortages, especially of tents. One invited us into his place of business for tea; he showed us cracks and other damage to his building. Others followed his lead taking us from building to building all of which were structurally unsafe (Figure 7). An old man with one arm, whom the other villagers seemed to ignore, took us across the square and showed us what appeared to be a vegetable store. The roof was badly damaged especially where it joined the walls. His manner was frustrated and angry; he told us through the interpreter that he didn't have a tent. As far as we could understand most of the villagers needed tents. There was an undercurrent of frustration in all of them. Further enquiry showed that very little assistance had reached the area.

A committee of village elders admitted that there were shortages: they said that they had voluntarily given up their supplies to help Rudbar. Our guides examined their records, which showed that they had been resupplied with some relief goods. Half way through the discussion three new faces appeared; we were informed these were the leaders of the Committee. The Chief was Mr Sadeghipour and the officer in charge of Relief Supplies (merchandising) was Mr Khailiy.

The Committee appeared to be on the defensive about not issuing tents that they had. We said there could be a catastrophe if a large aftershock occurred, or if there was a heavy rainstorm. Some of the Committee appeared to care very deeply about what was happening. Others, in our opinion, were using the relief supplies and the situation to their own local political advantage. Briefly, it seems that the Governor of Gilan Province had asked for the original relief supplies on Day Three to be redirected to the worst hit areas. He had promised to resupply the village by Day Eight. Seventy tents were eventually issued but thirty families had not received one as they had run out. As soon as it was polite to do so we walked back to our vehicle, the Committee attempted politely to keep us talking. As we reached the main road a tractor pulling a large trailer piled high with tents was being driven out of the village. We all understood the implications.

As we left Spili on the road to Daylaman about a mile from the village, we

246

FIGURE 6 *A vernacular timber and mud house that sustained severe structural damage in Spili, Gilan Mountain Province*

FIGURE 7 *A close-up view of a mud-wall collapse in Spili*

FIGURE 8 *In this collapse two people died in Daylaman, Gilan Mountain Province*

came across a small Iranian medical unit from Mushhad University, that we had not been informed about, being run by volunteers under the direction of Dr Edany. Apparently he was the only doctor working in the area. Quite understandably he was totally exhausted. He asked us for assistance and listed tents, toilets and baths and a Disinfectant Team as an urgent need, as well as a Red Crescent presence to assist in the proper distribution of relief supplies.

18.30 hrs. Daylaman. Here our visit contrasted sharply with our experiences in Spili. Survivors gathered round us and began to tell us of their grievances. They claimed that there was unfair distribution of relief supplies and this was caused by the Local Committees. We drove into the village and then walked along its narrow roads. A number of buildings had been totally destroyed, while others had been badly damaged.

In the front yard of one such building we met an old man whose wife and another member of his family had died (Figure 8). He told us that his wife had gone into the building three times to rescue people and on the fourth time the building had collapsed killing her and a relative. We tried to comfort the old man by saying that many rescue workers died doing their job and he should be proud of his wife's courage and honour her memory because her life had not been in vain. The old man was visibly moved and understood what had been said. He and other villagers then took us to the school to see the Chief of the Local Committee.

FIGURE 9   *The family that lived here was lucky: although structurally unsound the house survived*

The partially damaged school contrasted markedly with its surrounding mud and timber houses as it was constructed of reinforced concrete. The school-yard was full of relief supplies (except tents), with little sign of their proper management and of distribution. We discussed the problems with the people in the yard and as we left the villagers were being issued with tents from another building along the road (Figure 9). We saw at least a dozen people carrying tents with them smiling and thanking us by laying their right hand across their heart. A woman gave us two loaves of bread and a villager said 'Please get help for us', another passed more bread through the window of the truck saying 'Thank you, thank you, thank you'.

23.00 hrs. We were all concerned that the information that we had gathered should be passed on to the Red Crescent at the earliest opportunity, but radio-communication in the area seemed non-existent. We decided to return to a town so that we could pass on the message that tents and other resources should be air-lifted into the area as soon as possible.

Reza was adamant that we should first visit another village nearby and he stated that it was not far away. Dark was coming on quickly as we left Daylaman for Kuhara and the village that was reported to have sustained damage. We hoped the Japanese team would be there by now. Rescue Officer Stanton told Reza that some of the villagers we had spoken to had in fact come from other villages and we knew the problems. However, the vehicle began to

249

climb further into the mountains. Shortly afterwards we passed an undamaged village only to find that Reza had picked the wrong road. In the end Rescue Officer Stanton had the bus turn round and we drove down the mountains until we reached the town of Langabad at 22.30 hrs. Here we tried to telephone the Red Crescent headquarters but we were unable to get through. Our driver by this time was exhausted and had done an incredible job. Our translator and our other guide were also very tired, as we were, so we decided to stop for a few hours' sleep. Reza eventually found us shelter in a Revolutionary Guard barracks outside the town. Here they were friendly and hospitable and let one of us watch a World Cup football match on their television. It helped to dispel the frustration we felt.

Thursday 28 June 1990

During the night the building was shaken by a number of strong aftershocks. Most of us were too tired to move.

05.00 hrs. We left the barracks and waited for twenty minutes for Reza to appear; when he did he said he'd been trying to find a radio (lorries loaded with relief supplies were parked outside).

05.45 hrs. We drove into Langabad town and had to wait for the Red Crescent manager to arrive at their Centre. Meanwhile we had some bread for breakfast and stretched our legs in an adjacent local park.

07.50 hrs. The Red Crescent manager was an Islamic priest, the first we had met. He greeted us with warmth and evident sincerity. We told him what we had discovered the day before. He said he was aware that there was a shortage of tents and explained that people would need tents while carrying out repairs and reconstruction. He also stated that money was needed for repairs and that, because of the harsh winter weather in the mountains, special winter tents would soon be required. He reassured us that he had done his best to sort the problem out and asked us to inform Tehran of his difficulties.

Our journalist left us this morning. We found him a kind and sensitive man who had supported us when Reza was being difficult. He gave us a traditional goodbye. We decided that we should return to Tehran to debrief as quickly as possible if the people of the mountains were to be helped.

On our way to Tehran, a journey of nine hours, we were delayed by a puncture and had to stop to have the damaged tyre repaired. We were also held up for some time at a river bridge that was blocked by a minor traffic accident which we cleared.

20.00 hrs. We eventually arrived at Red Crescent headquarters in Tehran but there was nobody there to debrief us. We arranged with the officials on duty to be debriefed at 08.30 hrs the following morning. Red Crescent workers got us a room at the splendid Azhadi Grand Hotel where we had a bath and something to eat before beginning work on our debrief report.

Friday 29 June 1990

08.00 hrs. Though none of the Red Crescent officials at the hotel knew about our debrief session, we were told that a car would pick us up. Despite Reza's assurances to the contrary it did not arrive. However, we did eventually get a lift and arrived at headquarters at 08.30 precisely. It appeared that no one there knew of our appointment either, so they took us to a nearby hotel for breakfast while the problem was sorted out.

15.00 hrs. Our debriefing to the Red Crescent Rescue Officers began at 09.30 hrs. The whole session, including peripheral matters, took four and a half hours. We agreed that the debrief should be tape-recorded.

We found that our ideas and our training were similar; however, we felt that we did have something positive to offer our Iranian colleagues. Half-way through the debriefing session we were told that a Red Crescent official and a team of four workers were to be dispatched to the mountain villages as soon as it could be arranged. We hope that from the conversation we had that we may continue to assist the Red Crescent Society in the training of their workers.

Saturday 30 June 1990

We made contact with Dr Akbar Zargar and over dinner we passed on to him the information we had gained. We also expressed our gratitude for his assistance.

Sunday 1 July 1990

00.30 hrs. We boarded the coach to the airport with the French Search and Rescue team (COSI).

02.00 hrs. We were informed that we were not on the flight list for the aircraft to London but the French were, though they wanted to fly to Paris. From this moment on the whole business of our departure was chaotic. Eventually, the French and ourselves embarked for London at 05.00 hrs.

10.30 hrs. (BST) We arrived back at Heathrow. The French team now found themselves in severe difficulties. Their airline tickets were from Paris to Tehran and from Tehran to Paris, but the airline had flown them to London with no tickets to take them on to Paris. Our team, although tired, spent the next eight hours trying to sort the mess out. We had seen the excellent response to the disaster in Iran and feared that such a stupid mistake by the airline workers in Tehran would cause an incident that the media could use for their own negative purposes. Air-Iran staff at Heathrow worked very hard to sort out the problem. Eventually, at midnight, thirteen hours after arriving, the French team finally embarked on an Air-France aircraft for home, minus their equipment.

Conclusion

We were very pleased to have worked with the Iranian Red Crescent Society; our overall impression was that the relief effort was quick and efficient. We were pleased to have had the opportunity in the debriefing to offer our guidance and positive criticism.

Our overall findings are listed below:

(1) We found that the Iranian Red Crescent Society and the work of ordinary people, as well as the efforts of Central Government, brought as much order as possible from the chaos of the first six days. As far as we are aware this has never been achieved before. The average time taken to 'control an incident' is usually between ten and fourteen days. There is no doubt that the tremendous suffering of the people was alleviated at the earliest opportunity. There are two major contributing factors that should not be ignored. The first was the state of preparedness of the nation due to the experience gained in the eight years of war with Iraq. The second was the time of year. If the disaster had occurred in winter, there is no doubt that it would have taken much longer to achieve 'control'.

(2) It is clear that the initial response to the disaster in the impact zone was conducted by the survivors themselves using locally available resources. It was their efforts that answered the immediate Search and Rescue needs, and their efforts that began the huge clear-up operation.

(3) The initial external emergency intervention was, according to many witnesses, slow and because of this many of the injured and trapped died. However, we feel that no blame can be attached to any of the authorities involved because, in the initial hours, darkness and blocked roads prevented rapid intervention. This meant that personnel outside the impact area were largely unaware of the conditions until damaged communications could be brought into use again.

(4) Once the formal and professional response gathered momentum, it was swift and effective. We have recorded our findings as to the handling and distribution of resources as follows:

Food. It seems from the evidence gathered that in most areas the supply and distribution was effective. In many communities this was supplemented by local resources. In Gilan Province though, some survivors from mountain villages had to travel some distance in order to obtain basic supplies.

Water. There appeared to be no shortages of water, although by Day Seven statements were being made by Red Crescent workers and others that this was becoming a problem. Local water supplies had been affected by the earthquake and not enough had been done to protect existing water supplies, especially where there were high levels of population.

Medical Aid and Search and Rescue. As previously described, the formal response was slow; however, we found that in the field, medical resources and Search and Rescue resources were adequate. We also found that the international resources were largely underused and too often wasted. We also found that search areas had not been properly mapped or gridded. Damaged and collapsed structures had not been marked, leading to confusion as to which had been searched.

Small tools. Unlike many previous situations in other countries, we found there was no shortage of picks and shovels, although small tools such as hammers and chisels seemed to be lacking. They may have been available in the first few days and since disappeared.

Large plant. Survivors reported that initially there was a shortage of heavy machinery. By Day Six we encountered no shortages in this area. In fact many large machines were unused, though many survivors could have made use of plant and personnel to clear sites, but instead they were doing the job manually.

Shelter materials. In the lowland areas we found no shortages of tents or other shelter material. In the mountain communities however we found both a shortage of tents and some mismanagement of resources. This could have been avoided by having Red Crescent officials overseeing the supply and distribution. *A longer term problem may be encountered if reconstruction is not undertaken quickly, as most tents were not winter weather quality.*

Clothing. On the face of it there seemed no shortages; however, small numbers of survivors said they could not obtain sufficient to change their clothing regularly so as to be able to wash what they had already used and to cope with approaching winter conditions.

Domestic utensils. Most survivors recovered some utensils from their collapsed or damaged houses. It did seem though that there were shortages, especially in Rudbar and Manjil.

Financial support. We are unable to comment on this matter especially in relation to direct financial assistance. Indirectly though, it was obvious to us that considerable financial support had been made available for the relief effort.

Transport and fuel. By Day Six we could find no shortages in either transport or fuel. This made a welcome change from most impact areas in other countries where both are normally in short supply. We were impressed by the standard, use and management of this resource.

Disaster relief managers. We found almost without exception that Red Crescent managers were highly motivated and carried out their tasks extremely efficiently. We noticed that many managers by Day Six were exhausted and were making some mistakes. Management personnel should be allowed to rest and recover wherever practical, preferably as soon as possible after the first 48 hours have elapsed. We hope that the Iranian Government and the governing body of the Iranian Red Crescent acknowledge the wonderful work done by their managerial personnel.

Their dedicated contribution was considerable, but experience in past disasters world-wide show that such personnel may suffer psychological and physical health effects long after the disaster.

Distress and stress counsellors. Modern disaster mitigation methods usually include distress and stress counsellors. We ask that *this resource should be made available as soon as possible both for emergency personnel and survivors,* to aid the recovery process. It is vital that this work is carried out by in-nation experts both working in centres and in the field. *This is the only area of the mitigation effort that gives us great concern for the future.*

Facilities for the disposal of the dead. We encountered no problems in this area, nor did we receive any complaints or negative statements, although we were concerned that in some areas the recovery of bodies for burial had not been achieved.

Documentation. At no time, from any source, could we be sure of reliable information as to how many people had died; or were injured; or were missing; nor how many survivors there were. Survivors we spoke to were confused about how many people had died in their own street. It is imperative that in future mitigations this should be dealt with at the earliest possible opportunity and that such information is disseminated amongst the population. Many people will have a difficult time trying to trace relatives and loved ones if documentation isn't carried out in a professional manner.

Emergency veterinary services. We were informed that emergency veterinary services were available in some areas. However, we cannot confirm this as we did not speak with anyone involved. In the larger areas of damage a number of animal carcasses were seen lying in the open. It is vital that these are disposed of quickly either by burial or by incineration in order to help prevent the spread of disease. Most living animals that we encountered appeared to be in good health.

Storage of relief supplies. In many areas that we visited relief supplies were adequately stored. However, on a number of sites they lay in the open exposed to the weather. We realise the difficulties of supplying adequate storage, but in many cases relief supplies were not raised off the ground or even covered with polythene sheeting. This can obviously lead to unnecessary wastage.

Emergency headquarters. With the exception of the Red Crescent personnel and the international French team, *no one had created a proper headquarters system.* In the mountain villages we found that not only was there an absence of an emergency headquarters but also the response was being run by 'ad hoc' committees who were either inefficient or using the relief resources to strengthen their own political power: *this undoubtedly caused survivors unnecessary worry and suffering.*

Disinfection and sanitation units. Most of the disinfection units encountered were either military or Revolutionary Guard in origin and were extremely efficient. We were, however, concerned that in Manjil *children were seen carrying out the function*. It was also observed that *they did not use masks or gloves*. Field latrine facilities were adequately dug and constructed to give a reasonable amount of privacy, but they were generally not kept clean and could be a serious source of disease.

Statement by the Team

This report was undertaken at the request of the Iranian Red Crescent Society. We hope that we have shown our genuine and sincere desire to assist the Iranian people in their recovery. We also wish to record our sincere thanks to the many people that contributed to our efforts, not least to our Iranian Red Crescent colleagues who accompanied us on our mission. We regret that we were unable to make a more in-depth assessment, but this was mainly due to the fact that we were being continually pressured (by one of the Iranian volunteers) to return to Tehran as quickly as possible.

Our enduring memory is of the kindness, hospitality and genuine openness of the vast majority of Iranians. Added to this is our impression of the survivors whose strength, courage and forbearance shone through their personal suffering. We are also aware that the world could learn much from the Iranian people's experience in responding to this disaster. We hope that in time this experience may be written up and shared, so that the lessons learned in Iran can be used by others when disaster occurs.

We realise that some of our conclusions are critical; however, we were asked to be honest in our findings according to our experience. Furthermore, we would like to reiterate that *the overall mitigation effort was, in our opinion, quite exceptional.*

We are aware that media interest in the Iranian people's disaster has already faded and that the world at large will quickly forget the suffering and death in the Zanjan and Gilan Provinces. We know that the Iranian Government will continue with its wonderful support through the months of reconstruction, so that the survivors may hopefully find peace of mind and return to a more normal life as quickly as is humanly possible.

Conclusions and Recommendations for the International Decade for Natural Disaster Reduction (IDNR)

YASEMIN AYSAN

Disaster Management Centre
Oxford Polytechnic, UK

During the two days of the Workshop participants formed groups to discuss the following themes: Training and Education, Risk Mitigation, Emergency Planning, Risk Assessment. The purpose of the discussions was to make recommendations for the Decade on the selected themes. The following are edited from these group reports.

Training and Education

The recommendations of this group were to:

- promote the disaster culture through formal education channels and the media
- explore the possibility of creating or preferably strengthening existing information focal points
- translate and widely distribute a handful of key publications which already exist
- integrate disaster planning into development planning
- shift the emphasis from disaster relief to decreasing the vulnerability of families and communities
- undertake research on former and current building education projects with a view to determining factors of long-term sustainability
- where possible, integrate building education projects into existing long-term development programmes
- design and structure building education to suit the administrative system and the community structure to which it is addressed.

Risk Reduction (Mitigation)

The working group on this theme chose to present its findings under a series of sub-headings.

Justification

To professionals, practitioners and to localised communities who feel themselves to be exposed to danger, the adoption of risk reduction practices may seem both wise and of high priority. However, for political leaders, administrators, civic leaders and the population at large, mitigation has to compete as an idea with a medley of other voices and causes.

The concept of risk reduction has to be advocated, defined, and linked to the protection of assets as a necessary underpinning of development actions.

Use of the word *mitigation* needs to be revised in the coming Decade as it is not in common usage and implies different actions in different contexts. To clarify its meaning it has to be mentally translated into *risk reduction*, which may be a more effective term.

Institutionalisation

Institutionalisation of 'risk reduction' needs to be addressed at various levels:

- political philosophy of risk reduction as a national objective
- in relation to other national objectives and development strategies, five year plans and the annual budget
- as a series of ministerial actions with a budget line for risk reduction activities
- through leadership and demonstration by departments and agencies, private business, professional bodies of health, engineering, architecture, etc., public awareness programmes, publicity given to local community efforts
- with media co-operation, there is a need to build on political commitment and encourage the participation of all parties
- through the work of representative committees (national/provincial/civic), technical sub-committees and 'key persons' in preparing a strategic overview of risks and possibilities of risk reduction: what is needed, who should do what, when
- through the preparation of practical guidelines via a cascade of guidance manuals, visual demonstrations and training at a wide range of levels from the professional to the public
- by encouraging dialogue and information exchange at all levels
- through establishing responsible bodies in a co-operative management system
- by facilitating the establishment of a 'safety culture'.

Management

The management tasks at various levels (national, provincial, departmental and community) include:

- the development and prosecution of risk reduction measures in existing built environments; in undertaking new projects and programmes; in post disaster situations (repair, resettlement, reconstruction etc.)
- actions that are structural in nature (roads, bridges, buildings, services distribution); agricultural and industry based; non-structural (laws, building regulation, public awareness programmes, insurance)
- setting priorities for risk reduction
- establishing development plans, preparedness plans, hazard monitoring, evaluation of performance of mitigation measures
- establishing incentives.

Community based mitigation

The group felt strongly that unless risk reduction measures targeted the community level, they would not be effective. There is much evidence that this is so:

- communities should be integrated into decision making on their safety, and local development projects should be used as vehicles to reduce risks
- economic acceptability of the risk reduction measures by the target communities should be a part of mitigation strategies.

Insurance

This is perhaps a neglected area outside developed countries. Insurance thinking does not form part of the culture of the public and the administrators. There are problems assessing risks, making recommendations on how to reduce risks, maintaining inspection procedures of properties, establishing relevant procedure, reinsurance, all of which need to be addressed and explored throughout the Decade.

Technical know how

There is a considerable accumulation of knowledge within the research community. However, the 'how and when' of application – the making of appropriate choices – is not as strong. This is a key area that needs to be developed over the Decade. Affordability and replicability of the technical choices are also critical issues.

There are communication gaps to be closed in the professional 'disaster community' between researchers, philosophers, educators, trainers, Government officials, consultants, advisors and community level workers. If we do not improve inter-communication we cannot expect it of others.

Emergency Planning

For the purposes of discussion, emergency planning is defined as a process involving the interaction of human behavioural, organisational, governmental and technological elements at all levels, but giving special emphasis to the community. The process includes time periods covering both pre- and post-disaster.

Equally, shelter, and the community's or individual's relationship to it, is a process and therefore any discussion of issues related to shelter should have a long term perspective.

In many situations, the dynamic, everyday shelter condition is in crisis, displaying extreme vulnerability. In this context disaster is an extraordinary social disruption. Emergency planning, as a concept confined to the immediate post-event period, may act against the disruption but will not affect the dynamic condition.

Thus there must be a link between emergency planning, reconstruction and development. Long-term planning institutions need to be involved in emergency planning discussions. There is a need to integrate disaster management structures within general planning mechanisms to ensure that emergency and long-term considerations are part of the same continuum. Special emphasis should be given at all stages to community participation and a 'grass roots' approach.

In the planning stage the question of whether disasters can be used as a means of achieving basic change in societies must be on the agenda. On the other hand, planners should be aware that decisions taken early in an emergency are likely to remain in place over the long-term even if their effects are counterproductive.

Two further issues were identified:

- aid frequently does not reach the real victims at the lowest levels of society. On the other hand, some aid programmes that do reach the lowest levels and promote self-help can become paternalistic. This concept needs to be defined closely to avoid imposed self-help. Whatever happens, aid interventions must be made with care to avoid dependency and long-term problems
- the needs and priorities in shelter and housing reconstruction will obviously vary depending on whether the context is urban or rural. However, emphasis must be put on increasing urbanisation and the urgency of addressing its major problems.

Finally, in any discussion of these issues it is important to remember that

259

the community is the major actor in any emergency and shelter may not be the highest priority.

Risk Assessment

The discussion group focused on issues of risk acceptability and choices about risk levels. Who makes decisions on risk? Engineers currently make unilateral decisions on levels of protection needed. Feedback is needed from the community into this process. Also, who imposes the risk and who bears it? People, even the middle classes, have little control over settlement site, building form and quality. However, individual control over building is closely related to individual power.

Those bearing the risks rarely do so in ignorance or due to other priorities. But, the need to cope with reality frequently means that a variety of coping mechanisms from the psychological to the social are used. Acceptable levels of risk are likely to be different for individuals compared with larger communities: their amount of choice and power to change things is different. Higher levels of risk may be acceptable for higher community benefits (for example, living on a flood plain for economic benefits). Risk assessment should move towards the empowerment of communities to protect themselves and the encouragement of self-protection.

Many attempts to reduce vulnerability simply replace one sort of risk with another, shift the risk to another group, or result in different behaviour which negates the aim of the programme. These factors are usually ignored even in sophisticated analyses, and often result from the views of those making the decisions rather than those bearing the risk.

Vulnerability is closely linked to recoverability – the capacity of a community to recover. The dynamics of a community – where it was heading economically before the event – are critical to post-disaster recovery and for mitigation planning.

Index

adobe buildings 242
Armenia 26

Bangladesh 88, 92, 97, 110
block structure 24
building
  codes 1, 125, 128, 227
  content 189
  education 159
  improvement 52
  material 1, 36, 123, 201
    availability 186
    low-cost 39
    small-scale 39
    procurement difficulties 103
  quality 203
  techniques 185
bureaucracy 242

California earthquakes (1978, 1979, 1983) 191
Caribbean 45
collapsed buildings 242
community
  development 27, 208–9
  organisation 74, 221
  participation 75, 106, 172, 201
construction
  costs 102, 186
  low-cost 223
  non-engineered buildings 125
  programme 210
  safe 125, 238
  speed 103
  technique 2, 36
controllability of hazards 192
coping mechanisms 31
cost effectiveness 228
cultural issues 32, 41, 67, 70, 74, 77, 85, 225

disaster
  aid 146
  as social disruption 68
  and development 6, 27, 43, 45, 72–3, 148
  management 5
  mitigation 72, 162, 171
  planning 18, 47, 77, 114, 227
  preparedness 5, 252

disaster (*continued*)
  prevention 45
  protection 36, 119
  relief 47, 72–3, 167
  relief managers 253
  resistance 40
  resistant construction 183
  response 184, 231
  risk 1
    high-damage potential 16
    low-damage potential 16
Dominican Republic 207

economic issues 26, 122
  income group 95
  poverty 88
Ecuador earthquake 1987 41, 146
El Salvador 218
emergency
  and relief services 234
  housing 94
  procedures 114
  response 82
  shelter 93
evaluation 27, 99, 171, 224

flood 19, 88, 97, 110
  Action Plan 117
  Alice Springs 77
  damage 81, 112
  embankment 113
    breaches 112
  flash 81
  protection scheme 90
  rehabilitation 97
  seasonal 110
  settlements 111
  types of 111
  warning 82–4, 113
flood-resistant house 106

Government
  public awareness programmes 11
  reconstruction 199
  role of 23, 50

state agencies 75
Guatemala earthquake 1976 62

housing
  community focus 24
  costs 101
  design 102
  improvement 88
  intervention 90
  model 158
  needs 89, 104
  permanent 185
  programmes, design of 225
  provision 97
  recovery 127
  rural 3, 36–7, 88, 94, 100, 108,
    220
  safe 13, 94, 227
  universal 26–7
Hurricane House 179–81

income
  generation 210
  group 93
infrastructure, damage to 99
interdisciplinary approaches 47
Iran earthquake
  1972 59
  1990 120, 231
Iraq 194

Kalamata earthquake 1986 136

land
  pressure 38
  shortage 115, 221
  tenure 3, 89
loss estimation 11
low-cost
  design 97
  structures 107
low-income
  communities 32
  housing 221

Mexico City 25
Middle East 59
mitigation 10, 12, 14–15, 45, 110,
    115, 127, 224, 255
  and development 49
  earthquakes 227
  Government role 117, 126
  individual measures 115
  options 227
  role of NGOs 116
model houses 158

NGOs 28, 97, 172
  and public awareness programmes
    11
  role in disaster work 23, 72

occupant
  behaviour 189
    cultural differences 190
  safety 189
    educational materials 191

Peru Earthquake 1990 162
Philippines earthquake 1990 121
political
  context 173
  empowerment 63
Popayán 25
population 3, 111, 207
post-disaster
  resettlement 58
  stress 242
post-earthquake
  housing 14
  resettlement 59
  shelter 14
prefabricated houses 137, 144, 227

reconstruction 92, 119, 162
  cultural issues 124
  earthquake 119
  plan
    and development 169, 205

impact of 170
post-war 194
programmes 122
projects 224
rural housing 146
war 26
recovery 12
  planning 122
  rate 130, 131
Red Crescent Society 231
rehabilitation and development 104
relief 94, 154, 171
relocation 124, 220
resettlement
  community participation 62
  cultural issues 61
  design 61
  development issues 62
  failure 60
  housing and community services
    64
  unplanned 63
risk 32
  assessment 10, 15
  communication 69
  identification 126
  reduction 9, 12, 16
river erosion 114

search and rescue teams 231, 235
selection of beneficiaries 105
self-help
  programme 221
  project 94
  reconstruction 26
shanty towns 219
shelter
  design 90
  instant 13
  materials 253
  provision 9
  strategy 137
site
  development 141

site (*continued*)
  layout 140
  social problems 143
slums 3, 207
social
  needs 133
  networks, recovery of 69
  organisation 88
social scientists, role of 67, 74
social viability 183
Solomon Islands 183
structural inequality 215
sustainability 11, 48

target groups 229
technical
  cooperation 45, 53
  knowledge, and availability 53
technology
  improvement 147, 173
  intermediate 37, 38
  transfer 45, 55
temporary
  accommodation 13
  housing 136
  shelter 221
Tongan Hurricane House 175, 179
traditional construction 148, 238
training 45, 54
  programme 41–2
Turkey earthquakes (1970, 1971, 1976) 59

urban 1, 3, 74–5
  development 14, 207
  housing 94, 108, 220
  migration 24, 218
  poor 50

population 79, 114, 124
reconstruction 29
tenement 25
vulnerability 29
urbanisation 2, 64

vulnerability 9–11, 30, 36, 45, 49, 59, 81, 110, 212
  analysis 32
  and poverty 50
  cultural 34
  ecological 35
  economic 33
  educative 34
  fire 212
  floods 213
  high winds 213
  ideologic 34
  institutional 35
  landslides 213
  man-made disasters 214
  marginalised groups 85
  natural 33
  physical 33
  poverty 37, 212
  reduction 51
  social 34
  small dwellings 40
  technical 34
  urbanisation 37–8, 166

winds 176–7
  building to resist 175
  cyclone 183
  housing testing 178

Yemen 25